Sudden Infant Death Syndrome
Who Can Help and How

Charles A. Corr, Ph.D., is Professor in the School of Humanities, Southern Illinois University at Edwardsville and Chairperson, International Work Group on Death, Dying, and Bereavement. Previous volumes he has coedited include *Helping Children Cope with Death: Guidelines and Resources* (second edition, Hemisphere Publishing Corporation, 1984), *Childhood and Death* (Hemisphere Publishing Corporation, 1984), and *Adolescence and Death* (Springer Publishing Company, 1986).

Helen Fuller, M.S.W., is Executive Director, SIDS Resources, Inc., St. Louis, Missouri. She has been working in the area of Sudden Infant Death Syndrome since 1977, has been an active member of the Association of SIDS Program Professionals since its beginnings in 1986 (serving both as Vice-President and as Treasurer), and has co-authored articles and brochures on SIDS.

Carol Ann Barnickol, M.S.W., is a SIDS parent who has been involved in SIDS counseling and education both as a volunteer and (since 1975) professionally, as Coordinator, first, of the Missouri SIDS Information and Counseling Project and, currently, of SIDS Resources, Inc., in St. Louis, Missouri. She has co-authored articles and brochures on SIDS.

Donna M. Corr, R.N., M.S.N., is Associate Professor of Nursing, St. Louis Community College at Forest Park, St. Louis, Missouri. With her husband, she is coeditor of *Hospice Care: Principles and Practice* (Springer Publishing Company, 1983), *Hospice Approaches to Pediatric Care* (Springer Publishing Company, 1985), and *Nursing Care in an Aging Society* (Springer Publishing Company, 1990).

Sudden Infant Death Syndrome

Who Can Help and How

Charles A. Corr
Helen Fuller
Carol Ann Barnickol
Donna M. Corr
Editors

Springer Publishing Company
New York

AAZ1327

In memory of Mary Beth Barnickol
(January 28, 1969—February 23, 1969),
and for all the other children and families
who have been affected by
Sudden Infant Death Syndrome

Springer Publishing Company, Inc.
536 Broadway
New York, NY 10012-3955

91 92 93 94 95 / 5 4 3 2 1

Printed in the United States of America

CONTENTS

Part III   SIDS—Guidelines for Helping

Part IV   SIDS—Summing Up and Looking Ahead

PREFACE

Sudden Infant Death Syndrome (SIDS), commonly called "crib death" in the United States and "cot death" in Great Britain and some other countries, is the leading cause of death in infancy after the neonatal period. SIDS is a personal and family tragedy, a frustrating puzzle for researchers, and a daunting challenge for clinicians, counselors, and a wide range of community helpers. In the midst of these difficulties, however, there are ways to help and opportunities for a broad range of interventions. The purpose of this book is to draw attention to those who need help, to identify those who can offer help, and to suggest practical guidelines for constructive assistance. We hope to provide a useful resource for parents and family members, for professional and lay helpers, and for students of all sorts with primary concern for SIDS, but also with some potential value for other forms of infant death.

Many people helped us in the preparation of this book. These include SIDS parents and family members, together with a wide variety of professional caregivers. We owe a debt of gratitude to all who shared with us their experiences and expertise. A very special group of these people agreed to take time from busy schedules to contribute chapters. They deserve particular thanks. In addition, we want to mention the assistance that we have received from those associated with SIDS Resources, Inc., in Missouri, from Southern Illinois University at Edwardsville, and from St. Louis Community College at Forest Park.

CHARLES A. CORR
HELEN FULLER
CAROL ANN BARNICKOL
DONNA M. CORR

CONTRIBUTORS

Pasquale J. Accardo, M.D., is Associate Professor of Pediatrics and Adolescent Medicine, School of Medicine, Saint Louis University, and Director, Knights of Columbus Developmental Center, Cardinal Glennon Memorial Hospital for Children, St. Louis, Missouri.

Joan Hagan Arnold, R.N., M.A., is Assistant Professor, Marion A. Buckley School of Nursing, Adelphi University, Garden City, Long Island, New York, and Consultant, New York City Information and Counseling Program for Sudden Infant Death.

Connie J. Cunningham, M.H.A., is a Pharmaceutical Representative for Syntex Laboratories in Jefferson City, Missouri, where she was Program Coordinator for SIDS Resources, Inc., from 1985 to 1990.

Betty Davies, R.N., Ph.D., is Associate Professor, School of Nursing, The University of British Columbia, Vancouver, British Columbia, Canada.

Beverley De Bruyn, B.Sc., is Executive Director, Canadian Foundation for the Study of Infant Deaths, Toronto, Ontario, Canada.

Penelope Buschman Gemma, R.N., M.S., C.S., is Research Nurse Clinician, Columbia-Presbyterian Medical Center, New York, New York.

Connie Guist, R.N., M.S., C., is Field Services Manager, Multnomah County Health Division, Portland, Oregon. She was Weld County (Colorado) Regional SIDS Coordinator (1977–1980), Interim Nurse, Colorado Sudden Infant Death Syndrome Counseling and Information Project (1980), and Coordinator, Wisconsin Sudden Infant Death Syndrome Center (1980–1986).

Laura S. Hillman, M.D., is Professor of Child Health and Professor of Human Nutrition, Medical School and Graduate School, University of Missouri, Columbia, Missouri, and President and Medical Director, SIDS Resources, Inc., St. Louis, Missouri.

Judy E. Larsen, R.N., E.M.T.-P., is Educational Coordinator, Milwaukee County Paramedic System, Milwaukee, Wisconsin.

Sheila Dayton Marquez, R.N., B.S.N., P.N.P., is Executive Director, Colorado SIDS Program, Inc., Denver, Colorado.

Marion McNurlen, M.S.W., L.I.C.S.W., is a pediatric oncology social worker at Children's Hospital of St. Paul in St. Paul, Minnesota. In addition, she is a leader of support groups for the Minnesota Sudden Infant Death Center, and a developer and leader of group leadership training programs in the Minneapolis/St. Paul area.

Teresa Roberson Mullins, is a SIDS parent, a volunteer counselor with SIDS Resources, Inc., and a Pastoral Associate at St. Francis De Sales Parish in St. Louis, Missouri.

Richard A. Pacholski, Ph.D., is Professor, Department of English, Millikin University, Decatur, Illinois.

Milda Dargis Ranney, M.A., was Project Coordinator at the Sudden Infant Death Syndrome Center, Loyola University Medical Center, Maywood, Illinois, from 1976 to 1989. She now lives in West Bloomfield, Michigan.

Sydney Segal, M.D., is Professor Emeritus of Pediatrics at the School of Medicine, University of British Columbia, Chairman of the Board of Consultants of the Canadian Foundation for the Study of Infant Deaths, Chairman of the Medical and Scientific Advisory Committee of the SIDS Alliance, and a SIDS parent in Vancouver, British Columbia, Canada.

Marie A. Valdes-Dapena, M.D., has served as Chairman of the Scientific Advisory Board of the National Sudden Infant Death Syndrome Foundation, and is Professor of Pathology and Pediatrics, School of Medicine, University of Miami, Miami, Florida.

Barbara Y. Whitman, Ph.D., is Associate Professor of Pediatrics and Adolescent Medicine, St. Louis University School of Medicine; Associate Professor of Social Service, St. Louis University; and Director of Family Services, Knights of Columbus Developmental Center, Cardinal Glennon Memorial Hospital for Children, St. Louis, Missouri.

Susan F. Woolsey, R.N., M.S., C.S., before her retirement, was Director of the Maryland Sudden Infant Death Syndrome Information and Counseling Program and Assistant Clinical Professor, University of Maryland School of Medicine, Baltimore, Maryland (1976–1988), and served as a member of the Board of Directors of the National Sudden Infant Death Syndrome Foundation.

PART I

SIDS—Characteristics and Research

Sudden Infant Death Syndrome (SIDS) is a subject that sharply exemplifies human and professional limitations. It is neither predictable nor preventable. The first symptom of SIDS is a dead infant. The once popular phrase "near-miss SIDS" has now been recognized as an imprecise expression, if not an actual contradiction in terms, and has been replaced by the more neutral expression "apparent life-threatening event" (ALTE). In our society, SIDS itself is rightly perceived as one of the most untimely, unexpected, and unfortunate of all types of death.

In Chapter 1, Marie Valdes-Dapena describes historical and phenomenological characteristics of typical SIDS experiences. From this description, it is evident that we have much yet to learn about SIDS and its etiology. As a result, Chapter 1 communicates an unmistakable sense of the challenges presented by SIDS.

In Chapter 2, Laura Hillman surveys research that has been done in the area of SIDS and theories that have been offered to explain SIDS. Some 10 or 15 years ago, there was the tantalizing hope that research might soon identify the cause or causes of SIDS, thereby opening possibilities for screening of high-risk populations and for the eventual prevention of SIDS. Such hopes for a great, unique, and prompt step forward have faded as one theory after another has proven unsatisfactory. The result is a growing sense that the underlying origins of SIDS may be substantially more complex than previously suspected.

The two chapters in Part I of this book are intended as a broad framework for all that follows. They identify the events and the limitations in our understanding of those events from which all of the rest develops. In this way, the present situation is both a stage in the development of our knowledge in this area and a jumping off point for the long haul in terms of scientific research, the care of affected persons, and the development of organizational efforts.

1

CHAPTER 1

The Phenomenon of Sudden Infant Death Syndrome and Its Challenges

Marie A. Valdes-Dapena

In the past 30 years, the medical community and the public at large have become increasingly aware of Sudden Infant Death Syndrome (SIDS) as the major cause of postneonatal mortality in the United States. At least one-third of all infant deaths involving children between the ages of one week and one year are attributable to this phenomenon. In the United States, where the rate of occurrence is two SIDS deaths per 1,000 babies born alive, approximately 7,000 apparently healthy infants die of SIDS every year. In Canada, the problem is equally distressing—the rate there is virtually identical. There can be no doubt but that SIDS is a major public health problem for the people of this continent at this time, principally because we are unable to prevent it or to predict it.

SIDS does occur in third world and developing nations such as the countries of Central and South America, probably as frequently as it appears on the North American continent and in Europe. However, relatively little attention is paid to SIDS in third world and developing nations because diarrhea and infectious diseases take the lives of so many babies that SIDS is comparatively unimportant. After all, SIDS, often referred to in popular speech as "crib death" or "cot death," became a matter of public concern in the United States and in other developed countries only after infant diarrhea and other similar causes for morbidity and mortality among babies began to be controlled in the early 1900s.

In fact, SIDS occurs everywhere in the world. No country is immune to it. Some nations, such as Sweden and Japan, report very low rates as compared with those in the United States, while others, like New Zealand, seem to have surprisingly and inexplicably high rates (Valdes-Dapena, 1988). For many nations, there are no figures available. The reasons for that are the following: (1) in order to determine what is or is not a SIDS death, reliable infant autopsies

2

must be conducted routinely in highly organized, well-staffed medical examiners' offices; and (2) in order to count those occurrences, nationwide, comprehensive, and reliable systems for census-taking and tallying of causes of
death via death certificates must function accurately. Typically, developing
countries simply do not have the agencies to conduct the necessary autopsies,
nor do they have in place the data collection systems that would be required.
Hence, the fact is that no one knows the total number of SIDS cases annually in
the world as a whole.

DEFINITION

The definition of Sudden Infant Death Syndrome remains essentially what it
was when first formally defined in 1969, that is, the sudden and unexpected
death of an infant who has seemed well, or almost well, and whose death
remains unexplained after the performance of an adequate postmortem investigation including an autopsy, examination of the death scene, and review of
the case history (Beckwith, 1970). What officially constitutes "an adequate autopsy" was described in detail a few years later (Jones & Weston, 1976), and
the death scene and case history requirements were added in 1989.

HISTORICAL BACKGROUND

As far as anyone knows, SIDS is as old as humankind. It is said that the first
documented case appears in the Bible, in the Book of Kings, in the story about
Solomon's judgment which begins with the statement, "And this woman's child
died in the night because she overlaid it" (I Kings 3:19).

Later references appeared in the Middle Ages and reports can still be found
in quotations from newspapers of the mid-1800s. Although there is no way to
confirm that those references were to the entity known today as SIDS, it is
likely that a substantial number of them were, indeed, that phenomenon.

In the 1800s, little was written about SIDS in the medical literature. However,
everyone, lay persons and physicians as well, knew that it happened. Since in
those days infants under one year of age often slept with their mothers, most
of those deaths were attributed to accidental overlaying. Others were ascribed
to pneumonia or neglect. It must be remembered, however, that at that time
infant mortality in general was ever so much higher than it is now. Physicians
were turning all of their interest and energies to caring for infants with or
trying to prevent "summer diarrhea," which was then the most important

cause of infant mortality. In terms of numbers of cases, SIDS was, by comparison, a minor concern for those doctors.

The infamous "thymic theory" emerged in the mid-1800s in an article written by Dr. C. K. Lee (1842), "On the thymus gland, its morbid affections and the diseases that arise from its abnormal enlargement." Dr. Lee ascribed these infant deaths to a specific pathologic condition which could be identified at autopsy. The theory was that an "enlarged" thymus compressed the infant's upper airway, posterior to it, resulting in so-called internal suffocation. Hence, the condition was referred to, in medical circles, as "Status thymico-lymphaticus."

This error probably arose from the fact that anatomic pathologists, accustomed to conducting autopsies on infants who had died following serious illness, found the thymuses of infants who had died of "crib death" to be "abnormally" large. That temporarily popular hypothesis was slow to succumb. As late as 1945, an article, "Status thymico-lymphaticus," appeared in the *American Journal of Pediatrics* (Carr, 1945).

Now, of course, we realize that the thymus of the infant is normally large. We are also aware of one serious consequence of this mistaken theory. That is, in the early 1900s many pediatricians irradiated the thymuses of infants thought to be at risk, in order to prevent crib death. Sadly, some 25 to 30 years later many of these unfortunate patients developed carcinoma of the thyroid as a result of the irradiation.

In 1892, a physician by the name of Templeman published a remarkable article on his autopsy and investigational findings in 258 infant deaths which he ascribed to "suffocation" (Templeman, 1892). It was, in fact, a series of babies who had died suddenly and unexpectedly. Templeman reported that the greatest number of those babies died between October and March, and that the highest incidence was among infants from one to six months of age. He found those deaths to be most prevalent in families of low socioeconomic status. Templeman, like others before him, believed that the infants had died of overlaying, which he attributed to ignorance, carelessness, drunkenness, and overcrowding. Nevertheless, it is amazing how like our present information concerning SIDS his descriptions are. He must have been referring to the same phenomenon.

In addition to these investigational findings, Templeman's autopsy observations are impressive. They correspond exactly to what is seen in the typical SIDS necropsy today. "Frothy mucus, often tinged with blood, is generally seen about the mouth and nostrils. The hands are sometimes tightly clenched." Templeman also described, "more or less engorgement of the internal organs, especially the lungs and kidneys . . . ." Finally, he added that, "in about half the cases examined small punctiform haemorrhages were observed beneath the pleura and pericardium."

In 1934 and 1938, the eminent Dr. Sidney Farber, a pioneer in pediatric pathology, published two articles on the subject of sudden death in infancy (Farber, 1934, 1938). Fundamentally, and mistakenly it turns out, he believed that these sudden infant deaths were the result of unsuspected sepsis or infection.

The first systematic, documented, detailed, and objective analyses of a series of SIDS autopsies, including the histopathology, were those published by Doctors Werne and Garrow of the Office of the Medical Examiner in New York City in 1953 (Garrow & Werne, 1953; Werne & Garrow, 1953a & 1953b). In those days, it was the forensic pathologists who wrote what little there was concerning SIDS in the medical literature, because they were the only physicians who had to struggle with that enigma on a regular basis. No one else in medicine was much involved or even interested in studying the topic.

One of the finest and most dedicated of those rare forensic pathologists was Dr. Lester Adelson, whose classic description of the typical autopsy is preserved for us, excellent photographs and all, in the proceedings of the 1963 Conference on Causes of Sudden Death in Infants (Adelson, 1965).

The second of the landmark international conferences on SIDS, sponsored by the National Institute of Child Health and Human Development (NICHD), took place near Seattle, Washington, the site of the first meeting, in the year 1969 (Bergman, Beckwith, & Ray, 1970). Both of those gatherings accomplished a great deal in regard to arousing the interest of academicians in this subject. However, what ensued was even more effective.

In the early 1970s, Dr. Eileen Hasselmeyer, Director, Perinatal Biology and Infant Mortality Branch of NICHD, managed to capture the world's finest pediatric scientists and gather them into the arena of SIDS research by means of conducting a series of workshops concerning one after another potential mechanism for the causation of SIDS (Hasselmeyer & Knox, 1972–1976). It was a masterful feat, requiring not only imagination and courage, but diplomacy and hard work as well.

Two large, international conferences in the 1960s, together with Dr. Hasselmeyer's series of topic-oriented, invitational meetings at NICHD represent the true turning point in SIDS research. It was during those days that highly qualified, critical persons in a variety of scientific disciplines began to participate in relevant research that had been considered impossible before that time.

TYPICAL PATTERNS

There are typical patterns in regard to the phenomenon of Sudden Infant Death Syndrome. Included among them are certain generalities concerning, or common characteristics of, the infants who succumb to crib death, their mothers, their home environments, and even the events themselves.

Infant Factors

Ever since the early 1960s, it has been increasingly apparent that all babies are not at the same degree of risk for SIDS. For 30 years, it has been known that those infants who are between two and four months of age are at much greater risk than those under one month or between five and six months of age, and that very few babies die in this manner after the age of six months (Goldberg, et al., 1986). That fact obtains in all parts of the world and is usually interpreted to mean that, whatever it is in these babies that fails, it must have something to do with the developmental phase through which they are passing at the time. Some investigators feel that the key factor is a failure of maturation within critical portions of the central nervous system.

There is a slight preponderance of the male sex among the babies who die of SIDS, but in most series the difference between the two is something like 52% as opposed to 48%, and is usually attributed to the fact that, in the realm of pediatric disease, males seem almost always more vulnerable (Valdes-Dapena & Steinschneider, 1983).

In the United States, there is and always has been a higher rate among black than among white infants; in general, blacks are almost twice as much at risk as whites. However, the infant most at risk in this nation is the Native American (Valdes-Dapena & Steinschneider, 1983); in some published series the risk of those infants exceeds eight per thousand live births. Nevertheless, that is not true of all tribes. In the state of Oklahoma, the risk for Native American babies does not appear to be substantially different from that for caucasians (Kaplan, Bauman, & Krous, 1984).

When one considers the world at large in this regard, it becomes apparent that in any country the racial group which is most afflicted by SIDS is the group at the bottom of the socioeconomic ladder. For example, in Australia it is the aborigines. In Great Britain, it is the Indians who have migrated into the British isles from India. In New Zealand, it is the Maoris. Although that differential is not always apparent (there is at least one exception), it exists in most places and has caused investigators to surmise that the inadequate social or medical condition of the mother (probably during pregnancy and perhaps even before that) may have a part to play in pathogenesis of the SIDS phenomenon.

Cultural factors also play some role in risk for SIDS. It appears that infants born of oriental parents in the United States, whether they be Japanese or Chinese and even though they may be in lower socioeconomic strata, are uniquely protected. This seems also to be true in Hong Kong (Davies, 1985) and on mainland Japan. Interestingly, in Dade County (Miami), Florida, the rate of occurrence among infants with Spanish surnames (predominantly Cuban) is only 0.22 per thousand total live births (1979–1983), as compared to 0.68 for other caucasians and 1.99 for non-whites (Copeland, 1987). Similarly, a 1986 study in Cook County (Chicago), Illinois, based on an analysis of 1,233 SIDS deaths, showed the rate to be 5.1 among blacks and 1.3 among whites, but only 1.2 among Hispanics, even though, in that locality, Hispanics are socio-economically disadvantaged (Black, David, Brouillette, & Hunt, 1986).

Birth weight and parity both affect risk for SIDS. There is an inverse relationship between birth weight and the relative risk for SIDS; the higher the birth weight, the lower the risk, and conversely, the lower the birth weight, the higher the risk. Perhaps as a consequence of that relationship, twins are at much greater risk than singletons, and triplets are much more at risk than twins.

Just as SIDS infants seem not to grow and develop in utero quite as well as other babies do, so they appear to lose ground after birth as well. According to data gathered by Naeye, Ladis, and Drage (1976) from the cerebral palsy study, the SIDS infants followed in that project were born at only the 40th percentile and, in the first four months of life—if they lived that long—they dropped to the 20th percentile. Possibly also related to this, infant "graduates" of neonatal intensive care nurseries are said to be at a tenfold increased risk (Sells, et al., 1983).

Maternal Factors

The group of mothers at greatest risk for losing their babies to SIDS are teenagers (Hoffman, et al., 1988). This is another inverse relationship for, once again, the younger the mother the greater her risk, and the older the mother the smaller her risk. Also, mothers who are anemic are more apt to lose their infants to SIDS than those who are not anemic (Hoffman, et al., 1988).

The infants of mothers who use illicit drugs or alcohol during pregnancy are at markedly increased risk for SIDS (Hoffman, et al., 1988; Valdes-Dapena & Steinschneider, 1983). The exception to this rule, in regard to maternal drug abuse, seems to be cocaine. According to at least one recent report, the risk of SIDS for mothers who abuse cocaine during pregnancy is not increased (Bauchner, et al., 1988). However, women who smoke cigarettes during pregnancy do have a significantly greater risk than those who do not smoke (Hoffman, et al., 1988; Valdes-Dapena & Steinschneider, 1983).

Other Epidemiological Factors

Most crib deaths occur "in the middle of the night," so to speak, usually between midnight and nine o'clock in the morning (Valdes-Dapena, 1963). This observation has led many to believe that SIDS is closely associated with sleep, even though, in the great majority of instances, the death is not actually observed.

Day of the week is unassociated with incidence of SIDS deaths (Borhani, Rooney, & Kraus, 1973), but the time of the year has a definite bearing on the rate of occurrence of these deaths. All over the world, more SIDS deaths occur when the weather is cold than when it is warm. In all of the United States, even in relatively warm places like Miami, most SIDS events take place during the months of January, February, and March. And in Australia, where winter occurs in June, July, and August, the peak incidence of SIDS appears during those very same months. In places where the climate is more nearly constant, such as Seattle and southern California, the discrepancy between the numbers of SIDS deaths in summer and in winter is not so obvious, but it exists nonetheless.

TWO CASE EXAMPLES

Case History #1

Baby S.G. was the second child of loving parents and died at the age of only 55 days. Her older brother was two at the time. The baby was being breast fed and, although occasionally fussy, she was essentially healthy and happy.

The day before her death, Baby S.G. had been ill with a little bronchitis; the night she died, she had a little trouble going to sleep. Her mother stayed up with her until half-past midnight, rocking her in a rocking chair in the living room. Finally, mother became so tired that she laid the baby in the bassinet there and went upstairs to awaken her husband. She asked him to sit with the baby for a while. Just before she fell asleep, she heard the infant cry a bit and then become quiet again as her father picked her up.

The next morning, Baby S.G.'s mother awoke at five thirty and went down-stairs, thinking to herself as she did so, how thoughtful her husband had been in letting her sleep so long. When she arrived in the living room, she saw her husband asleep on the couch and the baby lying in the bassinet. Looking at the baby—even from three feet away—she knew instantly that something was wrong, despite the fact that the infant looked the way she always did when asleep. The blankets were not out of place, and the child was lying on her tummy, as usual, with her hands on the two sides of her head.

Her heart racing, Baby S.G.'s mother bent down to listen for the baby's breathing. Hearing none, she seized the infant and started shaking her crying out, "On, my God! No!" The baby's father jumped up and cradled the infant in his arms while his wife could only scream. Because their son had begun to cry upstairs, both parents ran up to him, the father carrying the baby.

Mother telephoned 911 and was given instructions on how to perform cardiopulmonary resuscitation, which she relayed frantically to her husband. He put the baby on the floor and began to breathe into her mouth while his wife, rigid with fear, sat on the bed holding her little boy on her lap.

A few minutes later, a police officer came to the house. The parents spent quite a long time with him explaining everything they could about their baby. They did not want to stop talking because that would have meant accepting the fact that the infant was dead. A little later, the mother telephoned her sister, asking her to come and be with them. Soon thereafter, the medical examiner arrived, pronounced the baby dead, and explained to the parents than an autopsy would be required. The mother held the baby again for a while; then the medical examiner took the infant from her and left.

Shortly thereafter, a chaplain came to the house to comfort the grieving family. He explained to them that Sudden Infant Death Syndrome, which was what it seemed to him had happened in this instance, is unpredictable and unpreventable, and that they were not to blame themselves. The parents had difficulty believing that. Both of them felt that there must have been something that they could have done—and failed to do—that had caused their baby to die.

These parents now say that their lives will never be the same again. Their infant was, and still is, their second child and a very important part of the family. They visit her grave often and take little toys and flowers there for her. Even though months have passed since she died, they think of her every day and know that they will never forget her.

Case History #2

Baby T.S. was four months of age and an apparently healthy baby when he died suddenly and unexpectedly. His father and mother were young professional people who had been married for only two years. Their infant son had just had his four-month, well-baby check-up the day before he died. The doctor had pronounced him healthy and ready to start eating solid foods.

The morning of his death, since both of his parents worked, they dropped Baby T.S. off with his sitter. Later that day, his mother received a telephone call from the babysitter's son who reported to her that the baby had stopped breathing and that the paramedics had taken him to the hospital with the babysitter. The mother left her office immediately and drove as quickly as she could to the hospital where she was met by a doctor and a social worker. They escorted her to a room, and, even as they did so, she knew that her son had died.

The physician explained to her that the baby had, indeed, stopped breathing and that the attending staff had done everything in their power to resuscitate him, but to no avail. The mother remained in the hospital room, telephoning her family and friends, because she just had to talk with the people she knew and loved about her devastating loss and had to say it over and over again. Repeatedly, she would blurt out the words, "The baby's dead. They took him away."

The baby's father was working out of town that day and could not be located immediately. When he returned to his office, his supervisors told him that his son was in the hospital. Since it never occurred to him that the incident was of major significance, at first he attempted to finish his work before leaving. However, his supervisors insisted that he go right away—and so he went.

The first person he encountered at the hospital was his wife's father who was standing outside the building "white as a sheet" and unable to speak. Together they hurried inside to find the baby's mother who had to tell them twice that the baby had died. They cried and held the baby for a long time, hugging and caressing him. The social worker gave them a card from the local chapter of the National SIDS Foundation and told them that someone from that organization would contact them soon, to offer them information and support—whenever they might want it.

When father and mother returned together to their home, they found it full of family, friends, and co-workers who had come to offer their sympathy. For weeks, they continued to receive that kind of support. In addition, cards and notes arrived from a variety of other people in other places.

An autopsy was performed. The infant's death was officially attributed to Sudden Infant Death Syndrome.

These parents contacted the National SIDS Foundation directly and spoke with members of that organization and office staff almost daily for weeks after their tragic loss. In addition, as a member of the Employee Assistance Program at work, the mother was counseled by professionals there.

With the passage of time, these parents have become active in trying to help other SIDS families and they have participated recently in an appeal to Congress for an increase in federal funds for SIDS research. They now have a two-year-old child, a subsequent sibling, but make it clear that they will never forget the baby they lost. They are emphatic in stating that he changed their lives and will live forever for them as a real part of their family.

WHY IT IS IMPORTANT TO IDENTIFY THIS EVENT AS A SYNDROME

The medical dictionary defines a syndrome as a set of symptoms which occur together or the sum of the signs of any morbid state (Dorland, 1988). In fact, the way physicians conceive of it is the manner in which a certain condition presents itself or the way it appears. As physicians, we use the term "syndrome" when we do not know the real nature, let alone the cause, of the medical condition to which we are referring.

In that regard, then, the term "syndrome" is appropriate for this entity. SIDS presents as the sudden, unexpected, and unexplained death of an infant. We really know little more than that about it, for certain. SIDS may be a group of phenomena "dressed in the same clinical clothing." That is, it may involve several different mechanisms which superficially look alike to us, clinically and pathologically, at this time. Hence, calling it a syndrome, in a sense, "keeps us honest." It says no more than we mean.

At the same time, there is a special power in being able to name any phenomenon. To speak of a sudden infant death *syndrome* is to identify a recognizable pattern or constellation of events. Although this pattern can be verified only by autopsy, its identification by experienced professionals carries great significance. For example, in 1979 "Sudden Infant Death Syndrome" was approved by the World Health Organization as a distinct and official cause of death, and in recent years both the phrase itself and its acronym, "SIDS," have become common. Such labelling may not appear notable to the casual observer, but it heralds the beginning of systematic record keeping upon which epidemiological and pathological research can be founded. Also, naming the syndrome is a powerful tool in counseling SIDS survivors and in seeking to relieve them of unjustified guilt.

SIDS AND ITS CHALLENGES

SIDS challenges all of us—physicians, scientists, counselors, helpers, and lay persons—in many ways. In the first place, SIDS remains an unpredictable, unpreventable, and unexplainable tragedy—a situation in which we are unable to do anything for the infant who has died. Thus, SIDS demands that we unravel its mystery, find its cause or causes, and learn how to prevent it from happening. In the second place, SIDS calls upon us to set aside inappropriate accusations of child abuse and to find ways to assist parents, family members, and all of those who are affected by the infant's death. Finally, the practical realities of the SIDS phenomenon challenge us to raise the funds that are essential for SIDS-related research, education, and counseling.

REFERENCES

Adelson, L. (1965). Specific studies of infant victims of sudden death. In R. J. Wedgwood & E. P. Benditt (Eds.), *Sudden death in infants: Proceedings of the conference on causes of sudden death in infants* (pp. 11–36). Bethesda, MD: U.S. Department of

Health, Education, and Welfare, Public Health Service, National Institutes of Health, National Institute of Child Health and Human Development. PHS Pub. No. 1412.

Bauchner, H., Zuckerman, B., McClain, M., Frank, D., Fried, L., & Kayne, H. (1988). Risk of sudden infant death syndrome among infants with in utero exposure to cocaine. *The Journal of Pediatrics, 113*, 831–834.

Beckwith, J. B. (1970). Discussion of terminology and definition of the sudden infant death syndrome. In A. B. Bergman, J. B. Beckwith, & C. G. Ray (Eds.), *Sudden infant death syndrome: Proceedings of the second international conference on causes of sudden death in infants* (p. 14–22). Seattle: University of Washington Press.

Bergman, A. B., Beckwith, J. B., & Ray, C. G. (Eds.) (1970). *Sudden infant death syndrome: Proceedings of the second international conference on causes of sudden death in infants.* Seattle: University of Washington Press.

Black, L., David, R. J., Brouillette, R. T., & Hunt, C. E. (1986). Effects of birth weight and ethnicity on incidence of sudden infant death syndrome. *The Journal of Pediatrics, 108*, 209–214.

Borhani, N. O., Rooney, P. A., & Kraus, J. F. (1973). Postneonatal sudden unexplained death in a California county. *California Medicine, 118*, 12–16.

Carr, J. L. (1945). Status thymico-lymphaticus. *American Journal of Pediatrics, 27*, 1–43.

Copeland, A. R. (1987). Sudden infant death syndrome (SIDS): The metropolitan Dade County experience, 1979–1983. *Medicine, Science and the Law, 27*, 283–287.

Davies, D. P. (1985). Cot death in Hong Kong: A rare problem? *The Lancet, 2*, 1346–1348.

Dorland's illustrated medical dictionary (27th ed.) (1988). Philadelphia: W. B. Saunders.

Farber, S. (1934). Fulminating streptococcus infections in infancy as a cause of sudden death. *New England Journal of Medicine, 211*, 154–159.

Farber, S. (1938). Unexpected death in early life. *New England Journal of Medicine, 219*, 836–841.

Garrow, I., & Werne, J. (1953). Sudden, apparently unexplained death during infancy. III. Pathologic findings in infants dying immediately after violence, contrasted with those after sudden, apparently unexplained death. *American Journal of Pathology, 29*, 833–851.

Goldberg, J., Hornung, R., Yamashita, T., & Wehrmacher, W. (1986). Age at death and risk factors in sudden infant death syndrome. *Australian Pediatric Journal, 21*, Suppl. 1, 21–28.

Hasselmeyer, E. G., & Knox, G. E. (Eds.) (1972–1976). Research planning workshops on the sudden infant death syndrome, Nos. 1–12. Washington, DC: Department of Health, Education, and Welfare.

Hoffman, H. J., Damus, K., Hillman, L., & Krongrad, E. (1988). Risk factors for SIDS: Results of the National Institute for Child Health and Human Development cooperative epidemiologic study. *Annals of the New York Academy of Sciences, 533*, 13–30.

Jones, A. M., & Weston, J. T. (1976). The examination of the sudden infant death syndrome infant: Investigative and autopsy protocols. *Journal of Forensic Sciences, 21*, 833–841.

Kaplan, D. W., Bauman, A. E., & Krous, H. F. (1984). Epidemiology of the sudden infant death syndrome in American Indians. *Pediatrics, 74*, 1041–1046.

Lee, C. K. (1842). On the thymus gland, its marked affections and the diseases that arise from its abnormal enlargement. *American Journal of Medical Sciences, 3*, 135–154.

Naeye, R. L., Ladis, R., & Drage, J. S. (1976). Sudden infant death syndrome: A prospective study. *American Journal of Diseases of Children, 130*, 1207–1210.

Sells, C. J., Neff, T. E., Bennett, F. C., & Robinson, N. M. (1983). Mortality in infants discharged from a neonatal intensive care unit. *American Journal of Diseases of Children, 137*, 44–47.

Templeman, C. (1892). 258 cases of suffocation of infants. *Edinburgh Medical Journal, 38*, 322–329.

Valdes-Dapena, M. (1963). Sudden and unexpected death in infants: The scope of our ignorance. *Pediatric Clinics of North America, 10*, 693–704.

Valdes-Dapena, M. (1988). Sudden infant death syndrome: Overview of recent research developments from a pediatric pathologist's perspective. *Pediatrician, 15*, 222–230.

Valdes-Dapena, M., & Steinschneider, A. (1983). Sudden infant death syndrome (SIDS), apnea, and near miss for SIDS. *Emergency Medical Clinics of North America, 1*, 27–44.

Werne, J., & Garrow, I. (1953a). Sudden, apparently unexplained death during infancy. I. Pathologic findings in infants found dead. *American Journal of Pathology, 29*, 633–675.

Werne, J., & Garrow, I. (1953b). Sudden, apparently unexplained death during infancy. II. Pathologic findings in infants observed to die suddenly. *American Journal of Pathology, 29*, 817–827.

CHAPTER 2

Theories and Research

Laura S. Hillman

WHY THIS CHAPTER?

This chapter provides a review of the principal theoretical accounts and research efforts in the area of Sudden Infant Death Syndrome (SIDS). Its aim is twofold: (1) to be sufficiently inclusive to be useful to physicians, nurses, and other caregivers in their own understanding of SIDS and in their roles as interpreters of scientific work to lay questioners; and (2) to be readable for SIDS families, students, and professionals whose primary concern is with psychosocial aspects of SIDS. As part of the effort to reassure families that they did not do or fail to do anything which resulted in the death of their infant, evidence is offered that many potential causes of SIDS have been investigated and shown not to be significant. This review can also be used to rebut bizarre theories and misinformation about SIDS which arise periodically in the popular media.

WHY HAVE WE NOT FOUND A SOLUTION TO SIDS?

One of the major frustrations for SIDS parents and professionals dealing with SIDS is why it is taking so long to find a solution. People see steady progress in the fights against cancer or heart disease. They observe rapid progress in the solution and treatment for diseases such as Legionnaires, and they wonder why the same has not yet happened for SIDS. The major difference is that in SIDS there are no *living* patients to study. It is only fortuitously (or with an extraordinary mass effort) that a SIDS infant is studied prior to death. There is no way to "look at" the disease and its effects prior to death. There is no way to do sophisticated testing or to obtain reliable samples. Most of the classical pathways of medical research are blocked by the lack of a living subject to study.

Once medicine has a good idea of a problem, then animal models can often be used to work out its detailed pathophysiology. There are inbred strains of rats and mice which clinically manifest many disease entities. However, there are no naturally occurring animal models for SIDS, and our level of current knowledge is just now getting to the point of identifying a number of artificially created models which could possibly be related to SIDS. In other diseases, scientists have been able to identify "high-risk groups" as subsets of the general population in which the natural history of a disease can be followed with smaller numbers of subjects. In SIDS, the "risk factors" are not strong enough or, more importantly, specific enough to allow identification of a very-high-risk group. For example, siblings of SIDS infants, although they represent the general population, probably have a risk for SIDS of less than 1%. Other groups with a significant but still small increased risk of SIDS (e.g., premature infants and Apparent Life-Threatening Events [ALTE] infants) do not represent the general population or the general population of SIDS, and therefore may lend only more confusion to the issues.

Thus, the study of SIDS has been hampered without: (1) living patients; (2) an animal model; or (3) an appropriate high risk population. This is not to say that progress has not been made. Large numbers of SIDS infants can and have been studied in two areas: (1) epidemiology; and (2) pathology. Also, small numbers of SIDS infants have been studied prior to death either fortuitously or through large studies of the general population.

WHAT HAVE WE LEARNED FROM EPIDEMIOLOGY?

Through epidemiologic studies of vital records, interviews with parents, and review of previously recorded medical records, an attempt has been made to describe those to whom SIDS happens (unfortunately almost anyone) and to try to piece together the "medical history" prior to death. This data collection seeks to identify a high-risk group for intensive study. Unfortunately, most SIDS cases happen to *low-risk* people. Epidemiologic study occasionally yields the "magical clue" or "the red flag" that will allow the unraveling of the mystery. So far, that clue has not shown up, has not been recognized, or does not exist. Still, epidemiological data bases are most helpful in designing and testing hypotheses. If a given theory does not fit with the known epidemiology of SIDS, then it is not a very promising theory. For example, the fact that fewer SIDS infants were immunized and that the time distribution from immunizations to death were the same as from immunizations to interview for control infants made a causal relationship between DPT and SIDS essentially impossible. So what has epidemiology told us about SIDS?

The most characteristic finding about SIDS is the *age* at death (Goldberg, et al., 1986). The age range of SIDS deaths is far more narrowly focused than the age range for most disease processes. The incidence of deaths due to most diseases either steadily falls with increasing age (e.g., all the problems of prematurity, prenatal insults, and congenital malformations) or steadily increases with age (e.g., accidents and malignancies). SIDS has a distinctive peak. It is rare in the first several weeks of life, rapidly peaks at two to four months, and then rapidly falls until six months, with a slow fall in the risk of cases out to about two years of age (more than 95% are within the first year).

The most incredible aspect of this distribution of age at death is that it is not altered by other risk factors (e.g., babies of young mothers die at the same age as babies of older mothers). Usually, gestation at birth (was the infant term or premature, and, if premature, how premature?) is the most important of these other risk factors, but SIDS researchers (Goldberg, et al., 1986) found that at least birth weight did not change the age at death. Another recent study (Grether & Schulman, 1989) shows a partial shift of premature infants to an older age at death. Death from SIDS appears to be timed more from when the infants are born, than from when the infants should have been born. This is important for theories that SIDS happens at a critical stage of development (in which case premature infants should be older when they die) or theories that SIDS is a function of immaturity (and thus premature infants should die even sooner).

The second major epidemiological factor is the *time* of death. There is a seasonality to SIDS with the highest incidence being reported either in the late fall or winter, intermediate numbers of cases in the spring, and lower incidence in the summer (Steele, 1970). This factor is so pronounced that SIDS professionals soon learn to plan their vacations and non-counseling projects accordingly. This seasonal incidence is important in theories of viral infection triggers or theories of temperature regulation. Some studies have suggested that the incidence of SIDS is higher on weekends, which might suggest a careful look at family dynamics and "stress" situations as triggers of SIDS.

SIDS most often occurs between midnight and 6:00 A.M., the most common long-sleep period for the three-month-old and certainly for his or her parents (Bergman, 1970). Since this long-sleep period usually involves a long period of "fasting" and several important hormones have day/night cycles, this may play an important role in theories of possible metabolic derangements or nutritional deficiencies. Finally, and most importantly, the timing of the SIDS death appears related to the state of activity of the infant, with most and probably all of SIDS deaths occurring during sleep. It would be very helpful to know during what sleep state(s) SIDS occurs, but these data are not available. A great deal of effort has been spent to define the maturation of sleep physiology during the SIDS age range. Suffice it to say that during this age range many changes are taking place and that many crucial relationships to the control of both respirations and cardiac function are evolving (Harper, et al., 1978).

To Whom Does SIDS Happen?

Beyond age at death and time of death there are a number of very unspecific risk factors for SIDS. Race appears to be a risk factor with rates among the black population being twice that of the non-black population, and with oriental populations having equal or lower rates (Grether & Schulman, 1989; Hoffman, et al., 1988). Clearly, "race" is highly confounded by multiple aspects of "life styles," so that the meaning of this risk factor remains unclear. Males are at somewhat higher risk than females, with about 60% of SIDS infants in a recent, large-scale series being males (Hoffman, et al., 1988). Again, no reason for the increased risk in males is apparent.

One of the highest risk factors shown in many studies is young maternal age (Kraus & Borhani, 1972). This is a risk factor for much of infant mortality and applies more specifically to SIDS when one looks at age of first pregnancy. This relates to another risk factor—high parity. In SIDS, there is a relative sparing of the first-born, but risk increases steadily with increasing parity. There is a synergistic effect of maternal age and parity, that is, the risk will be higher for the 18-year-old with her third infant than for the 16-year-old with her first infant. Multiple, closely spaced pregnancies at a time when the mother may herself still be growing and developing could set the stage for a number of potential prenatal or postnatal insults and could fit with a number of types of theories, such as, nutritional deficiencies, sexually-transmitted infections, or being emotionally overwhelmed.

By most markers of socioeconomic status, such as maternal education, income, legitimacy, or housing, the risk of SIDS is higher among lower socioeconomic segments of the population (Biering-Sorensen, Jorgensen, & Hilden, 1979). Additionally, ramifications for access to health care, nutritional adequacy, adequacy of emotional support, effects of crowding on infection, etc., are great. Countries with socialized health care systems (e.g., Sweden, England, and Israel) have traditionally had lower SIDS rates. Thus, many initially thought that SIDS would decrease (as has much of the rest of infant mortality) just through social reforms and provision of adequate health care. Unfortunately, SIDS rates have not fallen and in many of the countries with lower rates, such as Scandinavian countries and England, rates are actually rising. The problem with socioeconomic status and all of the other risk factors is that they are either not changeable or not easily changed. However, over and above that, they do not apply to the majority of SIDS cases. The great majority of SIDS cases happen to *low*-risk people, such as first infants of middle class, white women in their mid-twenties who have had excellent prenatal and postnatal care.

Researchers have looked at recurrence risk of SIDS in attempts to deal with the question of whether there is a genetic predisposition to SIDS. Clearly, there is no classical inheritance pattern in SIDS. Although SIDS rates are higher in twins, there is no increased incidence in monozygotic (identical) versus dizygotic (non-identical) twins, which suggests that there is not a strong genetic inheritance (Peterson, Chin, & Fisher, 1980). While an increased recurrence risk of SIDS has been reported for many years, in more recent studies this seems to be falling, with the largest and most recent study showing a recurrent risk of about 0.8% (3–4 times the national rate) (Peterson, Sabotta, & Daling, 1986). Even this increased risk was not statistically significant. J. Goldberg (personal communication, September, 1988) examined the previously described risk factors, particularly those reflective of socioeconomic status, in a large Chicago population and found that families with recurrent SIDS were even more "high risk." That is, whatever adverse factors were present during one pregnancy and infancy may have been present during subsequent pregnancies and infancies.

Nevertheless, the large group of infant deaths associated with SIDS is certainly "contaminated" by *small* numbers of cases which look on the surface like SIDS but have a definable cause. For example, we learned from the botulism theory of SIDS that infant botulism can rarely masquerade as SIDS and thus "contaminate" SIDS (Arnon, et al., 1978). The most recent group of diseases seen as possible "contaminants" are a group of inborn errors of fatty acid metabolism which are inherited with a one-in-four (25%) chance of recurrence. If these can be properly diagnosed and thus separated from SIDS, it is possible that much of the apparent recurrence risk can also be removed from SIDS.

Are the Pregnancies Different?

The two strikingly increased factors related to SIDS are premature birth and in utero growth retardation. Prematurity and in utero growth retardation (IUGR) share much of the epidemiology of SIDS just described and it is possible that they may share predisposing factors. Prematurity, IUGR, and SIDS may all be viewed as poor pregnancy outcomes. Since it is possible that some of the roots of SIDS are prenatal, it is important to look carefully at the pregnancies that produce infants who ultimately die of SIDS. The two major studies where this has been done are the National Collaborative Perinatal [NCP] study done in the late 1950s which collected data prospectively from 50,000 pregnancies which led to the expected 125 SIDS deaths, and the NIH Collaborative SIDS [NIH] study of 800 SIDS and 1600 control infants which reviewed medical records retrospectively. Generally, SIDS pregnancies were unimpressive and differed little from control pregnancies.

Three potential complications deserve attention: blood pressure, anemia, and infection. In no studies has hypertension or toxemia been associated with SIDS, but Naeye's analysis of data from the NCP study suggested that maternal hypotension may play a role (Naeye, 1976). This could not be supported by the NIH study. Naeye also found significant maternal anemia to be a risk factor, but the NIH study showed only a mild, third trimester anemia associated with SIDS. The NIH study showed an incidence of urinary tract infection of 15% in SIDS versus 10% of controls. This had been previously reported in British studies (Carpenter & Emery, 1974) but had not been seen in the NCP study. The incidence of other infections in the mother or the infant or of predisposing conditions like premature rupture of membranes does not appear increased in SIDS.

The possibility of increased exposure to toxins or teratogens was raised by the finding that a high percentage of SIDS mothers smoked during pregnancy (70% SIDS vs. 40% controls in the NIH study) (Hoffman, et al., 1988). This has been seen in multiple studies. Soon after, the increased risk associated with drug use (methadone, heroin, marijuana, etc.) during pregnancy was appreciated (Chavez, et al., 1979; Rosen & Johnson, 1988). More recently, maternal use of cocaine has initially been reported to have a high incidence of sudden death, but subsequent reports have not borne this out. That maternal nutritional factors could play a role is suggested by both the mild anemia and an increased incidence of low maternal weight gain (gain less than 20 lbs.).

Delivery factors do not appear to play a role and there are no differences in routes of delivery, delivery complications, anesthesia, and so on (Naeye, Ladis, & Drage, 1976). Further, when corrected for gestation, there are no differences in the condition of the infant at birth as reflected by Apgar scores (Hoffman, et al., 1988).

The NCP study was undertaken in 1950–1960, and the NIH study was conducted in 1979. Over the last 10 years, there has been intense interest in developing better methods to measure fetal well being. Remarkable advances in ultrasound technology have led to the ability to watch infants move and breath in utero, to watch contractions of the infant heart, and to learn slowly how these are affected by stimuli such as noise or by adverse conditions such as lack of oxygen. This type of monitoring has led to the delivery "just in the nick of time" of many compromised fetuses, but is not sensitive enough to predict most clearly bad outcomes. Whether this type of technology will be capable of detecting more subtle, possibly transient, insults or developmentally delayed patterns remains to be seen. More sophisticated methods of measuring fetal heart rate patterns and of actually looking at umbilical artery blood flow by doppler technology may also shed new light.

Are the Infants Identifiable at Birth?

As a group, SIDS infants differ at birth from the general population by the high percentage of premature births (approximately 18%) and the high percentage of infants with defined IUGR (approximately 9%) (Hoffman, et al., 1988; Protestos, et al., 1973). Because of the high percentage of premature or IUGR SIDS infants, any sign, symptom, treatment, abnormal lab test, and so on, will be increased in the SIDS group compared to a randomly selected control group. Knowing this, the NIH study carefully matched case and controls for birth weight less than 2500 gms in 250 gm weight increments. This matching made the majority of differences between SIDS cases and controls disappear, although there were enough premature infants (less than 37 weeks gestation) who weighed greater than 2500 gms and enough marginally growth-retarded SIDS infants to leave some differences. Once both SIDS and control infants were separated into three groups—premature infants, term but growth-retarded infants, and term appropriately-grown infants—then essentially all differences disappeared. The premature SIDS infants acted as other premature infants and as a group did not seem sicker or less mature. IUGR infants were also similar. Most important, in the majority (approximately 70%) of the term appropriately grown infants there were no differences between SIDS and controls except for growth parameters. Even if not qualifying as growth-retarded, SIDS infants greater than 2500 gms who were not matched by birth weight were smaller and shorter than controls. Head circumferences were not different. This degree of in utero growth retardation has been reported in other studies (Peterson, et al., 1974). This effect is not totally accounted for by the contributing factor of a high incidence of maternal smoking. Studies by Peterson have shown that there is a failure to catch up of this IUGR, as is characteristic of the growth retardation seen with smoking, and that there is even additional postnatal growth retardation (Peterson, et al., 1974). The NIH data confirmed these findings. Many physicians, particularly in Britain, have focused on postnatal growth as an important monitor for following siblings of SIDS infants.

No differences were seen in symptoms once infants were divided by gestation and growth (Hoffman, et al., 1988). Very specifically, no increases in neonatal apnea or gastroesophageal (G.E.) reflux were seen when controlled for gestation and growth. Tachycardia also disappeared. Absolute values and variability of heart rate, respiratory rate, and temperature were all more related to gestation, growth, race, and sex than SIDS-control by analysis of variance. Laboratory values and treatments required were also similar. Clearly as individuals, infants who ultimately died of SIDS could not be picked out from other infants. Even as a group, the data did not allow for the generation of a high-risk profile with enough specificity to be of much use for prospective studies.

Are There Differences in These Infants' Short Lives?

As discussed, a mild postnatal growth retardation and a failure of "catch-up" growth in infants with IUGR has been seen in several studies. The potential etiologies for such growth failure postnatally are as varied as prenatally. Looking at the diets of infants who die of SIDS one finds no striking differences from control infants. In 1979 the percentage of infants who were totally breast fed was significantly lower in the SIDS group and this difference could not be abolished by controlling for other socioeconomic factors (Hoffman, et al., 1988). However, the percentage of totally breast fed infants was low in both groups, and the marked increases in breast feedings that have occurred in the ensuing 10 years certainly have not decreased the incidence of SIDS.

Infants who die of SIDS do seem to have an increase in gastrointestinal symptoms, such as vomiting and diarrhea (Hoffman, et al., 1988). However, these could not be linked to feeding practices. There also was not an increase in what would be considered gastroesophageal reflux, a common theory of SIDS in the late 1970s with the suggestion that surgical fundoplication could prevent SIDS. These symptoms were usually linked to other symptoms, such as fever or upper respiratory tract infection (URI), suggesting more frequent gastroenteritis in the weeks but not the 24 hours prior to death. Gastroenteritis was the leading cause of hospital admissions in both SIDS and controls. SIDS infants had more hospitalizations, but the distribution of the diagnosis was the same. It is unclear whether this increase in hospitalization was related to: (1) the infant being sicker; (2) there being a delay in seeking medical care; or (3) a reluctance to treat the patient as an outpatient because of the socioeconomic situation.

Much discussion has occurred regarding the role of viruses as "trigger mechanisms" in SIDS. The group of viruses of primary concern have been the respiratory viruses. Multiple studies of SIDS have shown that one-third to two-thirds of the infants have had URIs during the several weeks prior to death (Scott, et al., 1978). A surprise of the NIH study was that the incidence was equally high in the control groups and that the incidence is distributed over weeks, not immediately prior to death (Hoffman, et al., 1988). Over 50% of SIDS autopsies give supporting evidence that a respiratory virus has been present in the recent past. Multiple theories can be put forth as to how a virus could trigger death in a particular vulnerable infant while most infants make uneventful recoveries. These could range from acute changes in upper airway resistance to temporally delayed effects on broncholar reactivity. Several respiratory infections (RSV, chlamydia) have apnea as one of their more disturbing symptoms (Bruhn, Mokrohisky, & McIntosh, 1977).

Either with or without infection, evidence of increased apnea in SIDS infants was not found in the medical record (Hoffman, et al., 1988). Only two of 800 SIDS infants ever had a documented Apparent Life Threatening Event (ALTE). On interview, with an incredible bias, only 7% of SIDS parents (vs. 3% of controls) ever described an episode of "stopped breathing or turning blue." The descriptions of these events were not different from the control infants, with most episodes occurring while the infant was awake and/or feeding. Although this clearly represents the bias of when parents can be expected to be paying close attention to their infants, it is also consistent with the prospectively collected data of Steinschneider, Weinstein, and Diamond (1982) who found evidence of respiratory control difficulties during feeding in half of the infants who went on to die of SIDS. Clearly, coordination of eating and breathing requires more study. However, the conclusion of the NIH study and the experience of many people would lean toward considering SIDS and ALTE infants as two separate populations with an unknown but small degree of overlap (Hunt & Brouillette, 1987).

Finally, a major area of concern was the association of SIDS to immunizations. Several SIDS clusters and poorly controlled studies had suggested a causal link between DPT and SIDS (with further amplification by the lay press). Fortunately, the data were being collected by the NIH study and a special analysis showed no temporal or incidence association between SIDS and DPT (Hoffman, et al., 1987). Indeed, probably because DPT is a good marker of both the amount of "well baby care" and of "wellness" at the time of care, there is a statistically significant "protective" effect of DPT. Several other studies have now supported a lack of association between SIDS and immunizations.

This review of the epidemiology of SIDS may also be helpful in a programmatic sense in that it may tell the inexperienced SIDS professional what to expect. It is no accident that one: (1) frequently has to deal with very young parents; (2) has a whole intensive care nursery upset over the loss of one of their graduates; (3) has a surviving twin to worry about; (4) has clusters of SIDS; (5) has a pathologist who signs out the death as "viral pneumonitis"; or (6) has a family with no money for burial.

WHAT HAVE WE LEARNED FROM PATHOLOGY?

An autopsy is for the parents' benefit, to answer the questions that they have now and/or will have years from now. With the current definition of SIDS, an autopsy is the only way to truly say the death was SIDS and not something else. Given a SIDS history, it is rare to find something that someone could have done something about. Thus, counseling that the death could not have been predicted or prevented is usually relevant in either case. However, if the diagnosis is something other than SIDS, then there may be a causal explanation which will be far more satisfying to the family than what we are able to offer as the cause of SIDS. In a very few cases, a diagnosis will be made which has possible genetic implications and could be relevant to future pregnancies. This could particularly be the case if inborn errors of fatty acid metabolism do masquerade as SIDS and are as common as predicted.

From the scientific perspective, good autopsies keep our data on SIDS clean so that studies such as those already described can be done without extraneous data. In areas where specific research is ongoing on SIDS pathology, routine SIDS autopsies often provide the samples necessary for further detailed research study. Unless such specific studies are ongoing in a specific location, the routine autopsy cannot be expected to "contribute to medical knowledge." That is not its purpose. The purpose of the autopsy is to establish the diagnosis of SIDS.

What Is the Pathology of SIDS?

By definition, the SIDS autopsy fails to find recognized abnormalities which are *sufficient to cause death*. That does not mean that no minor abnormalities can be present. Clearly, by history many infants who die of SIDS have had a "cold" within the weeks prior to death. So it is not surprising to find evidence of a previous or ongoing viral infection on the postmortem examination. When attempts have been made to culture virus from SIDS infants at autopsy many different viruses are found. The same can be said for infants dying of other causes (Brandt, 1970). A severe bacterial pneumonia which might be expected to cause death can easily be distinguished from SIDS.

Some cases of SIDS still continue to be labeled as "viral pneumonitis," which is the pathologist's attempt to describe what is seen while clearly distinguishing the case from bacterial pneumonia. Unfortunately, parents are not trained to make this distinction and this diagnosis is often translated in their minds to "pneumonia" which they believe should have been recognized in their infant and prevented with a shot of penicillin.

Similarly, minor congenital abnormalities, such as a small Ventricular Septal Defect, which do not normally cause death can be incidental findings in a SIDS autopsy. It is the responsibility of the pathologist to establish the cause of death (SIDS or another process known to cause death) and to separate this from incidental or possible contributory factors. Pathologists are increasingly recognizing the importance of identifying SIDS as the cause of death on autopsy reports and death certificates. But in many areas, some review and interpretation of autopsy reports is still necessary. SIDS professionals can work closely with individual pathologists on a case-by-case basis to establish working understandings, but this takes time.

In 1976, an investigative and autopsy protocol for making the diagnosis of SIDS was developed (Jones & Weston, 1976) and distributed to serve as a unifying document for SIDS autopsies and a basis for future revisions. In medicine, both the *history* and the *physical examination* are necessary to make the correct diagnosis; in pathology, both the *investigation* and the *autopsy* are needed to make the postmortem diagnosis. One article (Bass, Kravath, & Glass, 1986) suggested that careful investigation could reduce all of SIDS to accidental (or not accidental) death. This article appropriately outraged SIDS professionals and parents alike, but it also caused some professionals to confess that in recent years workloads and budget crunches may have led to inadequate history taking and that this area possibly needed improvement.

Clearly, having an accurate diagnosis of SIDS is important for both epidemiologic and pathologic research. Each investigator needs to define very carefully the population studied (e.g., were infants with infection included, what age range was allowed), and uniformity among investigators is certainly desirable. However, there has grown up a myth in many people's minds that we have not solved SIDS because our study populations are "dirty," that SIDS is a "wastebasket" containing multiple diseases or causes, and that if we can just define a group of "pure SIDS" answers will be obvious.

We do know that there are other causes of death that can masquerade as SIDS, but these are far less common, and awareness and ability to sort those other causes out is increasing. In the NIH study of SIDS, all cases had both the investigation reports and autopsies reviewed by a panel of three forensic pathologists. In 97% of cases referred to the study as SIDS, the panel concurred that they were indeed SIDS (Hoffman, et al., 1988). Had the panel not existed, the 3% of infants who were referred as SIDS but were something else would not have altered the data. The "answers" to SIDS have not been hidden or buried; they either are not there, or perhaps we are not asking the right questions or using the right technology *yet*!

What *is* a problem in SIDS is the heterogeneity and paucity of *control* infants, infants who have died of something other than SIDS. The only truly appropriate controls are sudden death accident victims who were known to be healthy prior to death. These are very rare in the SIDS age range where infants are not mobile and are in close contact with adults. A number of erroneous conclusions about SIDS have been made because of inadequate control groups. Establishing banks of specimens from appropriate control infants to be used by multiple investigators has long been thought necessary and may one day become a reality.

Are There Positive Findings in SIDS?

Having defined what SIDS is not, can one make a *positive* diagnosis of SIDS? Currently, there is no pathological hallmark of SIDS. That is, there is no single finding observed in all cases clearly confirming that they are SIDS. However, most pathologists who do many SIDS autopsies seem to have a positive "Gestalt" in most cases. The factors which contribute to this are largely in the lungs, with edema, hemorrhage, and the unique distribution of petechiae prominent. Between 50 to 85% of SIDS cases have petechiae (small broken blood vessels) found on the surface of the heart and lungs, and on the surface of the thymus gland adjacent to the lungs (Beckwith, 1970). Much speculation has been given to what terminal mechanism could produce this unique distribution (such petechiae are not found elsewhere in the body). The leading candidate is one form of upper (or lower) airway obstruction. In almost all cases, the lungs are heavy with pulmonary edema fluid and often this is seen coming from the nose or mouth at the death scene. This has long been dismissed as a nonspecific finding, but investigators are now looking at possible mechanisms that may be specific.

The rest of the "positive" findings in SIDS require a microscope and usually special techniques to process the specimens and examine them. Much of the controversy that has surrounded some of the "positive" findings in SIDS has revolved around which is the appropriate technique to use. Naeye (1980) led the search for microscopic abnormalities in an attempt to confirm or refute a theory of chronic hypoxia consistent with the then-popular theory of sleep apnea. His seven markers of chronic hypoxia have stood the test of time to varying degrees. Increased retention of brown fat around the adrenals has been confirmed, but only in the older SIDS infant (Valdes-Dapena, 1983). However, the adrenal glands themselves appear normal. Increased hematopoiesis in the liver has been found, but only in less than 20% of SIDS infants (people have begun to focus on fatty infiltration or fibrosis of the liver as possibly important, and the area of liver histology needs more work) (Valdes-Dapena, 1983).

Evidence for pulmonary vascular hypertension was reported as both increased thickness of the pulmonary artery walls and increased muscle mass of the right ventricle. While the changes in the right ventricle have not been confirmed, the presence of increased vessel wall remains a battle of methods, with variable results depending on the method of quantitation (Singer, 1983). It is certainly not an easily recognizable abnormality. While abnormalities of carotid body size have not been confirmed, closer examination of carotid bodies from SIDS infants has suggested both electron microscopic differences (Perrin, et al., 1984a) and an increase in dopamine concentration (Perrin, et al., 1984b); however, both of these findings await confirmation after five years because of the difficulty of the methodology. By far, the most exciting of these potential findings has been the brain stem gliosis (Naeye, 1976).

When nerve cells are hurt they become surrounded by glial cells, primarily the astrocytes or "nursemaid cells." Several investigators have now described increased gliosis in areas of the brain stem in infants dying of SIDS, and evidence of actual neuronal dropout (death) may be on the way (Kinney, et al., 1983). This could be due to some sort of injury (hypoxia being only one possibility) or it could be a developmental abnormality. In and of themselves, these findings are non-specific; they could represent part of a cause or a consequence. Attempts are being made to identify the specific areas involved in order to try to predict what physiological consequences such areas of damage might have. So far, the distribution of injury does not make obvious sense.

These findings have prompted a closer look at neuroanatomy in SIDS. A number of abnormalities have been reported, but none have been confirmed: (1) failure of dendritic spines to regress (Quattrochi, et al., 1980); (2) an immature distribution of cells in the cerebellum (unpublished); and (3) decreased myelinization and abnormal fiber size distribution in the vagus (Sachis, et al., 1981). All of these could represent maturational delays or the effect of many different types of injury (e.g., hypoxia, toxins, infections, nutritional deficiencies). The type of abnormalities would suggest that the "injury" would have needed to be present over weeks and that it would have needed to be present in the SIDS age range. This does not preclude that it was present earlier, even before birth, but it may not be consistent with an early in utero insult which then went away. However, all of these data need to be confirmed and greatly extended, and much more *normal* neuroanatomy known before even these speculations can be entertained.

Several histological investigators have looked carefully at the cardiac conducting system and proclaimed it healthy. However, this is probably the best example of how anatomy cannot predict physiology. Abnormalities of functional conduction can only be studied in the living infant.

Similarly, investigators have had limited success trying to look at metabolic and endocrine problems postmortem. Postmortem enzymes are degraded or stimulated, and substances change compartments—in particular, cellular components leak out of dead cells. It is hard to predict ahead of time what will happen to a given hormone, enzyme, or cofactor, and it becomes exceedingly important that adequate samples from appropriate dead control infants be available. A prime example of this was the thyroid story.

Whereas reverse T_3, and TSH are stable postmortem, T_4 is converted to T_3 postmortem by increased enzyme activity, so that T_3 is elevated in postmortem blood. In infants who have been sick prior to death T_4 is decreased (the sick euthyroid syndrome) so that there is less substrate for the enzyme to work on and T_3 is normal. Thus, dead control infants who were sick prior to death have normal T_3 levels and dead control infants who were healthy prior to death have elevated T_3 levels comparable to the SIDS infants. In short, the elevation of T_3 confirms that the SIDS infants were generally healthy prior to death (Schwartz, et al., 1983). Some hormones are stable, and cortisol and parathyroid hormone appear normal (Hillman, Erickson, & Haddad, 1980; Schwartz, et al., 1983). Vitamins E and D as measured by 25-hydroxy vitamin D appear normal (Hillman, Erickson, & Haddad, 1980; Schrauzer, Rhead, & Saltzstein, 1975).

Thiamin deficiency has been considered because of its importance in neurological function and the similarity of the age distribution of SIDS and infantile beriberi. It was felt that normal postmortem measurements of the thiamin dependent enzyme transketothiolase ruled out deficiency (Peterson, et al., 1981). However, measurements of postmortem serum thiamin were markedly elevated and the question of thiamin excess was even raised. The elevation was another postmortem artifact (Wyatt, et al., 1984). Unfortunately, it interferes with the assay used to rule out deficiency, so that the question of deficiency remains unanswered. A marginal deficiency of biotin in liver has been reported but not confirmed (Johnson, Hood, & Emery, 1980). Other vitamins remain to be studied and postmortem effects are unknown.

Minerals can be studied in tissues and extracellular minerals in serum. So far, deficiencies of calcium, magnesium, copper, and zinc have probably been ruled out (Erickson, et al., 1983b). Increased levels of lead, but not cadmium, have been reported, but the significance of this remains unclear (Erickson, et al., 1983a).

PEPCK, a key enzyme in the production of glucose in the liver, has been reported in a non-peer reviewed publication to be low in SIDS (Silverstein, et al., 1983); however, this has not been confirmed. Attempts have not been made, probably with good reason considering the chance of success, for multiple other enzymes. Recently, investigators have begun to look for defects in fatty acid metabolism in SIDS by looking for buildups of precursors. The most common enzyme deficiency in this family of defects is MCAT, and initially researchers estimated that about 10% of SIDS cases could be MCAT deficiencies. Recent evidence has dropped this to 2 to 3%, and final figures will probably be even lower. However, because these disorders are inherited with a 25% chance of recurrence, it will be important to establish systems of identification in infants who die suddenly (but who by virtue of having a recognized cause of death are not SIDS). As noted earlier, it is possible that the elimination of MCAT deficiency and possibly other inherited disorders (such as Wernick-Hoffman) would significantly decrease the apparent recurrence risk of SIDS.

WHAT ABOUT ANY STUDIES OF SIDS INFANTS WHILE THEY WERE ALIVE?

In order to get adequate numbers of SIDS cases to study, very large prospective studies of normal infants must be undertaken (1,000 infants for every two SIDS). Such a study was undertaken in Britain by Southall and his colleagues (1983) to test the hypothesis that these infants could be identified by 24-hour "pneumocardiograms," measurements of heart rate and respiratory rate. Eleven thousand infants were given 24-hour recordings in the home at four to six weeks of age. Of these, 26 died as predicted. The term infants' recordings were compared to term controls who did not die. No differences in respiratory rates, periodic breathing, short or long apneic episodes, and so on, were found. On the surface, heart rates were unimpressive, but more recent, very sophisticated computer analysis has suggested differences in the coupling of heart rate and respirations which could reflect abnormalities of autonomic nervous system control (Schechtman, et al., 1988). Some investigators have suggested that they can define a prolongation of the repolarization phase of the electrocardiogram relative to the heart rate in these tapes. If true, this could predispose to arrhythmias (Sadeh, et al., 1987). Others feel this is just an artifact of the slightly higher heart rate in SIDS infants and that the tapes are not of adequate quality for this analysis (since they were never collected for this purpose).

Another prospective study is ongoing in Italy, specifically to look at the question of a prolonged QT interval in infants dying of SIDS (Schwartz, 1987). Fifteen thousand infants have been studied, but since the incidence of SIDS in Italy is only .5/1,000 live births, this has produced fewer than 10 SIDS cases, some of which do appear to have a prolonged QT at the time of the study. Nevertheless, a subset of the infants studied prospectively on several occasions who did not die showed that there was an increase in the QT interval over the first three months and then a return to more normal. Thus, infants with apparently normal or slightly prolonged intervals when studied at four days of age could have markedly prolonged values at the time of death.

These two studies make two very important points that must be considered in any future large-scale prospective studies. First, one must know exactly *what* one wants to study and have the appropriate methodology. Second, one must know *when* to look for the abnormality. A study conducted with the wrong methodology or at the wrong time could represent an enormous waste of money and energy. More importantly, it could lead to the abandonment of a productive avenue of research. So far, the suggested abnormalities are not of a great enough magnitude or specificity to be of any use for predicting who will die of SIDS. (Indeed, if that possibility exits, there are many steps between research tools and practical screening methods.)

Steinschneider, Weinstein, and Diamond (1982) studied thousands of infants with polysonograms, measuring heart rate, respiratory rate, EEG, and airflow in an artificial setting (elevated temperature) designed to induce apnea both during sleep and when awake. They found that of 10 infants who died of SIDS, fewer than half had abnormalities during sleep, and half had abnormalities during wakefulness, especially when feeding. Many studies of infants who present as "near miss" infants have shown that developmental abnormalities of respiratory control and developmental abnormalities of feeding coordination often occur in the same infants (infants who did not go on to die). Thus, markers for the lethal condition which appears to occur during sleep may well be found in other systems during other states, and many areas of infant physiology need to be studied carefully.

Many of the infants studied by Shannon and his colleagues (Shannon & Kelly, 1982; Shannon, Kelly, & O'Connell, 1977) who ultimately died have been shown to have respiratory abnormalities, but most of these are infants who have been sent for study because of a "near miss" episode. Thus, they represent a selected group. Remember in the NIH study only 7% of SIDS cases (3% of controls) ever gave retrospective (and biased) history of stopping breathing or turning color, and only two of 800 were ever sent for medical attention because of a concerning episode.

As some screening tests for other abnormalities become more common, there will become larger collections of inadvertently studied SIDS infants. One such type of testing is fetal heart rate monitoring. One careful study in California showed no differences in infants dying of SIDS (Hoppenbr uwers, Zanini, & Hodgman, 1979). Also, the NIH study reported no gross abnormalities in fetal heart rate tracings. However these data have not been studied with the great detail given to the British tapes and may not have been collected in such a way as to allow this. In the future, it is crucial that such "routine" studies be stored in retrievable fashion. Schechtman and colleagues (1988) reported that the elevation of heart rate and decreased coupling of heart rate and respiratory rate can be seen as early as the first week of life.

During the large NCP study 125 infants who died of SIDS had been prospectively followed for neurological development. Unfortunately, that study was not designed to study SIDS and little evaluation was done in infancy. Examination of the infants at birth did show a decreased responsiveness to nasal occlusion as part of a behavioral scale (Rosenblith & Anderson-Huntington, 1975). The infants otherwise appeared normal.

All of these studies put together suggest that early subtle differences may exist. However there are no consistent findings and none of enough strength or specificity to be useful in screening. In the NIH study (Hoffman, et al., 1988), observation in the newborn nursery by experienced observers of newborn behavior did not yield higher incidences of signs or symptoms which could be considered worrisome. These observations were at least recorded prior to the infants' deaths. Observations of infants who died of SIDS reported retrospectively by their mothers who were nurses, and thus trained observers, suggested that these infants may have had differences of temperament and respiratory control (Mandell, 1981). However, these data again may be highly biased by their retrospective nature, even if the mothers were trained nurses. Indeed changes, or magnifications of abnormal behavior, should be expected between the newborn period when most infants are observed in semi-controlled settings and two to four months later when they die. This is a time of very rapid behavioral as well as physiological change about which much needs to be learned concerning the range of normal behavior. Clearly, the closer to the SIDS age range infants are studied, the higher the chance of finding relevant abnormalities. But this is an "inconvenient" time to study infants, and one risks missing the SIDS infants who die on the earlier side of the age range.

WHAT THEORIES ARE RESEARCHERS WORKING ON?

SIDS has hardly been researched in any systematic way. Indeed, "the theory of the month club" is not too inaccurate a description. All this is understandable given the problems noted previously. One approach is to try to work backwards from terminal mechanisms. At present, no one knows whether the terminal event is a cardiac arrest or a respiratory failure. Attempts to determine if there has been a period of hypoxia or lack of oxygen have failed. Recently, there has been a report of increased hypoxanthine in the vitreous humor of the eye suggesting a period of hypoxia, but this remains to be confirmed (Rognum, et al., 1988). Based on the occurrence of "near miss" infants, most investigation over the last 10 years has focused on respiratory control mechanisms. More recently, as infants have been found to die of SIDS in hospital newborn intensive care units and at home on monitors, researchers have begun to focus on more rapidly lethal and non-reversible causes of death. Obviously, arrhythmias were the first non-respiratory cause to be reinvestigated. However, mechanisms that are more complex than the stopping of respirations or heart beat are now being entertained, especially as newer technology shows that infants in NICUs may drop the oxygen content of the blood dramatically while appearing to breathe with a normal heart rate. Initially, spurred on by the petechial distribution already discussed, researchers focused on upper airway obstruction. More recently, bronchospasm of the terminal airways and "end expiratory apnea" have been postulated to produce similar effects. Hypoxia due to shunting through fetal channels is now well recognized in young infants and would be consistent with pulmonary arteriolar hyperplasia if it can be agreed to exist in SIDS. Profound vascular collapse has become a familiar sight in infants infected with the group B strep, and the young infant's ability or inability to control vascular tone has recently become of concern, as has the total function of the autonomic nervous system.

All of these systems, it turns out, can be rapidly changed by an ever-increasing number of mediators (leukotrienes, thromboxains, prostaglandins, the compliment system, etc.), which can be triggered by multiple factors, such as infections and toxins. The list of neurotransmitters and endogenous opiates is also rapidly increasing.

Thus, over the last few years we have finally seen a broadening in the areas of concern. As this has happened, it has become clear that our knowledge of normal physiology in this age range is still woefully lacking. The focus on respiratory control over the last 10 years has markedly increased our knowledge in that area, and our knowledge of sleep physiology has also been greatly expanded. However, there are many areas where knowledge is scant, and it may be helpful to review the most prominent of them.

A recent postmortem finding which has raised hopes of a screening test is an elevation of fetal hemoglobin when this is measured using individual globulin chain analysis (Giulian, Gilbert, & Moss, 1987). Previous measurements of HbF using the alkaline denaturation method for intact hemoglobin had not found differences, and now two additional methods which measure intact hemoglobin, HPLC and an antibody against HbF, also have failed to show a significant difference (Kline, et al., 1989). Why different results were found with the individual globulin method is unclear. Had the original data been substantiated, the use of HbF as a screening test would have been questionable, since the major differences were seen after 10 weeks of age when many SIDS infants would have already died and when screening is not convenient. However, the major problem would have been what to do with all the infants identified as positive (the SIDS and all of the false positive infants), since the abnormality did not suggest a method of prevention. Again, the lesson to be learned is that one needs to know what one will do with the information which one collects and one needs to anticipate the potential problems caused (e.g., large numbers of false positives).

Respiratory Control

After many years of work in this area, it has become clear that even in infants this is an incredibly complex system (Hunt & Brouillette, 1987). There are multiple stimuli which appropriately stop respirations, and several feedback systems which restart respirations. The result is that the normal infant has multiple respiratory pauses but rarely fails to resume respirations. This is particularly true during sleep, and the final safety system is the arousal from sleep. The control of respiration centered in the brain stem appears to be markedly influenced by input from the forebrain and even lower centers. Chemoreceptor function is both central and peripheral (e.g., carotid bodies, lung chemoreceptors). In infants, all of these systems are developing and the relative importance of these different inputs is changing. For example, in rats, rabbits, and pigs severing the nerves to the carotid body in the early neonatal period results in the sudden death of almost all of the young animals after a delay period, but the same deenervation only a few weeks later has little obvious effect (Henderson-Smart & Cohen, 1988). This appears to relate to the changing strength of inhibitory input from the forebrain. Whether this is a relevant animal model for SIDS remains to be seen, but it serves to illustrate the complexity and rapidly changing nature of the system. Some of the neuroanatomical lesions noted and the proposed abnormalities of the carotid bodies are consistent with respiratory control problems. However, they could be effects as easily as causes, given the feedback nature of these systems.

Whereas the early focus was on triggers of apnea, the current focus is probably on the arousal mechanism. Although "near miss" infants, now appropriately called ALTE infants (Apparent Life Threatening Events), may not have a great deal of direct relevance to SIDS (i.e., are probably not aborted SIDS), they have taught respiratory physiologists a great deal about what can go wrong with the infant respiratory system. This model of learning as much as possible about what is normal, then defining the possible ways in which the system can go wrong, and finally seeing if any of the possible abnormalities could be related to SIDS can hopefully be applied to other systems. Although as discussed earlier, easily discernible respiratory abnormalities have not been found in prospective studies and apnea monitoring has not always prevented SIDS, abnormalities in respiratory control have certainly not been ruled out. This area continues to deserve and receive much attention (Hunt & Brouillette, 1987).

Upper Airway Control

As complicated as the control of active respirations is, the control of the patency of the upper airways is even more complicated (Thach, 1983; Thach, Davies, & Koenig, 1988). Control of respirations involves control of the diaphragm and intercostal muscles; control of the upper airway involves at least 22 different pairs of muscles all controlled as muscles of respiration. The unstimulated state of the upper airway is closure and patency is only maintained by active stimulation of muscles. Failure of patency results in interruption of airflow in spite of respiratory effort or obstructive apnea.

It turns out that obstructive apnea is quite common in infants, particularly premature infants. A closer look, however, shows that obstructive apnea may not always be abnormal. Much of what appears as obstructive apnea may be normal protective airway responses, particularly in response to accumulation of secretions in the posterior pharynx. Indeed, solutions may trigger specific laryngeal receptors which stimulate airway closure while the infant swallows and clears the secretions. Non-physiological solutions may trigger particularly violent reactions in some animal models. Obstructive apnea is often followed by central apnea and vice versa, and this is referred to as mixed apnea. As with central apnea, obstructive or mixed apnea is even more of a problem during sleep, and arousal is a final common safety mechanism. Obstructive apnea is often followed by more rapid and severe bradycardia than central apnea and thus appears particularly dangerous.

As noted, the petechial distribution found in SIDS is suggestive of airway obstruction (Krous, 1984). Initially, researchers were concerned with causes of active airway obstruction, such as laryngospasm secondary to hypocalcemia. Support could not be gathered for an active laryngospasm and so the theory died out. However, increased knowledge of upper airway patency has led current researchers to postulate passive closure, a failure to actively maintain patency, as the cause of SIDS. Since the airway is always relaxed, and thus closed, postmortem, this is a difficult theory to confirm or refute.

Bronchospasm or End Expiratory Apnea

Active closure of the terminal bronchioles can rapidly result in reduced oxygenation of the blood, as can be seen in severe asthmatic cases. Conversely, failure of the terminal airways and alveoli to stay open, alveolar collapse, can result in severe deoxygenation. Alveolar collapse (with shunting) is characteristically seen in premature infants with Hyaline Membrane Disease due to a deficiency in surfactant. The surfactant in SIDS has been reported to be abnormal and thus predisposing to alveolar collapse (Morley, Hill, & Brown, 1988). However, if confirmed, this also could be an effect and not a cause. Southall and Talbert (1988) have reported infants who have had a tracheostomy (ruling out obstructive apnea), in whom rapid oxygen denaturation occurs, presumably due to terminal airway constriction or collapse, and have termed this "end expiratory apnea." Indeed, tracheostomy may predispose these infants to this outcome and the substitution of Continuous Positive Airway Pressure (CPAP) for normal glottic closure may markedly improve these infants. The importance of glottic (vocal cord) closure in stabilization of the respiratory system is just beginning to be appreciated and it is interesting that glottic closure which is present for several weeks after birth, wains during the SIDS age range then reappears (Johnson, 1988). This developmental process appears to be under strict neuronal control and is hopefully coordinated with the other respiratory control changes going on during the SIDS age range.

Severe bronchospasm can be induced by a number of mediators, such as the leukotrienes or Platelet Activating Factor, many of which are triggered by infection or a toxin. Increased bronchial reactivity is well documented in a delayed fashion after upper respiratory infection. The frequently heard story that the infant was just getting over a cold and was now doing better at the time of death is consistent with such increased reactivity. This whole area requires more study in infants, especially in relation to SIDS.

Cardiac Arrhythmias and Vascular Tone

Early in SIDS research, researchers worried about cardiac arrhythmias. There were initial reports of abnormalities in the conduction system of the heart, but subsequent studies showed that these were normal developmental changes in infants of this age range. Nevertheless, the conducting system is an excellent example of where something may "look fine" but function abnormally. The sympathetic and parasympathetic input to the heart is finely regulated to coordinate depolarization and repolarization of the cardiac muscle. Researchers looked for abnormalities of depolarization and repolarization on electrocardiograms of small numbers of "near miss" infants, SIDS infants, and parents of SIDS, but did not find abnormalities in these groups. Not finding support for a theory of cardiac instability in these studies, many researchers abandoned this avenue of research, possibly prematurely (Schwartz, 1987).

The group in Italy persisted and launched the large prospective study of electrocardiograms already mentioned. Their study suggests a developmental state of sympathetic imbalance between the right and left sympathetic inputs in all infants during the SIDS age range, which may be exaggerated in some infants actually dying of SIDS. Such an imbalance would increase the chance of development of sudden arrhythmias. As noted, because of the low SIDS rate in Italy, the numbers from this study remain small. Although other prospective studies, namely the British study, may not allow examination of electrocardiogram changes, they have been analyzed for heart rate variability, particularly related to respiratory rate changes. The SIDS infants appear to have higher heart rates, less general heart rate variability, and less variability related to respirations (Schechtman, et al. 1988). These changes suggest abnormalities in sympathetic and parasympathetic input. As noted earlier, these changes are not of a magnitude or specificity to allow identification of SIDS infants, but lend support to further studies of the neurological control of cardiac rhythm.

Several retrospective studies have found that some SIDS infants have histories of frequent "night sweats." (Unfortunately, this symptom was not specifically investigated in the NIH study, so that well-controlled data are somewhat lacking.) Investigators have postulated that this could represent a large sympathetic output which could be causative or which could be in response to a cause and indeed responsible for the infant's survival of that episode but not a subsequent episode. The sympathetic input is particularly important for the maintenance of vascular tone. It can be postulated that SIDS could result from vascular collapse (shock) associated with inadequate sympathetic tone either primarily or more likely as an inadequate compensating response to another vasodilatory stimulus. Many of the mediators discussed as having broncoconstrictive effects also have vasodilatory effects. This area has received very little study even in normal infants. Mathews and colleagues in Ireland are studying the sympathetic vascular tone response to the cold stress normally imposed on infants during the winter in Ireland, and they find a great variability in the ability of infants to respond (T. Mathews, personal communication, August, 1988).

Conversely, increased sympathetic tone could be associated with increased pulmonary vascular tone (pulmonary hypertension) which could result in right to left shunting of blood in infants with associated hypoxia. Except for the controversial data on pathological pulmonary arteriolar hyperplasia already discussed, this area has also not been well explored. Noninvasive methodology exists that can potentially detect pulmonary hypertension in infants.

WHAT ABOUT TRIGGERING MECHANISMS?

Although research has focused on terminal mechanisms and defining pathological abnormalities, there is an increasing realization that SIDS may occur when multiple factors coincide. Increasingly, researchers are considering that there may be a much larger population of vulnerable infants (potentially all infants) and that a certain trigger at a certain point in time will cause a subgroup of infants to die of SIDS.

The most frequently suggested triggering factor is infection, especially upper respiratory infection (URI). As noted, a history of URI in the few weeks before death is very common in SIDS. However, the NIH study found a similar high frequency of URI in control infants who did not die of SIDS. The question then is: can the same infective agent(s) which causes minor symptomatology in most infants, trigger death in a subset of infants? A number of possible triggering mechanisms have been postulated.

We know that URI increases the occurrence of apnea in infants with documented infant apnea. It is postulated that partial nasal occlusion due to secretions and edema increases nasal resistance and that this significantly affects many aspects of respiratory mechanics and respiratory control. Infection also causes a delayed increase in airway reactivity which can lead to increased bronchospasm. The immune response mounted to clear infections involves the production by the immune system of many mediators whose function is to communicate with, recruit, and stimulate other cells. Many of these mediators also have profound effects on smooth muscle, particularly in the bronchial tree and the vascular system, with potential for bronchospasm, pulmonary hypertension, and systemic hypotension.

A number of relatively common infections are acquired by infants in utero or at the time of delivery and do not result in symptomatology until later, if ever. Good examples of this phenomenon are chlamydia, Group B strep, and CMV. Some of these agents while otherwise asymptomatic can cause neurological damage, potentially consistent with the changes seen in SIDS (e.g., CMV or toxoplasmosis). Although serological evidence of exposure to CMV is not increased in SIDS, recent attempts to isolate CMV have shown an increased frequency of isolation in SIDS (about 10% of SIDS). Conversely, chlamydia titers are significantly higher in infants dying of SIDS, but attempts to isolate chlamydia postmortem were unsuccessful (Hillman & Gardner, 1981a & 1981b). These data together suggest a potential increased exposure to in utero or vaginally acquired infections, especially sexually transmitted infections. This would be consistent with much of the epidemiology of SIDS. Indeed, as additional sexually transmitted (or in utero acquired) infections are described, the possibility exists that a specific pathogen for SIDS could be found.

A large number of potential pathogenic bacteria normally reside in the intestine of infants who are not exclusively breast fed, but then decrease with increasing age. Particularly the anerobic bacteria produce a number of toxins which may get into the infant's blood stream and require neutralization by maternally-acquired or infant-generated antibodies. The age range of SIDS corresponds to the age when maternal antibodies to many infectious agents or toxins wains and infant production is still submaximal. In the late 1970s in California, a small number of infants who were reported as SIDS were diagnosed as having died from infantile botulism (Arnon, et al., 1978). Subsequent searches for examples of infant botulism in SIDS cases have produced very limited numbers. This has, however, stimulated many other theories of toxin production and SIDS which require study.

The seasonal distribution of SIDS has usually been felt to relate to increased exposure to infectious agents during the winter months, but the seasonability pattern is just as strong in small and large households, and therefore does not support this theory. Researchers have also focused on climatic changes, especially temperature, as a possible trigger. Although the incidence of SIDS remains constant within different latitudes in the United States, marked changes in incidence between mainland Australia and Tasmania (fourfold higher) have been postulated to relate to the colder temperatures with similar housing seen in Tasmania (Newman, 1988). In Los Angeles, the incidence of SIDS was seen to relate to peak times of air pollution with a seven-week time lag (Hoppenbrouwers, et al., 1981). These data were replicated for airborne lead in St. Louis (Erickson & Hillman, 1982). Thus, there may be a number of environmental factors which could act as triggers which require further study.

URIs have also been postulated to act as triggers through producing sleep deprivation, with the occurrence of SIDS as the URI resolves being related to a compensatory increase in sleep or depth of sleep state. Other environmental stimuli, such as moving or traveling, company, and family stress, have also been postulated to work through a sleep deprivation mechanism or merely disruption of normal sleep-wake cycles. The effect of environmental stresses on maternal-infant interactions and potential conditioning of infant behavior and autonomic nervous system states is just being considered as an area of investigation in SIDS.

WHEN WILL SIDS BE SOLVED?

There is always the chance of a monumental breakthrough at any minute in science. However, there is no suggestion that this is about to occur soon, and no area in which one would predict its occurrence. Solving SIDS will probably take a great deal more work. Even defining what is normal in this age range will require much additional work. The optimistic part is that there are more researchers than ever before looking at the problem of SIDS. In the past, a large "red flag" could have been waving and no one might have recognized it. Now there are enough researchers around who are knowledgeable about SIDS to recognize any clues that may exist and to use the scientific process to arrive at a solution.

REFERENCES

Arnon, S. S., Midura, T. F., Damus, K., Wood, R. M., & Chin, J. (1978). Intestinal infection and toxin production by *clostridium botulinum* as one cause of sudden infant death syndrome. *The Lancet, 1*, 1273–1276.

Bass, M., Kravath, R. E., & Glass, L. (1986). Death-scene investigation in sudden infant death. *The New England Journal of Medicine, 315*, 100–105.

Beckwith, J. B. (1970). Observations on the pathological anatomy of the sudden death syndrome. In A. B. Bergman, J. B. Beckwith, & C. G. Ray (Eds.), *Sudden infant death syndrome: Proceedings of the second international conference on causes of sudden death in infants* (pp. 83–101). Seattle: University of Washington Press.

Bergman, A. B. (1970). Sudden infant death syndrome in King County, Washington: Epidemiologic aspects. In A. B. Bergman, J. B. Beckwith, & C. G. Ray (Eds.), *Sudden infant death syndrome: Proceedings of the second international conference on causes of sudden death in infants* (pp. 47–54). Seattle: University of Washington Press.

Biering-Sorensen, F., Jorgensen, T., & Hilden, J. (1979). Sudden infant death in Copenhagen 1956–1971. II. Social factors and morbidity. *Acta Paediatrica Scandinavia, 68*, 1–9.

Brandt, C. D. (1970). Infectious agents from cases of sudden infant death syndrome and from members of their community. In A. B. Bergman, J. B. Beckwith, & C. G. Ray (Eds.), *Sudden infant death syndrome: Proceedings of the second international conference on causes of sudden death in infants* (pp. 161–174). Seattle: University of Washington Press.

Bruhn, F. W., Mokrohisky, S. T., & McIntosh, K. (1977). Apnea associated with respiratory syncytial virus infection in young adults. *The Journal of Pediatrics, 90*, 382–386.

Carpenter, R. G., & Emery, J. L. (1974). Identification and follow-up of infants at risk of sudden death in infancy. *Nature, 250*, 729.

Chavez, C. J., Ostrea, E. M., Stryker, J. C., & Smialek, Z. (1979). Sudden infant death syndrome among infants of drug-dependent mothers. *The Journal of Pediatrics, 95*, 407–409.

Erickson, M., & Hillman, L. (1982, June). The relationship of airborne lead to Sudden Infant Death Syndrome. Paper presented to the International Research Conference on Sudden Infant Death Syndrome, Baltimore.

Erickson, M. M., Poklis, A., Gantner, G. E., Dickinson, A. W., & Hillman, L. S. (1983a). Tissue mineral levels in victims of sudden infant death syndrome I. Toxic metals—lead and cadmium. *Pediatric Research, 17*, 779–784.

Erickson, M. M., Poklis,'A., Gantner, G. E., Dickinson, A. W., & Hillman, L. S. (1983b). Tissue mineral levels in victims of sudden infant death syndrome II. Essential minerals: Copper, zinc, calcium, and magnesium. *Pediatric Research, 17*, 784–787.

Giulian, G. G., Gilbert, E. F., & Moss, R. L. (1987). Elevated fetal hemoglobin levels in sudden infant death syndrome. *New England Journal of Medicine, 316*, 1122–1126.

Goldberg, J., Hornung, R., Yamashita, T., & Wehrmacher, W. (1986). Age at death and risk factors in sudden infant death syndrome. *Australian Pediatric Journal, 21*, Suppl. 1, 21–28.

Grether, J. K., & Schulman, J. (1989). Sudden infant death syndrome and birth weight. *The Journal of Pediatrics, 114*, 561–567.

Harper, R. M., Leake, B., Hoppenbrouwers, T., Sterman, M. B., McGinty, D. J., & Hodgman, J. (1978). Polygraphic studies of normal infants and infants at risk for the sudden infant death syndrome: Heart rate and variability as a function of state. *Pediatric Research, 12*, 778–785.

Henderson-Smart, D. J., & Cohen, G. L. (1988). Chemical control of breathing in early life. In P. J. Schwartz, D. P. Southall, & M. Valdes-Dapena (Eds.), *The sudden infant death syndrome: Cardiac and respiratory mechanisms and interventions. Annals of the New York Academy of Sciences, 533*, 276–288.

Hillman, L. S., Erickson, M., & Haddad, J. G. (1980). Serum 25-hydroxyvitamin D concentrations in sudden infant death syndrome. *Pediatrics, 65*, 1137–1139.

Hillman, L. S., & Gardner, M. (1981a). *Chlamydia trachomatis* seropositivity in sudden infant death syndrome cases (SIDS) and controls. *Pediatric Research, 15*, 613.

Hillman, L. S., & Gardner, M. (1981b). Cytomegalovirus (CMV) serology in sudden infant death syndrome (SIDS): Lack of correlation with *chlamydia trachomatis* serology. *Pediatric Research, 15*, 614.

Hoffman, H. J., Damus, K., Hillman, L., & Krongrad, E. (1988). Risk factors for SIDS: Results of the National Institute of Child Health and Human Development SIDS Cooperative epidemiological study. In P. J. Schwartz, D. P. Southall, & M. Valdes-Dapena (Eds.), *The sudden infant death syndrome: Cardiac and respiratory mechanisms and interventions. Annals of the New York Academy of Sciences, 533*, 13–30.

Hoffman, H. J., Hunter, J. C., Damus, K., Pakter, J., Peterson, D. R., van Belle, G., & Hasselmeyer, E. G. (1987). Diphtheria-tetanus-pertussis immunization and sudden infant death: Results of the National Institute of Child Health and Human Development cooperative epidemiological study of sudden infant death syndrome risk factors. *Pediatrics, 79*, 598–611.

Hoppenbrouwers, T., Calub, M., Arakawa, K., & Hodgman, J. E.. (1981). Seasonal relationship of sudden infant death syndrome and environmental pollutants. *American Journal of Epidemiology, 113*, 623–634.

Hoppenbrouwers, T., Zanini, B., & Hodgman, J. E. (1979). Intrapartum fetal heart rate and sudden infant death syndrome. *American Journal of Obstetrics and Gynecology, 133*, 217–220.

Hunt, C. E., & Brouillette, R. T. (1987). Medical progress. Sudden infant death syndrome: 1987 perspective. *The Journal of Pediatrics, 110*, 669–678.

Johnson, A. R., Hood, R. L., & Emery, J. L. (1980). Biotin and the sudden infant death syndrome. *Nature, 285*, 159–160.

Johnson, P. (1988). Airway reflexes and the control of breathing in postnatal life. In P. J. Schwartz, D. P. Southall, & M. Valdes-Dapena (Eds.), *The sudden infant death syndrome: Cardiac and respiratory mechanisms and interventions. Annals of the New York Academy of Sciences, 533*, 262–275.

Jones, A. M., & Weston, T. J. (1976). The examination of the sudden infant death syndrome infant: Investigative and autopsy protocols. *Journal of Forensic Sciences, 21*, 833–841.

Kinney, H. C., Burger, P. C., Harrell, F. E., & Hudson, R. P. (1983). "Reactive gliosis" in the medulla oblongata of victims of the sudden death syndrome. *Pediatrics, 72*, 181–187.

Kline, C. A., Ellerbrook, R. C., Goldstein, D. E., Monzon, C. M., & Hillman, L. S. (1989). Measurement of fetal hemoglobin (HbF) in sudden infant death syndrome (SIDS) and controls using radial immunodiffusion (RID) and high pressure liquid chromatography (HPLC). *Pediatric Research, 25*, 270A.

Kraus, J. F., & Borhani, N. O. (1972). Post-neonatal sudden unexplained death in California: A cohort study. *American Journal of Epidemiology, 95*, 497–510.

Krous, H. F. (1984). The microscopic distribution of intrathoracic petechiae in sudden infant death syndrome. *Archives of Pathology and Laboratory Medicine, 108*, 77–79.

Mandell, F. (1981). Cot death among children of nurses: Observations of breathing patterns. *Archives of Disease in Childhood, 56*, 312–314.

Morley, C., Hill, C., & Brown, B. (1988). Lung surfactant and sudden infant death syndrome. In P. J. Schwartz, D. P. Southall, & M. Valdes-Dapena (Eds.), *The sudden infant death syndrome: Cardiac and respiratory mechanisms and interventions. Annals of the New York Academy of Sciences, 533*, 289–295.

Naeye, R. L. (1976). Brain-stem and adrenal abnormalities in the sudden infant death syndrome. *American Journal of Clinical Pathology, 66*, 526–530.

Naeye, R. L. (1980). Sudden infant death. *Scientific American, 242*(4), 56–62.

Naeye, R. L., Ladis, B., & Drage, J. S. (1976). Sudden infant death syndrome: A prospective study. *American Journal of Diseases of Children, 130*, 1207–1210.

Newman, N. M. (1988). The epidemiology of the sudden infant death syndrome in Australia, with particular reference to Tasmania, 1975–1981. In R. M. Harper & H. J. Hoffman (Eds.), *Sudden infant death syndrome: Risk factors and basic mechanisms* (pp. 53–72). New York: PMA Publishing Corporation.

Perrin, D. G., Cutz, E., Becker, L. E., & Bryan, A. C. (1984a). Ultrastructure of carotid bodies in sudden infant death syndrome. *Pediatrics, 73*, 646–651.

Perrin, D. G., Cutz, E., Becker, L. E., Bryan, A. C., Madapallimatum, A., & Sole., M. J. (1984b). Sudden infant death syndrome: Increased carotid-body dopamine and noradrenaline content. *The Lancet, 2*, 535–537.

Peterson, D. R., Benson, E. A., Fisher, L. D., Chin, N. M., & Beckwith, J. B. (1974). Postnatal growth and the sudden infant death syndrome. *American Journal of Epidemiology, 99*, 389–394.

Peterson, D. R., Chin, N. M., & Fisher, L. D. (1980). The sudden infant death syndrome: Repetitions in families. *The Journal of Pediatrics, 97*, 265–267.

Peterson, D. R., Labbe, R. F., van Belle, G., & Chin, N. M. (1981). Erythrocyte transketolase activity and sudden infant death. *American Journal of Clinical Nutrition, 34*, 65–67.

Peterson, D. R., Sabotta, E. E., & Daling, J. R., (1986). Infant mortality among subsequent siblings of infants who died of sudden infant death syndrome. *The Journal of Pediatrics, 108*, 911–914.

Protestos, C. D., Carpenter, R. G., McWeeney, P. M., & Emery, J. L. (1973). Obstetric and perinatal histories of children who died unexpectedly (cot death). *Archives of Disease in Childhood, 48*, 835–841.

Quattrochi, J. J., Baba, N., Liss, L., & Adrion, W. (1980). Sudden infant death syndrome (SIDS): A preliminary study of reticular dendritic spines in infants with SIDS. *Brain Research, 181*, 245–249.

Rognum, T. O., Saugstad, O. D., Oyasaeter, S., & Olaisen, B. (1988). Elevated levels of hypoxanthine in vitreous humor indicate prolonged cerebral hypoxia in victims of sudden infant death syndrome. *Pediatrics, 82*, 615–618.

Rosen, T. S., & Johnson, H. L. (1988). Drug-addicted mothers, their infants, and SIDS. In P. J. Schwartz, D. P. Southall, & M. Valdes-Dapena (Eds.), *The sudden infant death syndrome: Cardiac and respiratory mechanisms and interventions. Annals of the New York Academy of Sciences, 533*, 89–95.

Rosenblith, J. F., & Anderson-Huntington, R. B. (1975). Defensive reactions to stimulation of the nasal and oral regions in newborns: Relations to state. In J. F. Bosma & J. Showacre (Eds.), *Development of upper respiratory anatomy and function: Implications for sudden infant death syndrome* (pp. 250–263). U.S. Dept. of Health, Education, and Welfare, Public Health Service, National Institutes of Health, DHEW Pub. No. (NIH) 75-941). Washington, DC: U.S. Government Printing Office.

Sachis, P. N., Armstrong, D. L., Becker, L. E., & Bryan, A. C. (1981). The vagus nerve and sudden infant death syndrome: A morphometric study. *The Journal of Pediatrics, 98*, 278–280.

Sadeh, D., Shannon, D. C., Abboud, S., Saul, J. P., Akselrod, S., & Cohen, R. J. (1987). Altered cardiac repolarization in some victims of sudden infant death syndrome. *New England Journal of Medicine, 317*, 1501–1505.

Schechtman, V. L., Harper, R. M., Kluge, K. A., Wilson, A. J., Hoffman, H. J., & Southall, D. P. (1988). Cardiac and respiratory patterns in normal infants and victims of the sudden infant death syndrome. *Sleep, 11*, 413–424.

Schrauzer, G. N., Rhead, W. J., & Saltzstein, S. L. (1975). Sudden infant death syndrome: Plasma vitamin E levels and dietary factors. *Annals of Clinical and Laboratory Science, 5*, 31–37.

Schwartz, E. H., Chasalow, F. I., Erickson, M. M., Hillman, R. E., Yuan, M., & Hillman, L. S. (1983). Elevation of postmortem triiodothyronine in sudden infant death syndrome and in infants who die of other causes: A marker of previous health. *The Journal of Pediatrics, 102*, 200–205.

Schwartz, P. J. (1987). The quest for the mechanism of the sudden infant death syndrome: Doubts and progress. *Circulation, 75*, 677–683.

Scott, D. J., Gardner, P. S., McQuillin, J., Stanton, A. N., & Downham, M. A. P. S. (1978). Respiratory virus and cot death. *British Medical Journal, 2*, 12–13.

Shannon, D. C., & Kelly, D. H. (1982). SIDS and near-SIDS. *New England Journal of Medicine, 306*, 959–965, 1022-1028.

Shannon, D. C., Kelly, D. H., & O'Connell, K. (1977). Abnormal regulation of ventilation in infants at risk for sudden-infant-death syndrome. *New England Journal of Medicine, 297*, 747–750.

Silverstein, R., Nelson, D. L., Lin, C-C., & Rawitch, A. B. (1983). Enzyme stability and SIDS: Studies with phosphoenolpyruvate carboxykinase. In J. T. Tildon, L. M. Roeder, & A. Steinschneider (Eds.), *Sudden infant death syndrome* (pp. 233–242). New York: Academic Press.

Singer, D. B. (1983, March). Small pulmonary vessels not thickened in sudden infant death syndrome. Paper presented at the annual meeting of the Pediatric Pathology Club, San Francisco.

Southall, D. P., Richards, J. M., De Swiet, M., et al. (1983). Identification of infants destined to die unexpectedly during infancy: Evaluation of predictive importance of prolonged apnea and disorders of cardiac rhythm or conduction. First report of multicentered prospective study into the sudden infant death syndrome. *British Medical Journal, 286*, 1092–1096.

Southall, D. P., & Talbert, D. G. (1988). Mechanisms for abnormal apnea of possible relevance to the sudden infant death syndrome. In P. J. Schwartz, D. P. Southall, & M. Valdes-Dapena (Eds.), *The sudden infant death syndrome: Cardiac and respiratory mechanisms and interventions. Annals of the New York Academy of Sciences, 533*, 329–349.

Steele, R. (1970). Sudden infant death syndrome in Ontario, Canada: Epidemiologic aspects. In A. B. Bergman, J. B. Beckwith, & C. G. Ray (Eds.), *Sudden infant death syndrome: Proceedings of the second international conference on causes of sudden death in infants* (pp. 64–72). Seattle: University of Washington Press.

Steinschneider, A., Weinstein, S. L., & Diamond, E. (1982). The sudden infant death syndrome and apnea/obstruction during neonatal sleep and feeding. *Pediatrics, 70*, 858–863.

Thach, B. T. (1983). The role of pharyngeal airway obstruction in prolonging infantile apneic spells. In J. T. Tildon, L. M. Roeder, & A. Steinschneider (Eds.), *Sudden infant death syndrome* (pp. 279–292). New York: Academic Press.

Thach, B. T., Davies, A. M., & Koenig, J. S. (1988). Pathophysiology of sudden upper airway obstruction in sleeping infants and its relevance for SIDS. In P. J. Schwartz, D. P. Southall, & M. Valdes-Dapena (Eds.), *The sudden infant death syndrome: Cardiac and respiratory mechanisms and interventions. Annals of the New York Academy of Sciences, 533*, 314–328.

Valdes-Dapena, M. A. (1983). The morphology of the sudden infant death syndrome: An overview. In J. T. Tildon, L. M. Roeder, & A. Steinschneider (Eds.), *Sudden infant death syndrome* (pp. 169–182). New York: Academic Press.

Wyatt, D. T., Erickson, M. M., Hillman, R. E., & Hillman, L. S. (1984). Elevated thiamine levels in SIDS, non-SIDS, and adults: Postmortem artifact. *The Journal of Pediatrics, 104*, 585–588.

PART II

SIDS—Loss, Grief, and Survivors

The first responsibility presented to students of SIDS and to potential helpers is to understand *who* is most likely to have been impacted by the death of the infant and *how* that impact typically expresses itself. This may seem obvious as we think immediately of the infant's parents. But that alone is insufficient, both in terms of the individuals who have been affected and the ways in which they are touched. Certainly, our foremost concern is for the parents of a child who has died of SIDS. But we also need to take into account siblings, grandparents, extended family members, and a variety of other significant persons (e.g., day care providers, babysitters, co-workers, friends of the family, the clergy, funeral directors, emergency responders, and health care providers) as potential members of the expanded group of human beings whose lives may be upset by the SIDS event. This helps us to appreciate the meaning of the claim that each SIDS death affects an average of 100 other persons.

Nevertheless, one cannot say that all of the individuals mentioned in the previous paragraph will inevitably be affected in powerful ways by the death of a SIDS infant. That depends to a large extent upon who they are, how they are related to the child or family, and what they have learned from prior experiences with loss and sadness. For any given individual, we must listen carefully to determine the precise nature and degree of the impact which he or she has experienced in the context of SIDS. But it is obvious that many persons in this expanded circle of concern will be touched by the harsh consequences of the infant's death and many of these are rightly regarded as "hidden victims" of SIDS. For example, some of these people will be professionals struggling with the inadequacies of their technical skills, some will be parents of children themselves, and all will be vulnerable human beings whose own safety and security may be threatened by the cosmic implications of SIDS.

Our task, then, is to strive for sensitivity to all of the individuals who might be affected by SIDS or by any sudden death of an infant, and to learn to appreciate the specific ways in which particular individuals are impacted. The five chapters in Part II explore implications of the death of an infant, both as regards specific individuals in the short term and in relationship to family systems over a longer time frame. Special attention is given to needs and concerns in three particular groups: parents; siblings and other children; and grandparents, extended family members, and other significant persons. Careful analysis of these populations and of ways in which they may be affected by SIDS establishes principles that are applicable to other individuals in less typical circumstances, whether related to SIDS or not. This analysis also constitutes a foundation upon which guidelines for helping can be explored in greater detail in Part III.

CHAPTER 3

Grief on the Death of an Infant

Joan Hagan Arnold and Penelope Buschman Gemma

INFANTS AND SOCIETY

A child has many, varied, and, sometimes, discrepant meanings to society and to the family into which it is born. In the United States, there is a romantic notion that every child will be beautiful, healthy, intelligent, perfect, and carry the ideals and hopes for future generations. Yet, little is done by our society to realize these hopes or to defend these ideals. There is no national policy on children in our society. There is little legislation dealing with the health or welfare of children. We barely recognize the importance of the child in our society as a valuable member with competencies and capabilities, as well as with future potential. There is little official recognition and protection afforded to children.

In the early years of this nation, infants and young children were born and died in large numbers. They died in difficult births, from diseases and problems for which there were no treatments, and of accidental injuries. Families produced many children in the hope that some would survive to carry the family's name and tradition. The birth of many children also served to provide a kind of insurance for families, improving the likelihood that some offspring would be alive to care for parents as they aged.

With advances in medical care, immunizations, and antibiotics, and with an increased emphasis on child safety, the death rate for children in this country has decreased. But overall infant mortality rates in a number of countries around the world are significantly better than those in the United States. Moreover, especially among the poor, Native American, black, and Hispanic populations in our society, infant mortality rates are as high as those of some underdeveloped nations. There are few effective programs aimed at remediating the social causes contributing to shameful infant death rates in the United States.

The body of knowledge about infancy is relatively meager. While there are massive research efforts supported by government and private industry directed toward health issues affecting the adult population, there is comparatively little interest in infant research. Small numbers of pediatricians, child psychiatrists, and others are exploring the resiliency, competency, and creative roots developed in infancy, as well as genetically linked diseases and other problems of infancy.

Infants are not valued by this basically narcissistic society because they are considered to be needy, costly, and dependent. They are unable to contribute in a productive fashion. Sadly, as nonproductive, noncontributing members, infants are considered to be rather insignificant and expendable by the society in which the family lives and works.

One very clear exception to this rule, a way in which infants are important in our society, is the effect that they have in turning their parents toward new modes of consumerism. That is, our society very much encourages parents to prepare in concrete, material ways for their baby. A whole new range of products and services will be offered to or pressed upon the growing family and its new or forthcoming child.

In part, this arises because the skills and tasks of parenting taught and learned informally within extended families and communities from a variety of caregivers are no longer the major focus of preparation. For many young, single parents and couples, the families of origin and good neighbors are not there. Friends, acquaintances with not much parenting experience, and the media have become the resources for and the educators of new parents. There is little social support for new parents and for healthy infants.

There is even less societal support for families of infants with developmental delays, illness, or disability—imperfect infants. In particular, parents of infants who die often go unrecognized by society. These parents struggle for recognition and seek validation for the breadth and depth of their grief. In response, they are sometimes advised to forget their child, to replace the infant with another, or to feel relief that they had not lost an older child.

Infants are not supposed to die! Their deaths repudiate all of the wishes and hopes of parents, all of their efforts to prepare and to care for newborn children, and all of their plans to nurture their children and care for them over their lifetimes. When an infant dies in our society, it is common for the family to be offered little understanding and to find few supports available in its grief.

The infant, all too insignificant in society's eyes, is his or her family's greatest treasure. When that infant dies, the family usually grieves with little recognition and support for its profound loss.

PARENTS AND CHILDREN

Within the context of the family, an infant is a cherished and vital member bringing new life and meaning. In the child are the hopes and expectations of the parents, their link to the future, their wishes for all they were not. The infant is of the parents and yet a stranger to them as a new, separate, developing self who contributes to and alters the family.

Many families plan for the number of children they can afford. Their expectation is that these wanted and planned pregnancies will produce children who are healthy, physically attractive, and intelligent. The media reinforce parental wishes and expectations by featuring photographs of healthy, lovely babies, and by advertising infant formula, food products, clothing, and equipment to be used by growing children.

The special relationship between parent and child is not comparable to any other relationship among human beings. There is the connectedness between parent and child that has its roots in the biological and emotional attachments that precede birth. This connectedness grows and is nurtured as the parent begins to know and care for the infant even before its birth. The infant is at once from the parent, part of the parent, and a separate self. As the child grows, the parent is active in encouraging and facilitating the developmental process. The child learns as the parent encourages learning. The child acquires and masters new skills as the parent creates a safe and challenging environment in which these skills can be practiced. The child grows as the parent encourages growth. The relationship, the bond between parent and child is enduring; it continues forever.

There is responsibility in the relationship of parent and child. The helplessness of the young child evokes in the parents an enormous sense of responsibility for sustaining and protecting the life they have created.

There is also vulnerability in this relationship and with it, the potential for hurt, disappointment, and loss. The parent is threatened by what might happen to the child, by ever-present dangers. There is a power and a powerlessness that exist in this relationship between parent and child. There is the power to make decisions, to determine directions and exert influence when the child is young. There is also a powerlessness to protect from all threats of harm.

SOCIETY, FAMILIES, AND INFANT DEATH

From a societal perspective, an infant's death is viewed as a tragedy for that particular family. After months and sometimes years of preparing, waiting, and wishing for a healthy baby, the baby arrives and parents feel a tremendous relief. Their fears and fantasies can be dismissed, for the reality is that the child is well formed and seemingly healthy. Relief is coupled with joy and satisfaction. For some, this sense of triumph is shattered shortly after life has begun when suddenly and unexpectedly death consumes all hope for this vulnerable child. The infant dies.

Infant death is a painful tragedy for all who are involved. Parents are overcome by confusion, guilt, and loss. Family members and friends feel helpless in any efforts to assist. Others feel threatened. An infant's death assaults our sense of safety and security. It awakens fears and fantasies that force us to acknowledge that we are all vulnerable, unprotected, and mortal. It makes us acutely aware of the presence and power of death.

An infant's death is an affront to unspoken expectations arising from our society and its achievements. The image of a small, white coffin or a tiny tombstone engenders helplessness and despair. The parents ask why this had to happen to them—why their baby died. They look to our advanced technology and ask how it is possible to explore space and transplant hearts, yet not be able to save their infant child from certain death by causes that remain unexplained. Parents wonder how scientific dilemmas can be solved when warning indicators that alert to danger and provide some way to anticipate, avert, or deter death cannot be found.

An infant's death is an injustice. An infant is pure and filled with hope and potential yet to be realized. Death wipes out this hope in a swift moment in time. Babies are not supposed to die. New life is the antithesis of death. Infant death is out of the natural order of developmental life events. Old age is a time of expected death in our society. Death among the elderly is anticipated. Elders can measure quality and purpose in their lives in terms of their accomplishments and the quality of their relationships over time. Living a long, full life means having had opportunities to contribute to one's family, friends, and community—to have made a mark. Death permits the mourners to remember these contributions and to reminisce about times shared together. Events and good qualities that are recalled in this way help to sustain mourners in their loss.

But when a baby dies, life is ended before it has really begun. The family is cheated not only of its infant member, but also of the small child and later the adolescent and the young adult that now will never be. Grandchildren that will never be born are mourned, as are the innumerable contributions to family and community that will never be known. From the perspective of those who are closely involved in this experience, the world will be sadder and less wise without this child. An infant child has been cheated out of a life and we have all been cheated in ways that we can never know, can never realize. Death has taken us by surprise and has shaken our faith. Death has reached out of the natural order and denied a life to a child and an important member to a family.

SOCIETAL RESPONSES TO THE GRIEVING FAMILY

Infant deaths arouse our sense of vulnerability and challenge what we would like to take for granted. We speak of such deaths as "unfair," as if the birth of a child was accompanied by some kind of guarantee on longevity and stability in family life. As members of society we are inclined to avoid any reminders of erratic, unexplained, and tragic death which tend to shatter our comforting assumptions of this sort. We want to insulate ourselves, to protect what we cherish, and to shield ourselves from any assaults, trying never to be vulnerable.

A child's death tells us loudly and clearly that we are all vulnerable, and, guard as we may, that we will never be safe from death. Nevertheless, every effort is made by our society and by many of its members to wipe the tragic picture of infant death from our minds and to avoid confrontation with the inner feelings with which we continually do battle.

Avoiding grieving families is a way to deny reminders of our own personal vulnerability. Avoidance feels justified as a way to protect our own boundaries from the invasiveness of death. We are fearful of the power of death to reach out from those whom it has directly affected and to touch us with its pain and agony. We fear contamination by death as though it were a communicable disease that is transmitted by touching and connecting with each other. We think that as long as we remain detached and disengaged we are helping ourselves. In fact, that is not the case, since we cannot live our own lives effectively while deliberately blinding ourselves to the shared realities of the human situation.

Moreover, it is important to realize that when we avoid and reject the bereaved, we give them some clear messages: "stay away," "keep out," "not wanted." Rejection signals, if not overtly, then at least covertly, that those who have been touched by death are tainted by it. That is, our actions convey to bereaved parents and family members that they are somehow contaminated by the very death they have suffered. They are, then, doubly burdened: first, by the loss that they have experienced and its implications; and second, by the sense of stigma imposed on them by a society which backs away from their pain at a time when they very much need social support and assistance.

It would appear that bereaved parents in our society are supposed to hide their pain and cover up their agony because they arouse uncomfortable feelings in the rest of us. We are horrified by the depth and extent of their anguish. We feel thankful that we were spared, and wonder why they were not. Perhaps, in some way, they did deserve the death. Perhaps they did something wrong.

Death can be and often has been viewed as a punishment. If so, it results in a decided lack of support from onlookers. Some feel they cannot risk giving support for fear of contamination. Others feel they cannot offer support because they do not know how. They feel overwhelmed and do not know what to say or do, as if paralyzed by their emotions. Others will not give support because they feel death may be deserved and justify that somehow it must be right.

Whatever the reasons, it is the testimony of many parents and families in our society that they experienced avoidance, rejection, and lack of support when their baby died. They also go unrecognized among us. There are words like "widow" and "orphan." But there is no single expression which describes the parent of a dead child. There is no word in our language to signify that "I am the parent of a dead child."

PARENTAL GRIEF

When an infant dies, parents feel shattered, broken, less than whole as if a vital part of them were ripped away. Their grief is complicated by the special meaning of the child and the nature of their unique relationship with that child. The baby may have been a long-awaited miracle, an untimely inconvenience to be accommodated, an unwanted accident, a device to save a marriage, a plan to extend a relationship. That special meaning of the living child forms and reshapes the relationship between parent and infant, between parent and parent. When the child dies, both this special meaning and the nature of the relationship with the parents exert profound influence upon the family's grief (Borg & Lasker, 1981; Peppers & Knapp, 1980).

Parental grief is boundless. It touches every aspect of the parent's being. Initially, upon the unexpected death of the infant, parents may experience shock, disbelief, and confusion. As the reality of the loss is appreciated, parents will respond with rage, horror, guilt, blame, and sadness. Somatic symptoms may be experienced, including pain in the chest and arms, generalized fatigue, fullness as the breasts fill with milk, and emptiness in the belly. Sleeplessness or the wish to sleep forever in order to avoid pain, loss of appetite or excessive eating, reminiscing about or quieting memories, spiritual comfort in faith or rage against God and fate are all among the wide range of possible responses that vary over time (Hagan, 1974).

The range of expression of parental grief is wide. These expressions are molded in part by culture and family expectations, previous losses, and the inner fear that exposing the intensity of the parents' grief will demonstrate to others their madness.

Some parents will express tears and hysteria openly. Others will silence these expressions and grieve inwardly. Parents may wish to join their dead child. They may be preoccupied with thoughts of the child's being cold, lonely, or frightened, and they may wish very much to hold and comfort their baby. They may hear the child's cry in the night and awaken to offer care as if the baby were still alive.

Rarely, if ever, are family members in synchrony in their expressions of grief. As unique and different persons, parents grieve alone, separately, and as a couple, recognizing that only so much of the grief can be shared and understood.

Parents are changed forever by the life and death of their child.

When a baby dies, parents grieve for the rest of their lives. Their grief becomes part of them, even though most eventually learn to live with their grief and with the certain knowledge that they are the parents of a dead child (Gunther, 1949; Lindberg, 1973). They grieve for their precious infant, the separate child that they were just beginning to know intimately by appreciating his or her special qualities, desires, and needs. They grieve for their baby that they cannot hold or soothe, cannot smell or kiss, cannot feel important to, cannot protect or watch grow through childhood into adulthood.

They also grieve for part of themselves that died, too (Furman, 1978). The infant is part of the parent and an empty space is created when the baby is stripped away (McClowry, et al., 1987). The parent is left with an inner cavity filled only with emptiness. Parents feel pulled apart and unwhole. They have been diminished and damaged by the death of their child (Arnold & Gemma, 1983).

Parental grief is so intense and pervasive that parents often feel they will never survive it. It consumes and changes them. As time passes, parents begin to appreciate that grief is the link to their child, that grief keeps the parents connected to their child. Grieving is part of one's being, it is a self-protective healing process. Grief facilitates healing by helping parents to maintain a connectedness to their child.

Through grief one realizes that parental ties need not be severed by death but can be extended beyond it. They will always be parents to this child. This child will always be a member of their family. The inner cavity is a special space that they carry with them, a space for this child. Grief provides the link between living with and living without. Memories of their child are incorporated into the lives of the parents. The dead child's space is maintained. Ultimately, the parents can reach out to form new relationships and to find meaning and purpose in such relationships. Memories can also provide comfort and healing.

Parental grief knows no bounds. It cannot be contained by time, cause, circumstances, family constellation, or culture. Grief is universal. Poetry and other art forms teach us that the experiences of a grieving parent are echoed in the experiences of parents from differing cultures in different centuries (Arnoid & Gemma, 1983; Sr. Mary Immaculate, 1966). Grief is a binding experience; its universality binds sufferers together. More is shared than is different. Grief is a link between people and experiences. Grief for an infant child is boundless.

Parents learn to live without the physical presence of their infant. Their baby will never grow up. Their infant will always remain a child. The relationship does not die and cannot be taken away. A parent when asked, "How many children do you have?", may say, "I have three children. Our first child died in infancy." Parents learn to live without the physical presence of the child, but to live with their memories of the child. Since this child lived for only a short time, each memory becomes a significant one. Having memories and reminiscing about the baby help parents to maintain that connectedness which is so vital for healing.

Parents learn to make meaning out of their child's short life and tragic death. They may choose to help others, for example, by serving as parent-to-parent contacts for others after a child's death, or by writing, teaching, or volunteering. Some will plant a tree in their child's name or start an annual candlelighting service, make a photograph album, or establish a memory chest. Others will save a blanket or piece of the baby's t-shirt and keep this treasure close to them always. Some will hang a picture of the baby in a prominent place in their home. Others will make frequent trips to the cemetery to visit and talk with their baby, while some will just find a private place where they can cry and be in touch with their feelings. Responses vary as much as individuals do. Grief is an expression of individuality and of the struggle to maintain integrity and dignity as meaning is made of loss. Comfort is found in memories.

SUDDEN DEATH IN INFANCY

Sudden Infant Death Syndrome (SIDS) by its very definition presents a special set of circumstances which surround the death and must be dealt with by the parents and family. SIDS means that an apparently healthy infant died suddenly and unexpectedly, and that the cause of death was assigned after a complete autopsy failed to determine any other known cause of death. Death occurs without warning, at a time of intense attachment between parent and child. A sense of oneness characterizes the relationship between parent and infant.

Parents respond with horror and disbelief to their infant's death. They engage in a panic-driven search to determine how and why this could have happened. They hope in some way that they can reverse the horror, that someone will tell them it is not true, their baby is not dead, they will be reunited as one with their baby. They are desperate to find a clue and may accuse each other, or whoever was the caretaker at the time of death. They are sometimes brutal in their self-accusations, certain that above all else they were remiss in their responsibilities as parents. They may feel and proclaim that they are failed parents, that they failed their responsibility to safeguard and protect their child or to anticipate a warning sign.

Usually in cases of SIDS, death takes place at home during a sleeping period. The parent or caretaker discovers the dead baby. Apart from the SIDS experience, death at home is an infrequent occurrence. Most deaths in our society occur in hospitals and other institutions, removing death from the immediate family. Many adults in our society have never seen a dead person—and surely not a dead infant. The postmortem changes that occur are often frightening and may be misinterpreted. Postmortem lividity may reveal blood-tinged froth and dependent pooling, resulting in bruise-like areas of skin discoloration, signs which can be confused with child abuse. In fact, child abuse must be ruled out and parents may be judged or held in suspicion. Shock, disbelief, confusion, and self-blame all collide (Hagan, 1974).

Parents call for help and often find themselves dismayed as first responders put their action plan into effect. Suddenly, strangers are handling their baby and making decisions at a pace so rapid that parents are left out and feel out of control. In addition, parents will be questioned about the circumstances surrounding their baby's death and may feel defensive in their explanation or cry out that they are responsible in some way just because they feel responsible. Babies are not supposed to die.

SIDS is a cause of death by exclusion. An autopsy must be performed. Unexplained deaths are investigated by the coroner or medical examiner, and the autopsy does not always require parental consent. Parents must confront a system with which they probably have never previously been involved, a system that generally investigates suspicious and criminal deaths. Parents must also deal with their feelings about the autopsy, which may include fear and horror at the violation of their baby's body. The results of the autopsy are often more distressing because there is no new information revealed; the unknowns remain. Parents continue to search for an explanation, feeling something was overlooked or misconstrued, feeling there must be a reason. Babies just do not die. Blame must be channeled in some direction, toward the doctor, the paramedic, the cold medication, the drafty apartment, the older sibling, the babysitter, the spouse, God, and always the self.

Parents ask, "Why did my baby die? Of all the people in the world, why my baby and me?"

THE NATURE OF GRIEF

It is difficult to describe or define grief though many have tried. Indeed, definitions and schema have been put forth to provide an understanding of grief. Raphael's work (1983) is a useful compendium on bereavement, providing a resource of definitions, explanatory models, and theories superimposed on a human developmental perspective. On this basis, one can distinguish among *bereavement*, the situation of those who have experienced a loss, particularly a loss through death; *grief*, the reaction of the bereaved to the loss; and *mourning*, the intrapersonal processes of coping with grief, together with the expected behaviors or interpersonal rituals of individual societies. Clearly, all of these experiences depend upon the complexities of human bonding and a variety of social, personal, and situational factors.

Some have sought to throw light on the shared human experiences of grief and mourning through models based on stages or phases, indicating a progressive ordering or series of successive steps. Mourning has been explained as an episode with a beginning phase, a working phase, and a terminating phase leading to resolution that may be understood as "recovery," "adaptation," or "completion" (Osterweis, Solomon, & Green, 1984). Further, Parkes (1987) has identified seven features of bereavement reactions: a process of realization; an alarm reaction; an urge to search for and to find the lost person in some form; anger and guilt; feelings of internal loss of self or mutilation; identification phenomena; and pathological variants of grief.

Others have preferred to speak about tasks of mourning, describing the work to be done and the accomplishments that must take place in order to live effectively with one's loss and grief. Thus, Worden (1982) refers to four tasks of mourning: to accept the reality of the loss; to experience the pain of grief; to adjust to an environment in which the deceased is missing; and to withdraw emotional energy and reinvest it in another relationship.

According to Freud (1957), living with grief means letting go of relationships lost and mourned. But many bereaved parents have been angered by the suggestion that this might mean that they should "forget" their dead child. And even the best scholars in the field acknowledge that it has not been easy to describe in any precise way the long-term outcomes of normal grief and mourning (e.g., Osterweis, Solomon, & Green, 1984).

This suggests that, despite the volumes of work on grief, the experience of grief seems to defy description, at least in some important senses. Definitions touch the fringes of grief but do not embrace its totality or reach its core. Despite the best efforts of their proponents, models represent imperfect attempts to highlight salient features of basic human situations and processes. In the end, grief is a fundamental human experience which continues to challenge our understanding even as it cannot be wholly contained.

Our language impotently attempts to translate the breadth and depth of grief into comprehensible terms, but our words are not powerful enough to approximate the true nature of grief. Grief is not a circumscribed reaction to loss or an event that one lives through and eventually overcomes or puts in the past. Grieving is a complicated, evolving human process. Grief is among the processes that make us human.

Loss, change, dying, and death are part of living, and, concomitantly, grieving is as much a part of living as breathing and thinking. Humans grow, develop, and change, taking on and giving up capabilities, values, and skills. Grieving is linked to these processes; it is in fact a human process. Losses are part of growing. Losses are also imposed upon us as those we care about leave or die. Grieving is a way of living with our losses, integrating them into our lives, and deriving meaning from those losses while we continue to grow and change.

CONCLUSION

Grief on the death of an infant requires closer attention. Not only is a baby's death a family tragedy but also a societal tragedy. Families need validation for their grief experience. A baby's death is not less significant because the infant lived for only a short time, but a major loss of far-reaching consequences for the parents, family, and society. Infant death tells us that we are not attending to basic needs for our nation's families and communities. When society negates the importance of an infant's life or death, it negates its own present and future.

REFERENCES

Arnold, J. H., & Gemma, P. B. (1983). *A child dies: A portrait of family grief.* Rockville, MD: Aspen Systems.

Borg, S., & Lasker, J. (1981). *When pregnancy fails: Families coping with miscarriage, stillbirth, and infant death.* Boston: Beacon.

Freud, S. (1957). Mourning and melancholia. In J. Strachey (Ed.), *The standard edition of the complete psychological works of Sigmund Freud* (Vol. 14, pp. 243–258). London: Hogarth Press.

Furman, E. P. (1978). The death of a newborn: Care of the parents. *Birth and Family Journal, 5*, 214–218.

Gunther, J. (1949). *Death be not proud: A memoir*. New York: Harper & Row.

Hagan, J. M. (1974). Infant death: Nursing interaction and intervention with grieving families. *Nursing Forum, 13*, 371–385.

Lindberg, A. M. (1973). *Hour of gold, hour of lead: Diaries and letters of Anne Morrow Lindberg, 1929–1932*. New York: Harcourt, Brace, Jovanovich.

Mary Immaculate, Sr. (Ed.). (1966). *The cry of Rachel: An anthology of elegies on children*. New York: Random House.

McClowry, S. G., Davies, E. B., May, K. A., Kulenkamp, E. J., & Martinson, I. M. (1987). The empty space phenomenon: The process of grief in the bereaved family. *Death Studies, 11*, 361–374.

Osterweis, M., Solomon, F., & Green, M. (Eds.). (1984). *Bereavement: Reactions, consequences, and care.* Washington, DC: National Academy Press.

Parkes, C. M. (1987). *Bereavement: Studies of grief in adult life* (2nd ed.). Madison, CT: International Universities Press.

Peppers, L. G., & Knapp, R. J. (1980). *Motherhood and mourning: Perinatal death*. New York: Praeger.

Raphael, B. (1983). *The anatomy of bereavement*. New York: Basic Books.

Worden, J. W. (1982). *Grief counseling and grief therapy: A handbook for the mental health practitioner*. New York: Springer Publishing Co.

SUGGESTED READINGS

Donnelly, K. F. (1982). *Recovering from the loss of a child*. New York: Macmillan.

Kirkley-Best, E., & Kellner, K. (1981). Grief at stillbirth: An annotated bibliography. *Birth and Family Journal, 8*, 91–99.

Sanders, C. M. (1980). A comparison of adult bereavement in the death of a spouse, child, and parent. *Omega, 10*, 303–322.

CHAPTER 4

SIDS and Parents

Milda Dargis Ranney

Although Sudden Infant Death Syndrome (SIDS) had a biblical reference in I Kings 3: 19–20, it has had a medical definition only since 1969, and has been able to be cited as an official cause of death on death certificates only since 1973. In addition, although SIDS can be diagnosed unequivocally by autopsy, and proper investigation, the underlying cause or causes of this elusive, silent killer still remain to be discovered. Logic reminds us, then, that if the cause of SIDS is unknown, the event of a SIDS death must be both unpredictable and unpreventable. Add to this the personal accounts of both bereaved parents and emergency medical professionals whose collaborative efforts at resuscitation prove unsuccessful. The result: SIDS is not subject to interruption; it is not reversible despite timely and appropriate intervention. The first symptom is death. This brief abstract, however grim, is the current state of the art in our knowledge of Sudden Infant Death Syndrome.

The purpose of this chapter is to explore the situation faced by SIDS parents, those very special survivors known as Mommy and Daddy. This account is based upon the experiences of a large number of SIDS parents and upon work with such parents over a 13-year period. Its aim is to describe the experiences of SIDS parents and to identify the issues that they face. One goal is to improve communication with and support for SIDS parents. Another is to avoid unintentional blunders on the part of the non-bereaved.

PARENTAL EXPECTATIONS

Let us examine the emotional impact on two people who have just become expectant parents. Nine months of preparation ensue. Prenatal classes, nutrition assessments, and monthly visits to the obstetrician all combine to provide a routine monitoring of the nurtured pregnancy. The mother, whether this is her first baby or the latest of several, plans jointly with the equally proud expectant father how best to welcome their forthcoming child.

The first trimester of the gestation passes. Risks for miscarriage are now minimized, and both parents reaffirm their commitment to preparing their baby's room. Soon, baby showers are given in loving anticipation and recognition of the big event. Siblings, if any, are coached by their parents regarding the rites of passage to status as Big Brother or Big Sister. Nurseries are stocked with infant paraphernalia. Prenatal classes are eagerly attended. An endless list of preparations is checked and rechecked.

The momentous day of the baby's birth finally arrives! Husband and wife are promoted to their new designations: Mommy and Daddy. Baby has made them a family, not just a couple. Both parents recognize that the biology of parenting has a certain inevitability. But the social aspects of parenting are learned, not inborn. Parents must sort out the immediately pertinent information regarding responsible caretaking for their infant that is shared with them by hospital staff and well-intentioned relatives and friends.

As the first month of life elapses, Mommy and Daddy become accustomed to their Little One's personality, their own chronic fatigue due to sleepless nights, and their efforts to accommodate impromptu visitors who want to welcome the newborn and share successful parenting techniques. The baby's first visit to the doctor confirms the good health of the infant. Both parents go home assured, relieved, and somewhat relaxed. Perhaps they no longer need to check their sleeping infant so many times during the night as parents at first often feel they must.

Little One's first three months come and go uneventfully. Routine visits to the pediatrician continue to declare the infant healthy. Winter comes; baby catches a cold. Minor symptoms prevail; no temperature, just a slight cough or runny nose. The attending physician sees no need to prescribe any medication and assures both parents that their infant should be back to normal in a few days. Parents proudly advise the pediatrician that before the onset of the cold, their Little One had already been sleeping through the night. They further reflect on past anxiety-ridden days that have now eased as confidence in their parenting skills has grown.

Reassured by the visit to the pediatrician, the parents have a restful night. While getting ready for work, Daddy glances into the infant's room for a routine check. Little One is still sleeping. Running late for work, Daddy finishes dressing and dashes into Little One's room for a quick goodbye kiss. Nearing the infant, a gut reaction signals that something is wrong. The ashen color in Little One's hands triggers a horror-stricken thought. He touches the baby and finds the previously warm and cuddly infant now cold, stiff, and unresponsive. The living nightmare of being a bereaved parent begins.

PARENTS—OF ALL SORTS

In the previous section, prenatal expectations and postnatal experiences have been depicted in the context of a parental couple sharing with each other and encountering no major difficulties prior to the death of their child. Not all parents are this fortunate. Some are unmarried; others are uncoupled or in new relationships as a result of widowhood or divorce. Some are still adolescents. Many were struggling with a variety of problems prior to the child's birth or during its short life. Even those who are happily married have a kind of dual status: they are both members of a couple and individuals in their own right. It will be useful, therefore, to begin by considering who these people are whom we call "parents" and by trying to get a sense of their diversity.

Couples

It takes two to parent, but grief can be simultaneously both a shared and an intensely private experience. As simple as that may sound, each member of a bereaved couple needs to know that the other is actively grieving. How the grief will be experienced or exhibited by each parent may differ (Fish, 1986). For example, grief may be marked by such features as a preponderance of sleep or lack of sleep, verbal expression of feelings or painful silence, religious fervor or extreme anger with God, or excess of alcohol or other drug usage. Grief is a daily unfolding of the ingredients of a new normal.

There is no previous practice for mourning the death of a child, unless a sibling has also died. The death of a child is not equivalent to the death of an adult (Sanders, 1980). Parents sometimes say that past adult deaths in their family "did not count." Mourning takes time, appropriately so. It cannot and should not be hurried by "outsiders," the non-bereaved.

Differences in grieving within the traditional family may in part be ascribed to masculine and feminine gender roles. Without addressing cross-cultural perspectives, it is important to note that although the social gap between the sexes is narrowing and indeed overlapping in some areas in recent years, certain biological givens remain. All human beings, whether male or female, will grieve. Anyone who loves grieves when the object of that love is taken away. Grief is a life-long legacy. However, individual coping mechanisms vary, as does the support that individual parents receive from the social systems around them.

Both genders recognize the importance of focusing on one day at a time. Moreover, this day needs to be broken down, by each individual, into successful coping intervals. At first, the intervals may be exceedingly short. Parents sometimes strive just to make it through the next 15 minutes. Manning (1979) stated that loneliness comes in only one size: extra large. Initially, grieving is extra lonely. Short intervals are a necessity. As time elapses, the intervals usually increase. Families report that dishes did not sit in the sink as long as they had before, that bathrobes were not worn all day, and that grocery shopping became less painful. But they quickly add that reminders or triggers exist in every aisle: Mickey Mouse straws, diapers, and pediatric drinking cups are strategically placed throughout stores by trained marketing experts. How parents wish that all infant-toddler paraphernalia would be promoted exclusively in one aisle! One mother said that she used to shop at midnight in hopes of not having to meet a newborn baby in tow by its proud parents.

Fathers

Traditional paternity—fathers as part of a marital couple—is being studied as the area of father-infant bonding germinates in Western culture. Davis (1988) identified the following fears and concerns of fathers-to-be: (1) queasiness; (2) increased responsibility; (3) ob-gyn mystique; (4) uncertain paternity; (5) loss of spouse and/or child; (6) being replaced; and (7) life and death. Davis also noted the importance of attachment and bonding which he described as involving: (1) fantasy; (2) association; (3) assimilation; (4) affirmation; (5) accommodation; and lastly (6) identification. In essence, fathers are noteworthy not only as biological counterparts, but also prenatally and postnatally in the life and death of their offspring.

Mandell, McAnulty, and Reece (1980) studied 28 fathers in 46 SIDS families and found patterns of behavior "peculiar" to men. These behaviors included attempts to deny the reality of the child's death and to avoid the pain of grief work; assumption of a manager-like role immediately after the baby's death; intellectualizing of grief and blame; increased involvement outside the home; a concern to have a subsequent child; and avoidance of professional support. Most fathers did not want to talk about the death and their feelings. Those who did typically expressed a decreased sense of self-esteem and remorse over lack of involvement in the care of their infant.

By contrast, mothers in this study were tearful, frequently incoherent, self-absorbed in grief, and seemingly unaware of much around them; needed to verbalize and express feelings; displayed a tendency to withdraw; and expressed fear of subsequent pregnancy. In general, fathers seemed angrier and more aggressive than mothers, who appeared more depressed and withdrawn. The issue of subsequent parenting was a source of conflict for some couples, and when mothers requested crisis intervention difficulties often centered around communication with the husband or specific concerns about his behavior.

Schatz (1986) argued that male roles arising from social conditioning can have a negative effect on fathers in dealing with their grief. Such roles include being strong or macho ("Big boys don't cry"); competing and winning in a crisis ("How can a man compete with death?"); protecting the family from harm (death brings failure to this role); being the family provider (which may require a rapid return to work); being the problem solver (death can't be "fixed"); being the controller (death makes life "out of control"); and, being self-sufficient ("Stand on your own two feet!"; "Men don't share feelings"). As a bereaved father himself, Schatz recommended making a conscious decision to grieve and suggested that one get the coping process started by such deliberate actions as: (1) lightening one's load; (2) talking to one's family; (3) setting aside time to think; (4) learning to cry; (5) expressing anger constructively; and (6) finding a support system. In fact, many SIDS fathers use these coping methods quite successfully.

SIDS fathers have reported that, although they chose not to talk about their son's or daughter's death when they were with non-bereaved parents, they still proudly wear the baptismal ring hung on a chain around their neck, or sleep with their son's hat or baby blanket. One father carries a picture of his deceased son, his firstborn, with his wife in his left breast pocket next to his heart "where they belong." Another father writes to his deceased daughter in a diary on sleepless nights. Reviewing this chronicle brings him comfort in reading about his own progression through finding a new normal.

Birth order of the SIDS child has affected some fathers. Those who described themselves as "Mr. Mom" with the first child, but not as active with a later child, now deceased, lament that they should have been as involved with the subsequent child. They compound their grief, relating that they never knew the deceased child as well as the first, and also grieve the loss of the father-child relationship which can no longer be developed. The infant's sex can contribute to a father's interest in passing on the family surname. A "Junior" or "the III" brings added reflections of lost futures, while the first male grandchild in exclusively female grandchildren has its own implications.

Mothers

Coping for mothers, as individuals within a parental couple, has different ramifications (Edelstein, 1984; Littlefield & Rushton, 1986; Peppers & Knapp, 1980). Traditionally, the mother is the primary caretaker of the infant who personifies the epitome of vulnerability. An infant is 100% dependent on the caretaker for his or her survival. Many mothers thus report a dual loss: of their infant and of their full-time mothering job. They sometimes describe themselves as "two-for-one" failures. Questioning one's competence in this way is understandable in the wake of unexpected tragedy; in response, we need to affirm that these people really were good parents and good mothers.

Upon the death of their infant, breast-feeding mothers are faced with a key decision. Some opt to take the prescribed medication to "dry up" the residual breast milk; others do not. Whether or not they have other children, many mothers say: "How can I take that pill? That's all the mothering for this child I have left! That's my only physical bond to that child!"

If the infant died before the customary six-week postpartum checkup, some mothers view this appointment as bringing an "end" to their connection with the deceased child. Some are angry that the physician did not even express condolences during the visit. Others, more fortunate, feel comforted by the doctor's sensitivity and support for their undeserved, bereaved status (Mandell, McClain, & Reece, 1987).

Mothers whose full-time work is in the home speak of the endless triggers that complicate their coping. One mother had just painstakingly sorted through the baby things and put them in storage when, in the next laundry load, she found a baby sock stuck in the sleeve of an older child's shirt. Since these mothers are at home, they are often confronted with endless questions and challenges from surviving siblings about the deceased infant.

For example, during a visit with another family, a five-year-old sibling reported that she had mailed a letter to her deceased sister. The child's mother explained that her daughter had previously written letters to Santa Claus and deposited them in the mailbox. One Sunday when the collection basket was passed at their church's services, her daughter placed a letter to her deceased sister in the basket, unknown to her parents. The letter was retrieved later, and when the daughter was asked about it, she said: "If I can write letters to Santa, then I can write my sister who lives with Jesus!" Children grieve in pediatric doses, and that letter sufficed for that day.

Another mother stated how she cherished the time with her infant when the other children, now all of school age, went to classes. She proudly remembered how her infant son liked to "dance" with her. Tearfully, she repeated over and over again how she "lost my dancing partner!"

Mothers who are primary caretakers often feel haunted by the clock. The time the infant was found, the feeding schedule, the nap time, the time the sirens started and the "rescue" crew arrived all serve as emotional triggers.

Mothers who are employed outside the home may have experiences very much like the above. In addition, they will be faced with all of the issues related to bereavement in the workplace. That is, they will be called upon to fit back into their work environment, deal with the questions of colleagues, cope with their own feelings, and somehow find the energy and attention span to do productive work. Another difficult issue may involve leaving surviving children in the care of someone outside the family, perhaps even in the care of the same child care provider with whom the baby died.

Special Circumstances: Single Parents, Adolescent Parents, and Blended Families

A variety of circumstances may influence the experiences of SIDS parents. For example, SIDS parents who are themselves professional caregivers, such as physicians, nurses, and emergency responders, often express outrage that the non-bereaved treat them as medical professionals instead of as parents first and foremost. By contrast, the interim parenting role of a surrogate, such as a grandparent, babysitter, or day care provider, is often ignored by helpers. For all of these primary or substitute parents, it is not their profession or original status that has been changed; it is their parental role that has been so drastically altered. Helpers need to focus attention upon these persons in terms of their roles as fathers, mothers, or surrogate parents.

Three special groups of SIDS parents deserve particular attention. *Single parents* suffer many of the same ups and downs of grief as do parents in marital dyads or traditional families. Both are riding a roller coaster gone wild. Both have lost the parenting status of that SIDS infant. The difference is not so much in the grief experience itself as in the lack of support from a partner and the potential presence of concurrent stressors.

For example, some parents, though unmarried, may live together and/or both be significantly involved in the care of the infant. In other cases, one parent may have had little involvement in either the life or death of the infant. Thus, it may be difficult to locate an absent father whose whereabouts are unknown. A single parent may have no one with whom to share problems and the burden of guilt. Who should make the funeral arrangements? What should be done about questions as to the parent's ability even to pay for the funeral?

For some single parents, an extended family provides a needed and welcome source of support before the baby's death and throughout the bereavement. For others, little support existed during the baby's life, and less may be available after the death. Outsiders may tacitly view the death as something that was for the best, thinking that the parent can now get on with life, work, or school. Some stigma or guilt may have been associated with becoming a single parent, and isolation after the death may now be more profound.

A single person may have been obliged to make many sacrifices in choosing to keep a child, thus forming a "one-on-one bond" that was intense and that excluded many others. As one parent said, losing a baby who was "only every-thing" was like finding one's self in solitary confinement. Such a parent may not have the option of a subsequent child or may carry deep-seated fears into a later marriage that are difficult to share. For example, a single, first-time parent may now lack confidence that any child can survive in his or her care.

Teenagers who become pregnant can also become bereaved parents while they are still adolescents (National SIDS Clearinghouse, 1988). Some of these *adolescent parents* are married, but most are a special subset of single parents. Often, such adolescents lack the depth of experience of more mature parents. Sometimes the pregnancy arises from inadequate decision-making abilities. For all young parents, the death of a child may have long-term consequences, since self-destructive behaviors, such as drug usage, alcohol abuse, and acting out, are common ways of resolving grief among teenagers.

Like many SIDS parents, most adolescents have not previously experienced the death of someone close to them. Such adolescents may exhibit a stronger aversion than older persons to death and to viewing or touching the dead child. In addition, their peer support group is unlikely to have previous experi-ence with supporting a grieving friend. Moreover, the experience of a teen who has already participated in the life cycle of her infant, both giving birth and providing a burial, establishes a special sense of identity which is at variance with her peer group.

The dual isolation of being a bereaved parent and being ostracized by their peers may make single adolescent parents less verbal and less assertive in seeking help. This need not be interpreted as rejecting assistance from knowl-edgeable counselors who can help put into perspective issues involving life and death. Thus, Barnickol, Fuller, and Shinners (1986, p. 146) recommend that professionals can be "most effective when they relate to the parents based not on stereotypes but on their value and needs as parents who have experienced the death of their child."

Another set of special circumstances involves individuals in *stepfamilies* or *blended families*. With the high rate of divorce and other forms of marital dissolution in our society, many adults and children find themselves in new relationships (Burgoyne & Clark, 1981; Visher & Visher, 1979, 1980). In such circumstances, stepparents (and other stepfamily members) may encounter unique difficulties in coping with a SIDS death. For example, the infant who dies may not be the child of its stepparent. More typically, the baby is the planned offspring of the new union. As such, the baby may be cherished in a unique way because of the symbolic significance which it holds for its parents and for the set of stepbrothers and stepsisters which each parent may have brought to the new relationship from a prior family system. Here the problems may not be those of lack of support or inexperience which face some single parents and some adolescent parents, but the complexities of the stepfamily relationships and the special role of the infant in the new family.

While recognizing these and other special circumstances and the many differences among SIDS parents, it may also help to consider some of the common issues and experiences that are faced by most parents following the death of an infant. In order to make this discussion manageable, these issues and experiences are organized here in a rough temporal order although they may not arise precisely that way in real life.

IMMEDIATE IMPACTS OF SIDS

Discovering the Dead Child

Death resulting from SIDS is unanticipated and certainly unwelcomed. It is also just the first in a series of difficult experiences for surviving parents. All of this begins with the discovery of the dead child and the first turbulent, confusing hours of bereavement.

Who among us has ever thought we would find raw death in our own home? We expect death to occur in hospitals after a prolonged illness or under the auspices of hospice care—anticipated death. Modern medicine has conditioned us to expect that old people will die, but not an infant who was declared healthy by a physician only days before.

Finding raw death is visually and emotionally devastating. Infants who succumb to SIDS are often found with their fists clenched. A white froth, sometimes blood-tinged, might be exuding from their mouths or nostrils. Since SIDS is a silent death, usually occurring during sleep, many hours may elapse before its discovery. During this time, lividity will occur due to the gravitational settling of the body fluids, causing irregular mottling on the anatomy of the deceased. The baby's position at death might be face down in the bed, misleading parents to think that their infant might have suffocated. A plethora of irrational ideas races through each parent's mind, like "Was I somehow accidentally responsible for my baby's death?"

The objective-subjective paradox also ensues. While attempting cardio-pulmonary resuscitation, parents recount thinking: "When the emergency crews arrive, they will be able to help my baby medically." But subjectively, in their hearts, and against all hope, they realize that their infant is dead. Pronouncement of death crystalizes the parents' worst fears. Their child has preceded them in death, and they do not know why.

The Emergency Room: Saying Goodbye

Grief-stricken parents, upon learning that their infant was dead on arrival at the emergency room, respond in a variety of very individual ways (Miles, 1977). For example, a mother of twins did not want to hold the deceased twin, but did want to nurture her surviving infant and, in turn, be comforted by that sibling. Most parents in this situation are bewildered by the baffling turn of events and strange new circumstances into which they have been so rudely thrust. Many do not have the presence of mind to identify and assert their needs, for example, to hold and say goodbye to the infant. Later, they may suffer additional regret if this was their unexpressed wish.

It will be important to parents that the body of their infant is treated with dignity and respect, and that he or she is acknowledged in conversation by name, not just as "the baby." These are ways of affirming that the infant did have a life, a death, and an identity all its own (Merritt, Bauer, & Hasselmeyer, 1975). Bewildered survivors may need to be held and comforted; certainly, tissues should be provided for weeping survivors. A second box of tissues placed directly in front of the father can convey compassion and grant permission for the paternal release of tears. Dads cry also, even though their tears are too frequently ignored.

Religious concerns may loom large in these hectic moments. For example, it may be important to have the baby baptized. Some parents whose baby had previously been baptized are gratified if the same minister can bless that child at death. For them, this consistency helps to bring closure to their infant's religious "life cycle." Other families find comfort merely in the presence of a member of the clergy or in an opportunity to visit the hospital chapel. In these ways, established resources can help bring order to this extraordinary situation. Of course, there may also be anger at God who allowed this bad thing to happen to good people and an innocent child.

There is no need to rush family members—including surviving siblings—in saying goodbye. For most, the next time they will see the infant will be in a baby-sized casket. Parents and other family members can all take part in this ceremonial leave-taking. In the case of siblings, for example, if they learn about death practically—that they no longer will need to bring the bottle for feedings or the diapers for changing, that the infant's body is no longer warm, that the baby will no longer coo or cry—this can crystallize the concept of death for them. Some siblings will opt to sing a favorite song to their brother or sister while holding the infant one last time.

Parents will usually welcome any offer to notify the family's other established sources of support, such as extended family members (e.g., maternal and paternal grandparents), the baby's pediatrician, the mother's obstetrician and gynecologist, employers, and best friends. The latter can especially be helpful in transporting the family from the emergency room to their own home or to a relative's house.

Even when parents do not request a picture of their child on the spot, a snapshot taken of the baby and put in the hospital chart can later—at the family's initiative—be a treasured addition to their photo album. Most of us took pictures when our firstborn arrived. But we may not have been so diligent for a later child. Sometimes we may have opted not to order the hospital birth picture. In any of these circumstances, and even when many other pictures are already available, the emergency room picture might later be an irreplaceable memento of the now-dead infant.

Medical-Legal Issues and Their Implications

Babies are totally dependent on their caretakers for survival from hour to hour. When infants die in the care of vigilant parents, the universal reaction is one of profound guilt. The comment, "Is there something I did or did not do that precipitated the death of my baby?", is echoed repeatedly. When a death is sudden, unexpected, and its underlying cause remains unexplained by scientists, it leaves in its wake an overwhelming feeling of emotional impotence, especially in one's parenting skills.

In the midst of profound feelings of helplessness and inadequacy, parents are catapulted into a new and unfamiliar world. Law enforcement officers ask questions and take photographs in their effort to protect society from harmful behavior, while health care personnel seek to obtain an accurate medical history. These interrogations may seem baffling and intrusive to anguished parents. In addition, the untimely, sudden death of an infant raises questions about an autopsy or postmortem examination which needs to be performed on the child to determine the medical cause of death and the legal manner of its death.

Bereaved parents are typically not seasoned medical professionals. Thus, attending law enforcement officers, emergency medical service personnel, coroner or medical examiner, or hospital personnel cannot assume that a parent will be familiar with their respective services or methods of operation. In each case, these need to be explained.

In particular, for most newly bereaved parents, the word "autopsy" is foreign and often frightening. An autopsy, simply explained, is surgery after death. This needs to be fully explained to parents in the emergency room. Otherwise, they will harbor visions of the television drama in which the pathologist, Dr. Quincy, undrapes a body and veteran police personnel faint. It must be emphasized that an autopsy is a thorough scientific procedure to determine the cause and manner of death. Parents need to be assured that an open casket *is* an option after this postmortem examination.

LATER IMPACTS OF SIDS

Awaiting the Autopsy Results: Blame and Guilt

Returning home from the hospital emergency room, the prevailing question for parents is, "What caused the death of my baby?" Awaiting the autopsy results is a study in frustration. Parents report mentally replaying memories of the death scene over and over again in their minds in search of clues to the cause of death. In addition, if the infant died late in the evening, parents often suffer the torment of waiting until normal business hours permit the attending pathologist to determine their child's preliminary diagnosis. Time becomes a catalyst for going back over memories of the death scene again and again.

In this process, hurt and pain often lead to anger and, in turn, to blame and guilt. Blaming others is a familiar way of "making sense" of the hurt which I am experiencing. Scapegoats are convenient objects for the projection of one's anger. Blame can be directed to the medical staff in both pre-hospital and hospital emergency room settings. Sometimes, blame is assigned to God or to the infant's carefully selected babysitter or surrogate parent. More often, parents, feeling culpable, blame each other. Frequently, they chastize themselves by taking on blame in the form of guilt for what has happened. All of these are ways of responding to deep-seated feelings of helplessness and vulnerability, and of honoring the conviction that there must be some rational framework or reason (in the absence of a known cause) for the occurrence of such a tragic event.

Father may say: "Why didn't I check on the baby when I passed her? I should have checked her sooner. At least, she wouldn't have died alone!" Mothers harass themselves with doubts specific to their own familial situation. "I only breast fed my baby. Should I have bottle fed?" Conversely, others will comment, "I bottle fed my child. Maybe I should have breast fed?" Some question their prior decision-making skills as parents. "My aunt raised six healthy children. She never took her infants to large social gatherings until they were four months of age. Should we have gone to restaurants so frequently? Perhaps that's where the baby caught her cold. But people at the restaurants commented on how healthy our baby looked. I can't believe she's dead!" These examples suggest that guilt and blame for SIDS parents can initially be symbiotic.

Guilt is the conviction that one has done wrong by violating some moral, ethical, or religious principle. Typically associated with such a conviction are lowered self-esteem and a feeling that one should expiate or make retribution for the supposed wrong. Hence, until the diagnosis of the cause of death is known—and often thereafter, in spite of the objective diagnosis—parents engage in a fact-finding search. Many researchers (e.g., DeFrain & Ernst, 1978; DeFrain, Taylor, & Ernst, 1982; Smialek, 1978; Weinstein, 1978) have stated that guilt is a particularly common and difficult emotional response when an infant dies of SIDS because of the lack of clarity about the cause of death, the fact that the death often occurs in the parents' home, and the fact that many of these parents are young, poor, and inexperienced.

Miles and Demi (1984 & 1986) suggested a theoretical model of parental bereavement guilt, according to which guilt arises from feelings of helplessness and responsibility. These feelings lead parents to ask how their past and present actions and feelings might have contributed to the child's death. Inevitable discrepancies between ideal standards and actual performance, along with perceived violations of self-expectations, culminate in guilt feelings. These researchers identified a typology of six potential sources of guilt:

1. *Death Causation Guilt* related to the belief that the parent either contributed to or failed to protect the child from the death
2. *Illness-related Guilt* related to perceived deficiencies in the parental role during the child's illness or at the time of death
3. *Parental Role Guilt* related to the belief that the parent failed to live up to self-expectations or societal expectations in the overall parental role
4. *Moral Guilt* related to the belief that the child's death was punishment or retribution for violating a moral, ethical, or religious standard
5. *Survival Guilt* related to violating the standard that a child should outlive his or her parents
6. *Grief Guilt* related to the behavioral and emotional reactions of grief at the time of or following the child's death.

Of course, guilt may lead to constructive outcomes. Thus, Bergman (1986) has observed that it was the intense guilt of parents and the experiences of parents being blamed for their infant's death that was the impetus in the United States for the national movement to develop a four-point program of intervention that included doing autopsies on all infants, using the term SIDS on the death certificates, informing parents promptly about the autopsy results, and providing follow-up counseling to help parents understand that there is no known cause of SIDS and that they were not to blame.

Struggles with pain, anger, blame, and guilt mark the beginning of a difficult journey experienced by SIDS parents. One part of that journey involves a search for the cause of their infant's death and a related attempt to make meaning out of the death itself. The other part of the journey involves a living through of the parents' own grief responses and an effort to establish a new standard of normality for ongoing living.

Preliminary Diagnosis: Understanding and Acting on Its Implications

SIDS parents share a need to have provisional information regarding the potential cause of death of their child. They should be advised that a qualified pathologist will perform the autopsy or postmortem examination, and that preliminary results will usually be known within a 24-hour period. Experience has shown that all parents should be treated as potential SIDS parents where review of the circumstances prior to the death are consistent with known facts about SIDS. Given the provisional diagnosis, parents can be given a SIDS fact brochure at the hospital. Reading the pamphlet can be helpful, but it still leaves the diagnosis as "pending" or "preliminary."

Feeling guilty, parents sometimes interpret these terms to mean pending investigation by police and medical examiner or coroner. In potential SIDS deaths, the term "pending" refers to "pending histological studies" in the laboratory of forensic medicine. Involved professionals need to be sensitive to misinterpretations on the part of families at this vulnerable time. Foul play is not to be suggested. Parents are usually relieved to learn, and others must keep carefully in mind, that SIDS is a natural cause of death. It is not to be confused with other modes of death, whether accident, suicide, homicide, or undetermined.

The issuance of a temporary death certificate allows for burial or cremation of the infant's body. The need to make decisions on these and other matters can present additional challenges to bereaved parents at a time when they are absorbed in their grief and have little energy to spare. Should the body be cremated or buried? Should there be a wake, a funeral service, or a memorial service? Should we make decisions now about what to do with the baby's things and his or her room, or should we decide to postpone decisions on these and a myriad of other matters?

Personal expression of grief can take many forms at this difficult time. Some parents feel the need for a private, family funeral or memorial service. Others find comfort in the support extended by a large group of family and friends at a wake and funeral. Likewise, some parents express the need to visit the cemetery often, even daily, while others feel that going to the gravesite is not at all helpful for them.

Davidson (1984) has described the importance of ceremonial leave-taking at the wake or funeral, emphasizing personal expression. For example, one grandfather wanted to dress his deceased grandchild, since he had not met the child before his death and needed to hold him. The parents had no interest in doing this. Some parents confess to coming late for their child's funeral because they knew it would be their last goodbye and wanted to postpone that event even for just a few moments. Again, each person must be given permission to express grief in his or her own individual way.

Final Diagnosis: Some Answers and More Questions

Following completion of laboratory studies, the final autopsy results reveal SIDS. This diagnosis brings both medical and legal exoneration. The doctors did not miss anything—the first symptom of SIDS was the death itself and there was nothing to notice prior to that time. Similarly, the parents were not remiss in their concern for or surveillance over their child. The caretaker at the time of death was equally vigilant. The law is not after anyone. No one is at fault. Some of these words are reassuring.

Nevertheless, the final diagnosis may kindle new questions. Some include: "Why is SIDS diagnosed by exclusion? Why are there no definitive pathological markers at autopsy? If SIDS is the number one killer of infants up to one year of age, why is its cause unknown? Why did it happen to my baby?" These are difficult questions to confront and difficult questions to answer. For newly bereaved parents, partial answers do not suffice. Often they only generate more questions and self-accusations, which usually begin with the phrases, "What if I had done . . .?" or "If only I had . . . ."

In the beginning, SIDS parents frequently say things like, "I never thought this would happen to me. I had heard about SIDS, but dismissed it." As they learn more about SIDS, many compare their own situation to the epidemiological risk factors that are associated with SIDS. They attempt to assign themselves on the continuum of low- to high-risk factors (Goldberg, et al., 1986; Peterson, 1988). Unfortunately, this is a fruitless quest. As Merritt and Valdes-Dapena (1984, p. 204) have said: "To date no risk analysis schemes have been found to have clinical usefulness." Risk factors for SIDS are descriptive and imprecise, not causal and predictive. Both high-risk infants and low-risk infants can die of autopsy-proven SIDS. Moreover, even a perfect match between an individual case and a risk factor profile would not bring back the dead baby. Grief remains and is not assuaged.

LONG-TERM IMPACTS OF SIDS

The Legacy of Grief

Newly bereaved parents often seek sanctioned guidelines for grieving. However, guidelines for grieving are not well defined (Demi & Miles, 1987) and the legacy of grief that is bequeathed to SIDS parents is characterized by parameters yet unknown to them. For example, the work of mourning entails not only grieving for the actual person who has died, but also for all of the hopes, dreams, fantasies, and unfulfilled expectations the griever held for that person and for that relationship (Rando, 1984). Another major complicating factor in accomplishing grief work is that the present loss may resurrect old issues and conflicts for the mourner, some of which were previously unresolved. In addition, unfolding of grief is concomitant and is in addition to one's regular job, whether the job be full-time in the home, as a lawyer, or as a public aid recipient. It is no wonder that what we call mourning or *grief work* is exhausting for parents.

The only guarantee is that if we love, then we will grieve. There is quite a variance as to how this will be manifested. Grief and mourning have many dimensions: cognitive, affective (emotional), physical (somatic), behavioral, and spiritual. Parents and others must attend to each. For example, physiological aspects of grief for SIDS parents include reports of sleep disorders, appetite disturbances, difficulty in concentration, and problems in decision making, even in decisions previously regarded as routine.

The basic cognitive issue for SIDS parents is their need to know what killed their baby. This question is posed over and over in an attempt to understand and purge oneself from ultimate blame. Different people—some professionals, some friends, some peers in parental bereavement—are asked the same questions. Reliability and validity of answers are sought. Each parent finds a self-paced manner of addressing his or her grief by obtaining information and facts about the lethal syndrome.

In this way, the medical cause of death becomes, in time, increasingly credible; but in an ever-hovering sense, incredulous. The seemingly sophisticated medical community knows how to diagnose SIDS accurately, but research has not been able to identify its cause. A plethora of theories about causation has been identified. But, as yet, no specific underlying cause has been found. Partial answers only foster more "what if" or "if only" queries. These are questions that need answers and questions that deserve answers, but questions for which answers are not now available.

In their quest for answers, some parents read and reread the literature that is offered to them by various SIDS-related resources. Other parents may have a need to conduct additional research or to search the libraries for journal articles addressing theories of causation. Findings are compared with their baby's prenatal and postnatal records. If there are surviving siblings, their records are sometimes reviewed also. Once the written autopsy report is completed, some parents consult with the deceased infant's pediatrician to gain additional insights, listening intently to his or her interpretations, ever questioning as the contents of the document are explained to them.

At some point in time, determined solely by each parent, there is submission to the accuracy of the diagnosis. This stepping stone in grief is sometimes accepted ruefully. During one peer support group meeting for SIDS parents, a mother resentfully exclaimed, "How come I became an unsolicited member of this select club?"

Some parents have expressed disappointment when they were advised that their infant's death was attributed to SIDS. Frustrated, they comment that if their child died of some cause other than SIDS, at least there would be clear pathological markers—*medical reasons*—to define the cause of death, instead of the dearth of such markers that characterizes the diagnosis of SIDS. Other parents feel some relief that at least a SIDS diagnosis exonerates everyone from blame in the child's death.

Rekindling the Search for the Cause

The parents' academic search for the cause of death is provisionally over. Provisionally, because only the current factual information has been temporarily catalogued in each parent's mind. This catalogue is reopened as media reporting—by radio, television, or the printed word—makes the parents evaluate the current proposed theory as to what causes Sudden Infant Death Syndrome. This is an agonizing process for parents which will cease only when the underlying cause or causes of SIDS are finally discovered.

Every new theory of causation leads SIDS parents to reexamine the death of their child in an attempt to gain control of an uncontrollable death. Some parents find these "new" theories hopeful; others are irritated by media coverage that does not yield the ultimate cause of SIDS, but only seems to rekindle past pain. Realizing the difficulties in SIDS research, some parents resolutely hope that the cause of SIDS will be found in their other children's lifetime, if not in their own. Parents often reflect on the death of their child by stating, "I wouldn't want this to happen to anyone else!"

Furthermore, just seeing another infant, toddler, or child reminds the bereaved parent of what was and what would have been. Parenting does not stop when a child dies. The parent is still a parent, but now of a deceased child. This is a permanent status and an irreversible one. Often, extended family, friends, and society do not recognize these parents as the parents they are. How many fathers receive Father's Day remembrances when their son is deceased? How many Mother's Day cards include the name of a now-deceased child?

The First Year: Seasons of Grief

The first year following the death of a child does not exhaust the legacy of grief left to SIDS parents, but it does have its own very special challenges. The full torment of a calendar year encompasses a series of anticipated and unanticipated difficulties. Grief is triggered by the most innocent of daily events: a toy found behind a piece of furniture; a roll of film finally developed yielding treasured pictures of the dead child; a family gathering that reveals an empty infant chair at the home of the grandparents—a chair that used to seat an infant who would now be crawling and saying, "Da-Da" and "Ma-Ma."

Halloween has prompted some first-time parents, now bereaved, to go to a hotel because they could not yet deal with smiling, giggling faces squealing "trick or treat." Thanksgiving comes—what is there to be thankful for? During the Yuletide season, some parents bring a Christmas tree, complete with functional lights, to their baby's gravesite monument because all children enjoy bubbling lights and shiny ornaments. Others leave unopened packages encased in plastic to protect their gift from nature's intervention. Later, the gift is often given to the pediatric floor of hospitals for distribution. Do you hang three Christmas stockings or two on the fireplace mantel? In Jewish families, Hanukkah and Rosh Hashannah may need to be re-evaluated. Families of all religious persuasions and ethnic traditions are touched in their own ways by memories and lost futures.

New Year's Day arrives. Parents often have no interest in celebrating. Easter also brings no revelry in Easter bunny antics. Some parents with surviving children state that they celebrate the major holidays held dear in their family traditions because of their surviving children's anticipation of the established rituals. But other parents state that this is done in a robot-like way. The previous magic of recognizing that day has abated. Mother's Day, Father's Day, and Grandparent's Day are difficult, especially during the first year after the death. Similarly, the anniversary of the baby's date of birth, date of death, and date they put the monument in place generate varied emotions. Each day needs to be recognized.

Zebal and Woolsey (1984) have examined key transition points in the long-term adaptation of SIDS families. Their description can be useful if it leads bereaved parents themselves and those who would help them to achieve heightened sensitivity to grief reactions over an extended period of time. But this portrait must not be frozen into a stereotypical framework which stifles individuality. No grief is created equal. Regardless of how close their relationship is, each bereaved parent needs to grieve individually, even when two parents must also grieve together as a couple.

According to Zebal and Woolsey, in the first several hours, days, or weeks after the death, shock and denial reactions give way to acute grief reactions. The latter include somatic reactions, hostility and anger, guilt and blame, anxiety and fear, depression and withdrawal, disorganization and difficulties in functioning, and preoccupation and searching.

Six to eight weeks after the death, Zebal and Woolsey note that the reality of the death is likely to be more clear, external support will often be withdrawn, and the abovementioned grief reactions will still continue.

The four- to six-month period brings a shift to future-oriented concerns. It is also a time in which periods of relief may alternate with recurrence of grief reactions.

Initial anniversary reactions include date of birth and date of death, holidays, and other significant times. Here, notable behaviors include intense memories and recurrence of grief reactions which had previously decreased in intensity.

The period from one to two years after the death is usually marked by a continued progression to family equilibrium, with mothers generally taking longer to recover. Also included are transient periods of sadness.

Confirmation of subsequent pregnancy brings a heightened anxiety and re-emergence of concerns about SIDS. At another key transition point, when the subsequent child's age surpasses that of the SIDS infant, anxiety usually begins to subside.

The final long-term adaptation point noted by Zebal and Woolsey concerns subsequent anniversary reactions. These kindle renewal of memories and fantasies about the deceased infant at that age if he or she had survived.

Handling the Holidays

In view of the importance of holidays in our lives and of the problems which they pose for bereaved parents, some writers (e.g., Conley, 1986) have developed guidelines for coping with such days and this is a familiar topic for peer support groups. The acronym which Conley used to focus on constructive ways of surviving the holiday roller-coaster of emotions is **C.O.P.E.** Let us examine each of these letters.

The letter **C** in **C.O.P.E.** entreats the bereaved to "clear" their minds by releasing frustrated feelings and bringing them to the surface where they can be dealt with. The letter **O** stands for "order" or "organization." This challenges the bereaved to examine their individual holiday concerns and then to prioritize them. The letter **P** stands for "planning" and refers to the "how" of the coping process. The letter **E** entreats the bereaved to "execute" the carefully considered plans which they, themselves, have created.

Within this framework, Melin (quoted in Conley, 1986) championed having a family conference to evaluate which holiday traditions, if any, should be continued, stopped, or amended. Practically, she recommended:

1. Eliminate the unnecessary and reduce the holiday pressures on yourself and others. Focus on the things that are really important to you and your family.
2. Don't over-extend. Don't over commit. Be realistic and you won't feel you have failed.
3. Give special consideration to what activities will help both you and the children. . . .
4. Finally remember the needs of others, and be aware that your greatest happiness may come in doing something for someone else . . . (p. 16).

Along with these activities, Conley urged bereaved persons to take time to pray; take time to worship; and take time to love and let yourself be loved.

Finally, Conley (1986) commented that handling the holidays involves so many personal variables that few bereaved persons can say exactly when or how the holidays eventually became easier and more enjoyable. But most, he continued, report that one day they found themselves laughing at things they had not laughed at for a long time. Suddenly, they realized an anniversary had passed and the anxiety did not totally overwhelm them.

In hindsight, most parents acknowledge that anticipation of a special date was worse than the day itself. One mother who had buried two children who had died separately of SIDS, commented that on one daughter's birthday the Women's Auxiliary of the hospital where the daughter was born had sent her deceased daughter a one-year-old birthday card. Of course, they had not known that the child was now dead. The mother said, "I'm going to keep that birthday card; it is the only one my daughter is going to receive!" Meanwhile, the ingredients for a chocolate cake with chocolate icing were sitting on the stove. The mother explained that her family would have birthday cake for dessert that evening. This same mother related that she often sees pieces of cake by the cemetery headstones of other infants, although that is not her family tradition.

Outcomes of Mourning

In recent years, researchers (e.g., Osterweis, Solomon, & Green, 1984) have questioned how we should properly characterize the outcome of grief work or mourning. Should we speak of "completion," "recovery," or "adaptation"? In a study of bereaved parents and siblings seven to nine years after the death of a child from cancer, McClowry and her colleagues (1987) reported that the central issue for these families was how to deal with the "empty space" in their lives. Three primary strategies were identified: (1) "getting over it" or putting the death in one's past; (2) "filling the empty space" by keeping busy or by undertaking new projects; and (3) "keeping the connection" or maintaining a place in the family for the dead infant.

Specifically in terms of SIDS parents, Wortman and Silver (1987) found little evidence that grief resolution increases over elapsed time intervals of three weeks, three months, and 18 months after the baby's death. They recounted data providing evidence that, contrary to popular belief, individuals are not always able to resolve their loss and come up with an explanation for the event that is satisfying to them. These researchers concluded that especially when the event is sudden, a majority of individuals appear to have great difficulty in coming to terms with what has happened.

SIDS parents often comment about having "empty arms" and physical aches, both in their arms and in their hearts for their deceased infant. They speak of an "empty space" in their heart which belongs solely to their SIDS infant. Although the subject has not yet been systematically studied, many SIDS parents state that they will never "get over" the death of their infant, nor will they "fill the space." Rather, they report that their task has been to learn to "maintain the connection" and live with this empty space.

The minds of most SIDS parents are dominated by thoughts and feelings about their deceased child as they make their way into a new universe. In the early hours, days, and weeks of learning what life is like as bereaved parents, it seems as if not an hour passes without their thinking about the child. The variable is not whether one will grieve. What varies is the individuality of the expression of grief. This is dependent on the parent's established repertoire of coping mechanisms and support systems, whether constructive (such as making a memorial scrapbook) or destructive (such as drinking to excess). Past mechanisms are challenged as parents struggle to develop more effective techniques of coping.

Frequently, parents report, "I think I am going crazy." Some describe hearing the dead baby crying. Others explain that they sometimes prepare the bottles or the bath water for the deceased infant, acting out of their normal parenting routines even though they know their child is dead. In short, the parenting rituals that were indoctrinated during the child's short life sometimes continue in the time following the infant's death. This is not surprising, since mourning is essentially "a process of unlearning the expected presence of the deceased" (Rakoff, 1973, p. 159). But if parents are not made aware of some of these common and normal behavioral manifestations, they may feel that their actions are abnormal. Such parents need to experience the full expression of their grief. Grief is normal. As Manning (1979) has said, it is nature's way of healing a broken heart.

In hindsight, parents report that they started feeling "better" when they suddenly realized that half a day or a full day elapsed without the thought of their child popping up in their mind. When grief work is effective and mourning productive, intensity of grief usually decreases for bereaved SIDS parents. However, every parent is a unique individual and the roller coasters of grief among bereaved persons are not always in synchrony. Nor should we expect that.

Where or how does a parent redirect the special love that each parent has for his or her deceased infant? If parents are allowed the dignity of grieving, each will find his or her own answer (e.g., Szybist, 1988). However, mourning takes time. There are no short cuts. Delayed or unresolved grief can be harmful. It is important to remember that each parent needs to establish a new "normal" after the death of his or her baby.

TWO RECURRING ISSUES FOR SIDS PARENTS

Surviving and Subsequent Children

Coping with surviving and subsequent children affects both parents (Mandell, Dirks-Smith, & Smith, 1988; Mandell, McAnulty, & Carlson, 1983). Each will reflect how he or she was engulfed by personal grief and found it difficult to have the energy to parent other children effectively. At the same time, parents are quick to state how lucky they are to have other children who help keep them busy and help comfort them: "I love you, Daddy, don't cry!"

It is important to note the difference between the bereaved parent commenting about having surviving siblings, and a counselor commenting. A non-bereaved professional offering the comment, "How lucky you are to have other children!", is likely to be viewed as insensitive and presumptuous, and the conversation with the parent will probably quickly end. Instead, the professional should be nonjudgmental and listen, sometimes offering no comment unless expressly petitioned to do so by the parents.

Bereaved parents speaking with each other often say how grateful they are that it was not their firstborn that died. Among themselves, they agree that in terms of birth order, the death of a firstborn ranks as "being the worst." The death of a child following permanent sterilization of either parent generally ranks second. First-time parents, having been promoted to family life and then "demoted" to being just a couple again, have no one left to parent. For them, there is no "living proof" that their other children were given identical parenting and lived.

Whether or not to have subsequent children is a question that affects the coping of both parents (Mandell & Wolfe, 1975; Szybist, 1976). Should I seek to become a parent again? If so, when? Issues germane to this question include prior ease in conceiving or complications of sub-fertility; mother's age balanced against other established genetic risks; permanent sterilization either by the father's vasectomy or the mother's tubal ligation; and availability of family finances to seek a reversal of either of these without future guarantee of conception. Difficult decisions about these issues must sometimes be made at a time when there is much indecisiveness. In situations where difficult decisions can be postponed until more energy is available, this is often helpful.

Once conception occurs, parents' anxieties again increase. Should they deliver at the same hospital where the previous child was pronounced dead? Should they change obstetricians so they can deliver at another hospital? Should they change pediatricians? These and other anxieties usually dissipate as decisions activate results. However, they dissipate more fully after the subsequent child passes the age at death of the deceased sibling. The emotional hurdles are large, whether a sibling died of SIDS at two months of age or at 16 months of age. Each day has its own victory of surviving the ordeal. Again, the focus needs to be one-day-at-a-time.

Decisions About Monitoring

Subsequent pregnancies resurrect the SIDS-apnea controversy. Given the demonstrated lack of control over a SIDS death, expectant parents vacillate on whether or not to use an infant monitor. Informed parents acknowledge that a monitor will neither prevent nor predict SIDS, but some nonetheless opt for its placebo effect. When indicated, the infant's pediatrician will appropriately test for apnea with results often falling within normal limits. Despite the positive feedback, a monitor may be prescribed, not for the healthy baby, but for the parents and relatives who might be on a 24-hour "watch." As monitoring caretakers, they often feel they are doing everything medically possible to ensure the life of their child. The decision to monitor or not to monitor rests with the bereaved parents, in consultation with their physician (Kelly & Shannon, 1988).

Monitoring can augment stress in an already stressful household (Slovik & Kelly, 1988). In monitoring, as in any new situation, there is the challenge of the learning curve. Monitors are machines; sometimes they set off false alarms. Yet, the emotional reaction of the attending parents will be a true one: an alarm for them indicates a danger to the baby, not an erroneous signal. All family members are affected. Who will babysit for an infant on a monitor? Will relatives and friends become intimidated and not even visit? Siblings often speak of their "bionic" infant sibling. Families complain about the ignorance of those unfamiliar with monitors. One father was frustrated when he, his wife, and the monitored infant went out to dinner. Someone asked him if the machine he was carrying was a video camera. He ignored the query, feeling the person did not deserve an explanation.

CONCLUSION

The role of a professional counselor or lay helper in any situation with bereaved SIDS parents should be to facilitate healthy grieving. This involves many things, including an affirmation of the bereaved parent's feeling of lost innocence, acting sometimes as a reflector back to the parent of his or her thoughts or feelings, but most of all just listening to the shared recollections of lost futures.

Counselors and helpers can assure that progress through grief and mourning is based in part on the reflected appraisals of others. The non-bereaved can help and should neither shun bereaved parents nor provide platitudes. For many newly-bereaved parents, it is the support of veteran peer parents that can be the most reflective of human mirrors. Peers have undergone and survived this terrible experience. They are living testament and a glimmer of hope to the newly bereaved who feel they are "going crazy" when in reality they are only grieving their beloved child.

The concept of "lost innocence" poses several questions that can be answered by the readers' silent show of hands. How many of us think: "It won't happen to me!"? How many of us have cemetery plots or a columbarium selected for our children? How many of us are prepared to listen earnestly to—not sit in judgment on—those bereaved parents who have had to answer "yes" to the first two questions? If we do listen actively and learn from both their positive and negative experiences, maybe together we can help them help themselves. The byproduct is that we will help ourselves become more effective counselors and more sensitive human beings through this process.

REFERENCES

Barnickol, C. A., Fuller, H., & Shinners, B. (1986). Helping bereaved adolescent parents. In C. A. Corr & J. N. McNeil (Eds.), *Adolescence and death* (pp. 132–147). New York: Springer Publishing Co.

Bergman, A. B. (1986). The *"discovery" of sudden infant death syndrome; Lessons in the practice of political medicine.* New York: Praeger.

Burgoyne, J., & Clark D. (1981). Parenting in stepfamilies. In R. Chester, P. Diggory, & M. B. Sutherland (Eds.), *Changing patterns of child-bearing and child-rearing* (pp. 133–147). New York: Academic Press.

Conley, B. (1986). *Handling the holidays* (rev. ed.). Elburn, IL: Thum Printing.

Davidson, G. W. (1984). *Understanding mourning: A guide for those who grieve.* Minneapolis, MN: Augsburg.

Davis, C. E. (1988). Male grief. Paper presented at a conference on Sudden Infant Death Syndrome: Its legacy of grief, Chicago, IL, June 9th.

DeFrain, J. D., & Ernst, L. (1978). The psychological effects of sudden infant death syndrome on surviving family members. *The Journal of Family Practice, 6*, 985–989.

DeFrain, J. D., Taylor, J., & Ernst, L. (1982). *Coping with sudden infant death.* Lexington, MA: Lexington Books, D. C. Heath.

Demi, A. S., & Miles, M. S. (1987). Parameters of normal grief: A Delphi study. *Death Studies, 11*, 397–412.

Edelstein, L. (1984). *Maternal bereavement: Coping with the unexpected death of a child.* New York: Praeger.

Fish, W. C. (1986). Differences of grief intensity in bereaved parents. In T. A. Rando (Ed.), *Parental loss of a child* (pp. 415–428). Champaign, IL: Research Press.

Goldberg, J., Hornung, R., Yamashita, T., & Wehrmacher, W. (1986). Age at death and risk factors in sudden infant death syndrome. *Australian Pediatric Journal, 22*, Supplement, 21–28.

Kelly, D. H., & Shannon, D. C. (1988). The medical management of cardiorespiratory monitoring in infantile apnea. In J. L. Culbertson, H. F. Krous, & R. D. Bendell (Eds.), *Sudden infant death syndrome: Medical aspects and psychological management* (pp. 139–154). Baltimore: The Johns Hopkins University Press.

Littlefield, C. H., & Rushton, J. P. (1986). When a child dies: The sociobiology of bereavement. *Journal of Personality and Social Psychology, 51*, 797–802.

Mandell, F., & Wolfe, L. C. (1975). Sudden infant death syndrome and subsequent pregnancy. *Pediatrics, 56*, 774–776.

Mandell, F., Dirks-Smith, T., & Smith, M. F. (1988). The surviving child in the SIDS family. *Pediatrician, 15*, 217–221.

Mandell, F., McAnulty, E., & Carlson, A. (1983). Unexpected death of an infant sibling. *Pediatrics, 72*, 652–657.

Mandell, F., McAnulty, E., & Reece, R. M. (1980). Observations of paternal response to sudden unanticipated infant death. *Pediatrics, 65*, 221–225.

Mandell, F., McClain, M., & Reece, R. M. (1987). Sudden and unexpected death: The pediatrician's response. *American Journal of Diseases of Children, 141*, 748–750.

Manning, D. (1979). *Don't take my grief away from me.* Springfield, IL: Human Services Press.

McClowry, S. G., Davies, E. B., May, K. A., Kulenkamp, E. J., & Martinson, E. M. (1987). The empty space phenomenon: The process of grief in the bereaved family. *Death Studies, 11*, 361–374.

Merritt, T. A., & Valdes-Dapena, M. (1984). SIDS research update. *Pediatric Annals, 13*, 193–207.

Merritt, T. A., Bauer, W. I., & Hasselmeyer, E. G. (1975). Sudden infant death syndrome: The role of the emergency room physician. *Clinical Pediatrics, 14*, 1095–1097.

Miles, M. S. (1977). SIDS: Parents are the patients. *Journal of Emergency Nursing, 3*(2), 29–32.

Miles, M. S., & Demi, A. S. (1984). Toward the development of a theory of bereavement guilt: Sources of guilt in bereaved parents. *Omega, 14*, 299–314.

Miles, M. S., & Demi, A. S. (1986). Guilt in bereaved parents. In T. A. Rando (Ed.), *Parental loss of a child* (pp. 97–118). Champaign, IL: Research Press.

National Sudden Infant Death Syndrome Clearinghouse. (1988). *Sudden infant death syndrome (SIDS) and other infant losses among adolescent parents: An annotated bibliography and resource guide.* McLean, VA: Author.

Osterweis, M., Solomon, F., & Green, M. (1984). *Bereavement: Reactions, consequences, and care.* Washington, DC: National Academy Press.

Peppers, L. G., & Knapp, R. J. (1980). *Motherhood and mourning.* New York: Praeger.

Peterson, D. R. (1988). The epidemiology of sudden infant death syndrome. In J. L. Culbertson, H. F. Krous, & R. D. Bendell (Eds.), *Sudden infant death syndrome: Medical aspects and psychological management* (pp. 3–17). Baltimore: The Johns Hopkins University Press.

Rakoff, V. M. (1973). Psychiatric aspects of death in America. In A. Mack (Ed.), *Death in American experience* (pp. 149–161). New York: Schocken.

Rando, T. A. (1984). *Grief, dying, and death: Clinical interventions for caregivers.* Champaign, IL: Research Press.

Sanders, C. M. (1980). A comparison of adult bereavement in the death of a spouse, child, and parent. *Omega, 10*, 303–322.

Schatz, W. H. (1986). Grief of fathers. In T. A. Rando (Ed.), *Parental loss of a child* (pp. 293–302). Champaign, IL: Research Press.

Slovik, L. S., & Kelly, D. H. (1988). Family reactions to home monitoring. In J. L. Culbertson, H. F. Krous, & R. D. Bendell (Eds.), *Sudden infant death syndrome: Medical aspects and psychological management* (pp. 198–226). Baltimore: The Johns Hopkins University Press.

Smialek, Z. (1978). Observations on immediate reactions of families to sudden infant death. *Pediatrics, 62*, 160–165.

Szybist, C. (1976). *The subsequent child.* Rockville, MD: U.S. Department of Health, Education, and Welfare, Public Health Service, (HSA) 76-5145.

Szybist, C. (1988). Sudden infant death syndrome revisited. *Journal of Developmental and Behavioral Pediatrics, 9*, 33–37.

Visher, E. B., & Visher, J. S. (1979). *Stepfamilies: A guide to working with stepparents and children.* New York: Brunner/Mazel.

Visher, E. B., & Visher, J. S. (1980). *Stepfamilies: Myths and realities.* Secaucus, NJ: Citadel Press.

Weinstein, S. E. (1978). Sudden infant death syndrome: Impact on families and a direction for change. *American Journal of Psychiatry, 135*, 831–834.

Wortman, C. B., & Silver, R. C. (1987). Coping with irrevocable loss. In G. R. VandenBos & B. K. Bryant (Eds.), *Cataclysms, crises, and catastrophes: Psychology in action* (pp. 189–235). Washington, DC: American Psychological Association.

Zebal, B. H., & Woolsey, S. F. (1984). SIDS and the family: The pediatrician's role. *Pediatric Annals, 13*, 237–261.

CHAPTER 5

Siblings and Other Children

Betty Davies and Sydney Segal

The sudden and unexpected death of an infant in a family provokes significant emotional responses in all family members. This is especially true for siblings because they are most often very young children and, as such, are intellectually and emotionally poorly equipped to cope with loss. Siblings are often frightened by the catastrophic nature of a SIDS death, and they may be unable to understand its meaning and its impact on the family. The situation of siblings is further complicated in that they experience not only the loss of the infant, but also the grief of their parents and changes in their relationships with the parents. Even though SIDS can create an especially difficult grief situation for bereaved siblings, until fairly recently there has been relatively little focus on such siblings. This chapter analyzes the impact of a SIDS death upon siblings and other children, and suggests ways in which adults can help.

WHY IS SIDS DIFFICULT FOR SIBLINGS?

Several features of SIDS and its aftermath present unique stresses to the siblings. In particular, reactions of parents and families, characteristics of children, and circumstances of the death all influence how siblings respond.

Parental Reactions

The impact of a child's death on its parents is profound. Parents are not at all prepared for the possibility of death in a presumably healthy baby. The death is unexpected and sudden, and there is no time for any preparatory work. The possible mitigating factor of anticipatory grief (Rando, 1986) is absent for such parents, unlike the parents of children who die following a fatal illness or as the result of severe, congenital defects. Regardless of the cause of death, however, the death of a child results in significantly higher intensities of grief in parents than occurs following other types of death (Sanders, 1980). Furthermore, parents of SIDS babies tend to be particularly young. They may never have experienced a death before, so are not prepared to cope with death. Similarly, they may not be well prepared to cope with the distress of their other children. Because the impact on the parents is so profound, the child's death is also particularly devastating for siblings.

In response to the loss of their baby, parents frequently feel increased anxiety about their remaining children. Not wanting to lose another child, they may perceive the surviving children as vulnerable, and become overprotective. They may feel a need to be physically closer to their children. Occasionally, some parents fear attachment and express a painful need for distance from their children (Cornwell, Nurcombe, & Stevens, 1977). Parents sometimes feel overwhelmed by the needs of surviving siblings for comfort and for explanations about the baby's absence. In addition, common parental reactions to the death of a baby include a variety of feelings, such as anger, helplessness, and loss of meaning in life (see Chapter 4). Feelings of guilt are universal and pervasive. There are often disruptions in routine behaviors and there may be frequent expression of hostile feelings toward close friends and relatives.

Given the parents' distress, their reactions are understandable. Nevertheless, these reactions cannot help but affect surviving siblings who are sensitive to changes in their parents. Siblings may be confused and frightened by the parents' despair and by their inability to offer comfort because of their own grief. Furthermore, parents' reactions last a long time; thus, they influence surviving children for a long time.

Family Reactions

Siblings are affected not only by individual grief reactions, but also by other aspects of the family unit. The nature of the relationship between the parents, for example, seems to be a potentially important variable affecting the responses of the family. In a study of Australian families where a baby had died, it was found that surviving children were more prone to developing problem behaviors when there had been a history of discord in the family (Williams, 1981). In another study of families following the death of a child, although the cause of the death was cancer rather than SIDS, it was found that surviving children in the more cohesive families demonstrated fewer behavioral problems up to three years following the child's death (Davies, 1988b). Another feature of the family that may influence the responses of siblings has to do with the degree of the family's involvement with individuals or groups outside of the immediate family. Again, in the study of siblings' responses following the death of a child from cancer, the family's active involvement in recreational, social, religious, or cultural events or activities increased the availability of social support for the family in times of crisis, and in families who were more active, the children had fewer internalizing behavioral problems (Davies, 1988b).

SIDS usually leaves a lasting effect on the family, which is forever changed as a result of the experience (Zebal & Woolsey, 1984). Although the family eventually may find ways to adapt to or learn to live with the loss, there will still be periods of sadness when subsequent anniversaries occur, when memories are renewed, and when the family fantasizes about what the infant "would have been like now." How the family handles these times affects surviving siblings (Spinetta, 1978; Williams, 1981). If the family encourages mutual sharing of memories and thoughts about the deceased baby, there is less chance for misperceptions to occur in the minds of siblings about what happened.

Assumptions about Children and Death

Through the immediate crisis and all subsequent transition points, how parents and other adults in a child's life view children and death is critical to influencing how children respond to the death of a baby. Many adults often react as though children have no feelings about death. Adults may assume that because children are so young, they are not affected by death. Such assumptions mean that surviving children are often the most neglected family members in cases of SIDS. They are frequently excluded from the family's mourning by being separated from immediate family members, which also prohibits them from discussing the death. Such exclusion only adds to a child's confusion and his or her sense of loneliness and isolation.

Characteristics of Children

Relationship with the Baby

In anticipation of the arrival of a new baby in the family, young children are prepared for assuming their new role of "big brother" or "big sister." Even before the baby's actual arrival, a relationship between the two children has begun. When the new baby dies, the older child loses this new role and relationship. Assumption of the older-sibling role has been interrupted and the child must deal with this (Weston & Irwin, 1963). The bond that has been established between the two children also affects the surviving sibling's reaction. The closer that the surviving child felt toward the baby brother or sister, the greater the likelihood that the sibling will miss the dead baby to a greater degree (Davies, 1988a). Jane, for example, was five years old when her brother,

Michael, was born. Jane was thoroughly excited about having a baby brother, and she loved to help her mother care for Michael. Jane eagerly ran to fetch clean diapers or Michael's bottle. Whenever Michael cried, she would rock his cradle and sing songs to quiet him. When Michael died at six weeks of age, Jane was at a complete loss.

Developmental Understanding of Death

Young children have understandings of death that are different from adult views. Each age group has its own characteristic way of perceiving death, and these perceptions are important factors influencing the ways in which surviving children respond to the death of a baby (Hostler, 1978; Wass, 1984). Children who are younger than two years of age do not have a formal conception of what "death" means, but they do fear separation from familiar people and miss someone who goes away and does not return. In a study by Burns, House, and Ankenbauer (1986), for example, parents believed that their children of less than two years of age were affected by the death of their baby sibling.

Preschool children (between three and five years of age) typically see death as temporary and reversible, similar to sleep or short absences. Thus, they have difficulty understanding why the deceased baby does not come back. Between six and nine years, most children are beginning to have an awareness of the meaning of death; they are beginning to see it as final. As a result, such children have many questions to ask about the death of a baby sibling. By the time children are 10 years old, they are usually able to understand that death is inevitable, irreversible, and final.

Before age 9 or 10, children typically look at death in terms of responsibility, that is, that someone or something was responsible for the death. Also characteristic of young children is magical thinking, in which it is thought that events are caused to occur by wishing them. These two features often predispose young children to assume responsibility for the death. A child may have lightly touched the infant on the night of the death, or may have taken away the baby's bottle, blanket, or toy, and, in this way, may feel implicated in the causality of the death.

Dependence on Others for Support and Information

In a description of factors which influence young children's responses to death, Bowlby (1980) indicated that young children really are at the mercy of their families. Children do not have the capacity or the freedom to seek assistance from outside the home; they cannot go elsewhere to have their needs met if their family is unsympathetic. Therefore, the kinds of assistance that are provided within their families are all that is available to them, and influence the children's responses to the loss.

Circumstances of the Death

Also affecting surviving siblings are the suddenness of a SIDS death and the ensuing events. In some cases, for example, a surviving child may be with the mother when she discovers the dead baby. A common reaction of mothers is to scream, and to cry. Not used to seeing such behavior in his or her mother, the young child may be very frightened. The mother may attempt to resuscitate the baby. In the eyes of the observing child, such efforts may appear violent, and the child may think that the mother killed the baby. In an explosion of confusion, fear, and anger, the mother may lash out to accuse the older child of doing something to the baby. Such reactions may be later repressed by the parent, but they remain vivid in the sibling's memory (Halpern, 1972).

The actual discovery of the death is followed by additional confusion: sirens may wail as the police or ambulance approach the home; uniformed police officers "invade" the home; other strangers, such as the coroner or an unfamiliar physician, ask Mom and Dad lots of questions. Often, a neighbor or relative "helps out" by taking the children away, and so they are left without opportunities to see how the confusion eventually settles and to ask questions. Instead of reality, their imaginations take over and conjure explanations that may be more scary than the truth. In moments of crisis, parents cannot be expected to think clearly about their reactions—they simply do the best they can. Later, however, parents can create opportunities to explain events to surviving children and to talk about their own reactions.

REACTIONS OF SIBLINGS TO A SIDS DEATH

The study of children's reactions to death has only relatively recently received the focus it deserves. In our Western world, death is not a popular subject for conversation, let alone for research, and to approach the bereaved has been avoided as a topic which is "too sensitive." Exploring childhood bereavement is considered even more "sensitive" and has, therefore, received even less attention than adult bereavement. Children, however, do grieve, and the effects of losing a loved one on even very young children can be profound and long-lasting. The largest proportion of the literature pertaining to children's bereavement has mostly to do with children's reactions to the death of a parent; literature that focuses on children's bereavement following the death of a sibling has only recently become available. Furthermore, the study of sibling bereavement pertains mostly to reactions following the death of a child from cancer. Very few reports are available that deal specifically with the bereavement responses of children following a SIDS death.

Information that is currently available falls into two categories. The first includes reports that focus on the responses of families to SIDS; here, in describing the reactions of various family members, the siblings are discussed. This literature begins with one article written in the 1960s (Weston & Irwin, 1963), and increases with additional reports throughout the 1970s and 1980s (Friedman, 1974; Mandell & Belk, 1977; Markusen, Owen, & Fulton, 1978; Smialek, 1978; Swoiskin, 1986; Zebal & Woolsey, 1984). The majority of these articles are clinically based; only two are research based (Cornwell, Nurcombe, & Stevens, 1977; DeFrain & Ernst, 1978). The second category includes reports of research that focuses directly on the siblings themselves; these reports have appeared only within the past few years (Burns, House, & Ankenbauer, 1986; Mandell, Dirks-Smith, & Smith, 1988; Mandell, McAnulty, & Carlson, 1983; Williams, 1981).

Most families who experience SIDS are young families with young children, and the majority of the children in each of the three research reports were between two and six years of age. Several limitations of research in the area of sibling bereavement are noted. For the most part, data were collected from the parents about their children. Williams' report (1981) is based also on direct observations of the children themselves. Most reports depend upon parental recall of their children's behavior. The passage of time may affect this recall, but, in addition, parents' perceptions of their children's grief may be affected by their own grief, and they also may underestimate the children's responses because painful memories are often suppressed. However, the consistency of parental reports about their children's behavior supports the validity of the data. In none of the studies was there an attempt to match the bereaved samples with a sample of children whose siblings did not die. Using control groups would help to differentiate normal developmental behaviors from grieving behaviors in young children.

Surviving siblings are generally very much affected by a SIDS death. The most difficult problems seem to be adapting to a sudden change in the family environment, understanding what happened, and coping with many disturbing feelings, such as guilt, insecurity, vulnerability, anxiety and fear, and regressive behavior (Zebal & Woolsey, 1984). These reactions may be summarized into the following categories of behavior.

Immediate Reactions

Immediately following the death of an infant from SIDS, surviving children may experience confusion and fear, particularly if they were present at the moment the tragedy was discovered. They do not understand what has happened, nor do they comprehend the events called into play as a result of what happened. They are fearful that the same thing may happen to them, or to Mom and Dad.

These reactions result in crying, withdrawal, or clinging behavior. Initially, surviving children are more frightened by their parents' reactions and by the events of the moment than by the fact that the baby has died.

If the child was not present when the baby was found, and is told about what has happened, his or her reaction may be surprising and upsetting to adults. Not fully comprehending the meaning of death, the child may react without any visible sign of sadness, and may even continue playing or ask to go to play. Such behaviors do not mean that the child did not "love" the dead infant, as some adults may tend to think. Instead, the child's wanting to play is an attempt to do something that feels comfortable since the gravity of the situation is sensed even though it may not be understood due to the child's immature conceptualization of death. Depending on his or her age, the child may ask questions, and this reaction may also be upsetting to adults who may have great difficulty answering questions such as: "Where did the baby go?"; "Why did the baby die?"; "Why did you let them take our baby away?"

Later Reactions

Questions

Children's questions continue for many weeks, months, and even years after a SIDS death. They are naturally curious about what happened, and asking questions is their way of trying to understand the death: "What happened to the baby's body?"; "How can the baby breathe in the ground?"; "Can the baby eat?"; "What toys does the baby have to play with in heaven?" Asking questions is also children's way of seeking reassurance for their fears that the same thing might happen to them, or to Mom or Dad: "Will I die too?" As children grow and mature, their conceptualizations of death and of what happened to the baby will also mature and change. With each new stage of development, then, children may ask more questions, attempting to integrate the events into their expanded understanding of death.

Fears and Anxiety

Children experience anxiety, insecurity, and uncertainty following a SIDS event. They do not understand what has happened, nor can they comprehend why it has happened. In this way, their reactions are similar to adult responses. The questions are unanswerable, but children do not realize this to be so. Thus, they persist with their questions, unless they are scolded for their curiosity. In such cases, children then begin to think that the situation is too awful even to talk about. Questions do not disappear, however. Instead of being verbalized, questions live on as worrisome concerns in the silence of the child's own mind.

In addition, children may be confused and frightened by their parents' de-spair, and this perception can add to their anxiety. Children are not accus-tomed to having Mom and Dad so upset, and they worry about what is wrong with them. Children wonder why they cannot make their parents feel better like they usually do. Their concerns center around what would happen to them or to their parents if they became sick, or if they went to sleep and did not wake up. Children seek comfort for their anxiety through physical contact and by wanting to be within sight of familiar adults. At a time when parents are having difficulty meeting their own needs and the needs of their children, these children want more attention. Often, they want this attention at bedtime, a common time for children's fears and anxieties to surface.

Sleep Disturbances

Problems with sleeping have been described in all research reports. Mandell, McAnulty, and Carlson (1983), for example, reported that over 69% of the sib-lings in their study had sleep disturbances that lasted from two months to over a year. The greatest difficulties with sleep were in the 24 to 30 month age group. These difficulties were manifested by resistance in going to bed and to sleep, by fear of the dark and of ghosts, and by nightmares.

Eating Disturbances

Many children were reported to have transient changes in eating patterns fol-lowing a SIDS death. Mandell, McAnulty, and Carlson (1983) noted that tran-sient changes in appetite occurred in over one-third of the children in their sample, but that this was not a major concern for parents.

Toilet Training

For young children, regression in toilet training was infrequently reported, al-though this may be due to the fact that the majority of children in the studies were over two years of age. For children younger than two, it can be expected that progress with toilet training would be interrupted following a SIDS death, since any major disruption in the lives of children affects their ability to con-tinue with acquisition of new skills. For preschool and young school-aged chil-dren, enuresis has sometimes been reported.

Social Interaction

Changes in social interaction occurred in 13 of 35 siblings as reported by Man-dell, McAnulty, and Carlson (1983). Such changes were especially true for chil-dren between the ages of two-and-a-half and four years. Changes ranged from quietude and withdrawal to increases in aggression. It is important to take into account the individual child's own personality in assessing changes in social interaction. Some children are usually quiet, and these children respond by becoming more so; other children are more vocal and active, and they respond by becoming more aggressive. Changes in social interaction often occur in relationships with parents and peers. Toddlers in particular may express anger with their parents for taking the baby away, or may have increased temper tantrums when separated from their parents (Cornwell, Nurcombe, & Stevens, 1977). Siblings test the limits of discipline for several months. Older children may often be reluctant to go to preschool or school, preferring instead to stay close to home and to Mom.

Guilt and Resentment

Guilt is frequently described as a common reaction among children following the death of a sibling. The assumption of guilt in children comes from our knowledge of the characteristic ways in which young children think. They are egocentric and engage in magical thinking, resulting in their tendency to assume responsibility for the death. Several of the clinical articles refer to children feeling guilty, but the research articles infrequently refer to this response. It may be that parents have difficulty interpreting guilt in their children and so did not mention guilt in their accounts of their children's behavior. Guilt, however, may be present and manifested in the children's fears and questions, and in the changes in their social interactions.

The behavior of the children in studies of sibling responses following the death of an infant to SIDS indicates that the children demonstrated a variety of responses, and that each child demonstrated several reactions. Mandell, McAnulty, and Carlson (1983) indicated that all of the children who experienced changes in peer relations also experienced sleep difficulties and changes in parent-child relations, plus a reluctance to go to school or to be separated from their parents. Children, therefore, respond with changes in several behaviors, rather than in just one area. The patterns of behavioral responses in grieving children are important to note.

Duration of Grief

The purpose of a study by Burns, House, and Ankenbauer (1986) was to examine the duration of grief within children whose younger sibling had died from SIDS. Most of the families had experienced the SIDS death in the past two to three years, though in some cases it had occurred as long as 16 years before. The results indicated that 54% of the children exhibited grieving behaviors for more than one year after the death of a sibling due to SIDS. An additional 6% were reported to be affected for six months to one year after the death. The proportion of children reported to grieve longer than one year is remarkably similar for children of all ages, which implies that the duration of grief is related to factors other than the age of the child.

Pathological Grief

A question remaining unanswered in relation to sibling grief has to do with differentiating between those children who are responding "normally" vis-à-vis those who may be showing pathological grief reactions. In some studies of childhood bereavement, about 25% of children demonstrated behavior problems at a level indicative of pathological grief (Davies, 1983; McCown, 1982 & 1987). In these studies, a standardized behavioral assessment tool was used to describe the children's responses to the death of a sibling. The development and refinement of assessment tools for clinical use with bereaved children would be of value. The use of such instruments would help in identifying the appropriateness of children's responses to bereavement and in identifying those children in need of some specialized intervention.

OTHER CHILDREN

Studies of siblings' responses to SIDS have been focused on siblings who were born before the SIDS event. None have referred to or included siblings born after the SIDS experience, nor have they referred to other children who may also be affected by the death of the infant.

Subsequent Siblings

Two factors must be taken into account when dealing with subsequent siblings. First, there is a danger of the child being considered a replacement child (Poznanski, 1972). In extreme cases, the new child is even given the same name as the child who died. But no child can take the place of the deceased baby, and for the parents even to hope that this might be the case is very unhealthy not only for themselves, but also for the child who may be deprived in this way of developing his or her own unique identity.

Second, the subsequent child may be subject to overprotectiveness. Parental concern for the well being of their other children is understandable following their traumatic experience with the SIDS event. Furthermore, their anxiety is increased by their fear that subsequent siblings could be at greater risk for SIDS (Valdes-Dapena, 1980). One study (Cornwell, Nurcombe, & Stevens, 1977) indicated that parents went to great lengths to protect their subsequent children: they planned for conception at a certain time so that the baby could be born when there was a statistically lower chance of SIDS death; they enrolled in first aid courses; and they quit smoking. When the new child was brought home, parents suffered great anxiety, particularly when the child was asleep.

They felt compelled to check the baby frequently, and were attuned to every whimper and cough. Some accidentally referred to the baby by the name of the deceased child. For most parents, there was a turning point when the new baby surpassed the age at which the other had died, and parents felt more confident thereafter.

Subsequent siblings never know the deceased infant, but they know about him or her and often regard the infant as "special" in some way. As they get older, they often have questions about what the baby was like, and are usually eager to hear stories about the baby. As time goes on, subsequent siblings sometimes wonder about what it would be like to have this older sibling. Their questions and thoughts must be answered, with reassurance that they, too, are very special to their parents.

Peers

Other children are often affected by the death of an infant, although they may not be directly involved in the situation. Nieces and nephews of the parents, or the children of parents' friends will surely hear about what happened, if not directly, then by overhearing adult conversations. They may witness the distress of their own parents, and, like siblings, become worried about what has happened. The best antidote for these concerns is open communication with such children, and reassurances that the same thing is unlikely to happen to them or to their siblings.

Babysitters

Another group of children affected by the infant's death is often forgotten: the infant's babysitters. Babysitters are usually older children of adolescent age, who may react strongly to the death of their infant charge. By pure chance, the death of an infant may be discovered by a babysitter in the parents' absence. The stress on this temporary parent-substitute may be felt with special potency for several reasons. The sitter would inevitably think about having provided less than adequate surveillance over the infant's breathing or crying. Having been asleep, or having given rapt attention to some form of entertainment, the babysitter may feel a failure in not hearing an assumed pre-mortem cry of distress. The routine interrogation by police, to rule out foul play in preparing their report, may open new areas of thought that provoke feelings of possible neglect as a cause of the death.

The young sitter, conscious of a lack of adult competence, may feel that the death might not have occurred if the baby had been supervised by an adult babysitter or by the parents themselves. The parents, overcome with the anger and guilt that are a part of grieving, may be unable to conceal their feeling that the sitter indeed had failed for some reason to prevent the death. The sitter may also fear that his or her reputation in the neighborhood will have been tinged by the event, causing a cessation of requests for services. Even without that damaged reputation, the sitter may feel too much uncertainty or danger to accept the trust of babysitting again, especially with the siblings of the baby who died.

Unless encouraged to grieve and weep in the presence of the affected family, and to share in grief counseling, the sitter may feel sufficiently outcast to assume that he or she is under suspicion for having permitted or caused the death. Although there is now general agreement that immediate efforts at resuscitation will be unsuccessful in a baby dying of SIDS, prior instruction in standard infant cardiorespiratory resuscitation for all babysitters would at least ease their conscience in the event of such an episode.

WHAT CAN WE DO TO HELP?

There are important guidelines for all adults to keep in mind when considering the needs of siblings in the aftermath of a SIDS death. The premise here is that parents are the best ones to help their children, so the suggestions that follow focus on parents. In addition, though, guidelines are offered for other significant groups of adults.

Parents

It is crucial that children be given opportunities to understand what happened and to express their feelings, fears, and concerns—especially since death may be a new and confusing concept for them. The groundwork is laid for helping children to understand what happened and to cope with the experience when they are first told of the death. Because children's conceptions of death may not be well developed, it is best to use words that are clear, direct, and simple. Children should be told that the baby "died" or is "dead."

Using euphemisms only adds to a child's confusion. Being told, for example, that God took the baby to heaven makes young children wonder when God might "take" them, too; or, later, they wonder why God does not bring the baby back. To young children, such an explanation can make God seem very frightening and cruel. This is not to deny the spiritual component of what parents believe and tell their children; rather, it is to emphasize that adults must take into consideration children's level of understanding. Young children may not find the same comfort as their parents in religious beliefs.

Similarly, to tell children that the baby is "lost," in a "deep sleep," or on a "long journey" is also potentially very confusing. Children wonder why the baby cannot be found if he or she is lost, and fear that they, too, may get lost. They worry about going to sleep; perhaps they, too, will go into a deep sleep and never wake up. Or they wonder when the baby will return home from the long journey, or how the baby even managed to travel alone. Therefore, it is best to be direct, saying simply that the baby has died.

Swoiskin (1986) recommended that we tell surviving children that the death represents a failure in the physical abilities of the baby; that there was something wrong with the baby's body that made it no longer able to live. She suggests that we also not tell children that the baby died because he or she was "sick" or had an "accident." Such explanations reinforce questions about whether or not the same thing could happen to surviving children, because they, too, have been "sick" and have had "accidents" of one sort or another. Children require reassurances about the healthy functioning of their own bodies and that the same thing will not happen to them. Such explanations are especially pertinent to children between two and five years of age.

In the same way that parents find it most aggravating to be told, "Don't worry . . . you can have another child some day," siblings find it just as aggravating to be told that they may "some day have another baby brother or sister." Telling this to children denies their right to miss their infant sibling. It denies the special relationship that existed between siblings and the dead infant. The topic of a new baby, however, may sometimes be introduced by children themselves, often as a way of trying to console their parents: "Don't cry, Mommy. We can get another baby." In such situations, it is best to tell the child that if they could get another baby, it would not take the place of the one who died. In this way, the child's suggestion is acknowledged, and the child is reassured that babies and children are not replaceable.

Children also need reassurances that they were not responsible for the death. They need to be told that nothing they said or did caused the baby to die. Some parents feel that mentioning such things might put the idea of guilt into children's minds, and so they shy away from discussing this aspect. However, it is a universal response of siblings, particularly those who are less than 9 or 10 years of age, to wonder if something they did or said may have contributed to the death. The combination of normal sibling jealousy and a child's magical thinking are natural ingredients for the child to feel responsible for the death.

Giving children opportunities to talk about the death also helps to alleviate their concerns and provides adults with opportunities for correcting children's misconceptions. When asked about what he thought happened to his baby sister, one four-year-old answered, "She died because she wouldn't stop crying." Others have been reported to say, "because I hit him," or "because Mommy dropped her on her head." Hearing the child's point of view is the only way to begin to correct such misconceptions.

Surviving siblings may find returning to the infant's room particularly difficult after the baby has died. This is even more likely if the child previously shared the room with the baby. Permitting the child to enter the room in his or her own time is important; do not force the child to do so. If the room was shared with the baby, giving the child a choice at some point about how to reorganize the room may be helpful in his or her adjustment. Permitting the surviving sibling to choose a memento from among the baby's belongings may also be appreciated, particularly as the child gets older. The key aspect of what to do with the infant's belongings has to do with the meanings that such belongings hold for various family members. Open discussion about belongings and their meanings facilitates healthy grieving for all family members (Davies, 1987).

Health Professionals

A variety of health professionals may be involved with the family following the death of an infant. Physicians are most likely to be involved at the time of the death; they may even be called to the scene, or the child may be brought into the emergency room. Nurses and others may also be involved if the child has been brought to the emergency room. It is vital that professionals show acceptance of the parents' and siblings' intense feelings and be willing to answer their questions. Do not suggest that the other children be taken away, but include them as much as possible in discussions with the parents. For physicians, make an appointment to see the family in a few days to share with them the autopsy results and suggest that siblings also come to the appointment. By including other children from the very beginning, parents are helped to see that their surviving children are also a part of the tragic event. Moreover, parents are presented with opportunities to discuss their concerns regarding these other children, and professionals are able to assess the reactions of the surviving children directly.

It is important for professionals to take an active role beyond the period immediately following the SIDS events. Professionals can encourage the parents to return to routine roles and tasks, such as cooking meals, doing laundry, and resuming family activities. These "normalizations" are helpful for siblings who can see that life will continue on (Betz, 1984). Even though parents are encouraged to resume their routine lifestyle, however, they still need to be reassured that feeling sad and crying are okay. Professionals can also serve as resource persons for the parents and the siblings, answering questions or being available just to talk about the death.

Professionals need to be aware that their support must continue for quite some time. Therefore, they must be patient and tolerant of parents' and siblings' concerns for many months after the death. It is helpful for physicians or community health nurses to note on the family record when the infant died as a reminder to inquire about how the family is doing. Some professionals are hesitant to mention the event or the dead infant. Yet, parents and siblings are most often grateful for opportunities to discuss their feelings. They are especially glad that someone cared enough to remember the baby. At such times, professionals can inquire about surviving siblings as well, and can use the time as an opportunity to share with parents some information about what to expect in their other children.

Funeral Directors

Funeral directors are in an excellent position to help surviving siblings, most often indirectly through their contacts with parents. Funeral directors can suggest that children be included in the funeral or that they be given the choice of being included. Families often worry about whether children should be included in the funeral and how this should be handled. In general, children should be allowed to attend the funeral, but their participation should never be forced. They should be told what to expect to see and hear if they attend the funeral, and, depending on their age, it is a good idea to have an adult companion who can look after the children if they become too disruptive or have questions to ask. It is unfair to ask parents to be attentive to the immediate needs of their other children during the infant's funeral.

Teachers

Teachers are significant adults in the lives of children, whether they be in day care, preschool, or school. Because they see children on a regular basis, teachers are in a position to note any changes in a child's behavior following the death, and can create opportunities to talk with the child about what has happened. Sometimes, the teacher is more uncomfortable than the child in discussing the death. In such cases, the teacher needs to recognize his or her limitations and seek assistance with helping the child. A preschool teacher, following an episode in her classroom, came to a workshop conducted by one of the authors to learn how to cope with loss. The baby brother of one of her five-year-old pupils had died from SIDS on the weekend. On Monday morning, the child was eager to have his turn for "Show and Tell." He stood up, blurting out to all, "My baby brother died on Friday, and nobody knows why!" The teacher felt overwhelmed by the news, told so matter-of-factly by the young child. In such cases, it is important for teachers to be open with children and to discuss their questions and concerns.

Talking about death by referring to nature is often helpful. Having several books geared to various reading levels may be useful for the library (Wass & Corr, 1984). Helping children to participate in some memorial activity may be helpful also, such as taking part in the creation of a sympathy card for the family. This kind of activity facilitates children's learning about death and about bereavement. It helps children realize that they can do something to help, rather than merely shy away from the bereaved.

Grandparents

Grandparents also experience acute grief when an infant dies. They feel not only the loss of the infant, but also the helplessness of not being able to take away the pain of their own children, the infant's parents. Grandparents, however, are often very helpful for surviving children, perhaps because both are "forgotten grievers" (Gyulay, 1975). Children can often talk to their grandparents in ways that they cannot talk to their parents. Encouraging them to have time together facilitates such communication. This is not to say, however, that young children should have prolonged visits with their grandparents or with other relatives during the acute stage of grief. The strangeness of such an unusual visit, particularly if it is an abrupt change for the child, may be more disturbing than the perception of disaffection within the family setting.

CONCLUSION

Helping children to cope with the death of an infant sibling is difficult for all adults. Involvement with the experiences of their surviving children emphasizes the adults' own feelings of grief and helplessness. However, helping surviving children can be seen as a constructive task for adults at a time when there seems to be so little to do that is really useful. Moreover, it is crucial that adults do attend to the needs of the surviving children, no matter how young they may be. Siblings and other surviving children must be reassured that these are difficult times, but that Mom or Dad, or Granny, or teacher, will be there to help. They must be permitted to express their feelings and concerns, whether verbally or through nonverbal play or drawing. They must be given extra doses of affection for many weeks and months following the death. In these ways, surviving children are helped to understand death and to learn that it is possible to manage grief constructively.

REFERENCES

Betz, C. (1984). Helping children to cope with the death of a sibling. *Child Care Newsletter, 3*, 3–5.

Bowlby, J. (1980). *Loss: Sadness and depression.* Vol. 3 in *Attachment and loss.* New York: Basic Books.

Burns, E. A., House, D., & Ankenbauer, M. R. (1986). Sibling grief in reaction to sudden infant death syndrome. *Pediatrics, 78*, 485–487.

Cornwell, J., Nurcombe, B., & Stevens, L. (1977). Family response to loss of a child by Sudden Infant Death Syndrome. *Medical Journal of Australia, 1*, 656–658.

Davies, B. (1988a). The family environment in bereaved families and its relationship to surviving sibling behavior. *Children's Health Care, 17*, 22–31.

Davies, B. (1987). Family responses to the death of a child: The meaning of memories. *Journal of Palliative Care, 3*(1), 9–15.

Davies, B. (1988b). Shared life space and sibling bereavement responses. *Cancer Nursing, 11*, 339–347.

Davies, B. (1983). *Behavioral responses to the death of a sibling.* Seattle, WA: University of Washington, unpublished doctoral dissertation.

DeFrain, J. D., & Ernst, L. (1978). The psychological effects of sudden infant death syndrome on surviving family members. *Journal of Family Practice, 6*, 985–989.

Friedman, S. B. (1974). Psychological aspects of sudden unexpected death in infants and children. *Pediatric Clinics of North America, 21*, 103–111.

Gyulay, J. (1975). The forgotten grievers. *American Journal of Nursing, 75*, 1476–1479.

Halpern, W. I. (1972). Some psychiatric sequelae to crib death. *American Journal of Psychiatry, 129*, 398–402.

Hostler, S. L. (1978). The development of the child's concept of death. In O. J. Sahler (Ed.), *The child and death* (pp. 1–25). St. Louis: C. V. Mosby.

Mandell, F., & Belk, B. (1977). Sudden infant death syndrome: The disease and its survivors. *Postgraduate Medicine, 62*, 193–197.

Mandell, F., Dirks-Smith, T., & Smith, M. F. (1988). The surviving child in the SIDS family. *Pediatrician, 15*, 217–221.

Mandell, F., McAnulty, E. H., & Carlson, A. (1983). Unexpected death of an infant sibling. *Pediatrics, 72*, 652–657.

Markusen, E., Owen, G., & Fulton, R. (1978). SIDS: The survivor as victim. *Omega, 8*, 277–284.

McCown, D. E. (1982). *Selected factors related to children's adjustment following sibling death.* Corvallis, OR: Oregon State University, unpublished doctoral dissertation.

McCown, D. E. (1987). Factors relating to bereaved children's behavior adjustment. *Recent Advances in Nursing, 16*, 85–93.

Poznanski, E. O. (1972). The replacement child—a saga of unresolved parental grief. *Behavioral Pediatrics, 81*, 1190–1193.

Rando, T. A. (1986). *Loss and anticipatory grief.* Lexington, MA: D. C. Heath.

Sanders, C. M. (1980). A comparison of adult bereavement in the death of a spouse, child, and parent. *Omega, 10*, 303–321.

Smialek, Z. (1978). Observations on immediate reactions of families to sudden infant death. *Pediatrics, 62*, 160–165.

Spinetta, J. J. (1978). Communication patterns in families dealing with life-threatening illness. In. O. J. Sahler (Ed.), *The child and death* (pp. 43–51). St. Louis: C. V. Mosby.

Swoiskin, S. (1986). Sudden infant death: Nursing care for the survivors. *Journal of Pediatric Nursing, 1*, 33–39.

Valdes-Dapena, M. A. (1980). Sudden infant death syndrome: A review of the medical literature, 1974–1979. *Pediatrics, 66*, 597–614.

Wass, H. (1984). Concepts of death: A developmental perspective. In H. Wass & C. A. Corr (Eds), *Childhood and death* (pp. 3–24). New York: Hemisphere.

Wass, H., & Corr, C. A. (1984). *Helping children cope with death: Guidelines and resources* (2nd ed.). New York: Hemisphere.

Williams, M. L. (1981). Sibling reaction to cot death. *Medical Journal of Australia, 2*, 227–231.

Weston, D. L., & Irwin, R. C. (1963). Preschool child's response to death of infant sibling. *American Journal of Diseases of Children, 106*, 564–567.

Zebal, B. H., & Woolsey, S. F. (1984). SIDS and the family: The pediatrician's role. *Pediatric Annals, 13*, 237–261.

CHAPTER 6

Grandparents, Extended Family Members, and Other Significant Persons

Sheila Dayton Marquez

It has been said that every SIDS death affects over 100 people! At first, that may seem incredible, but it is much more plausible when one considers that those who are directly affected include parents, siblings, grandparents, aunts, uncles, cousins, day care providers, babysitters, friends, neighbors, coworkers, members of the clergy, physicians, and other health care providers. In addition, associates and family members of each of these individuals are indirectly affected as they try to understand SIDS and identify their roles as friends and as support persons. Also, there are many people who become involved through the circumstances of the death: police officers, emergency responders, firefighters, coroners, and hospital staff. Each of these people, too, will share their grief with their families, friends, and colleagues.

On this basis alone, it is no wonder that the impact of SIDS deaths is felt so strongly throughout a community. Each of these individuals must deal with the death in his or her own way. That is, each of them has his or her own concerns and needs for support, even while, and at the same time, each of them may be drawn—willingly or unwillingly—into the tasks of giving support to the bereaved family. Many of these people will not only feel, but may also in fact be, ineffective in their support to the family.

This chapter looks beyond the immediate family to explore the impact of SIDS deaths on grandparents, extended family members, and other significant persons. Needs and concerns will be noted in each of these principal population groups as they are affected by the rippling implications of a SIDS death. In addition, suggestions will be made concerning ways in which to help these individuals and ways in which they can assist the bereaved family.

WHO IS AFFECTED AND HOW?

The most-dreaded call for most people is the unexpected one informing them of the death or impending death of someone they know or love. First reactions are similar to those of the immediate family: shock ("I'm numb, I don't know what to say."); disbelief ("I don't believe what I'm hearing. This can't be true. It just can't be happening."); and anger ("This is wrong! Why didn't somebody do something?"). Others, because of their own beliefs and experiences may see this as part of a master plan or one of those things that just happens—and life goes on.

Those who have been notified of the death of an infant from SIDS are particularly likely to be stunned by the suddenness and the finality of the death, and by its perceived untimeliness and inappropriateness. As a result, they may find themselves unable to take action or unsure of how to proceed. They ask: "What can I do now? What should I do in these circumstances?" Lacking much experience or confidence in these situations, sometimes they may do nothing at all.

In general, American society portrays life through descriptions of the young and beautiful, the fit and healthy, the achievers and successful. Despite the work of Kübler-Ross (1969) and the modern hospice movement, ours is a culture that is basically uncomfortable with aging, illness, and death (Gordon, 1986). As a result of busy schedules and discomfort both with the intensity of their own feelings and with those of the bereaved family, friends and relatives may all too soon appear to forget the bereaved. Families in grief often report that long-term support from their friends was not available. Unfortunately, when friends have forgotten or avoided calling for too long, they often fade from the bereaved person's life. In fact, many bereaved individuals form new relationships and friendships after or as a result of the death.

The ultimate goal of those who offer counsel or assistance in the area of SIDS is to promote a healthy response to the infant's death which will enable the family to go forward with their own lives and eventually to invest in other relationships. The support that the family receives from their friends and relatives is, therefore, a matter of primary concern. Worden (1982) has identified several factors which influence the impact of the death on various individuals and which, in turn, affect the support they can or will provide to the bereaved:

- Who the person was
- The nature of the attachment (including the strength and security of the attachment, as well as any ambivalence in the relationship)
- Mode of death
- Historical antecedents (how previous losses were mourned)
- Personality variables

- Social variables (including the social, ethnic, and religious background of the survivor).

In what follows, we will concentrate upon needs and concerns of the principal population groups outside the immediate family that are impacted by a SIDS death, together with some suggestions or guidelines for offering assistance to members of such groups. Of particular importance to those who offer SIDS counseling or assistance is to remember and respect that every person with whom they speak will reflect different needs. It is of the utmost importance that the ideas of the bereaved are respected even while they are provided with maximum support.

GRANDPARENTS

Needs and Concerns

Grandparents are especially affected by infant deaths. They grieve for their deceased grandchild and for their own child who is suffering (Raphael, 1983; Resolve Through Sharing, 1986; Schiff, 1986). They may feel that, for the first time, they cannot "fix" the pain of their child. There is nothing they can say or do to relieve the intensity of their child's pain. They may also be facing health problems of their own or of their parents, and may question why they, rather than an innocent infant, did not die.

With increasing life expectancies, more great-grandparents are also alive at the time of a SIDS death. They, too, may ask, "Why should one so young die when I have lived a full life and am ready to die?" If a family member has a life-threatening or terminal illness, the family may even be angry that death took the baby rather than the person who is already suffering and may be pleading for a timely death or freedom from pain.

Grandparents are often viewed as a source of parenting and infant care advice for the parents. These expectations can lead to conflicting opinions regarding the mother's pregnancy (Should the mother have gotten pregnant in the first place? Should she have run, exercised, swam, worked, hiked, etc., during the pregnancy?); infant care (Should the infant have been breast or bottle fed? Should the infant have been taken out of the house?); and plans for the infant (Should the mother have returned to work after the baby's birth?). These concerns, if expressed or implied, increase the pain and guilt of the parent whose child has died.

Grandparents, too, may have feelings of guilt and responsibility for the death, thinking they should have been more insistent on child rearing practices in which they believed, but were hesitant to discuss. They may also feel guilty for not having spent more time with the infant or in assisting with child care. Grandparents' feelings may cause problems in the relationship between the parents and grandparents as the death is reviewed or when additional children are born to these parents or to their siblings.

Another issue for grandparents may be that of namesakes. For example, an infant may be named after a grandparent or to carry on a family name through a title of Junior, the III, or the IV. There may be deep feelings that arise for grandparents in terms of the significance of the name, as well as whether the name can or should be used again, by these parents or by other siblings.

At the time of a death, grandparents may also be facing pregnancies, births, and/or new babies with their other children. Trying to be happy with one child while feeling overwhelming sadness with another can be very difficult. These feelings may be further complicated by the grandparents' feelings for a "favorite" child. Occasionally, the impact of a SIDS death is further complicated when grandparents had not yet seen the baby. They may have been waiting for a preplanned vacation or a special event (e.g., a baptism or holiday), or may not have had financial or other resources to make the trip. All of these circumstances may further complicate the feelings of those involved. In addition, many families live with internal or intergenerational stresses. Relationships may be further strained by such matters as child abuse, alcoholism, or other lifelong family problems and disagreements. Obviously, the more historical information of this sort that is available to the counselor or helper, the more effective he or she can be in providing support to the grandparents, as well as to the bereaved parents.

Guidelines for Helping

A counselor or other person working in the field of SIDS might do some or all of the following to help grandparents in a family impacted by SIDS:

- Provide accurate information regarding SIDS
- Address child-rearing practices which are of concern
- Acknowledge the loss experienced by the grandparents and encourage them to do the same
- Explore the grandparents' own resources for support and encourage them to utilize those resources as they are needed or as it becomes appropriate
- Offer supportive literature and counseling regarding their grief and mourning
- Explore issues that the grandparents identify related to other children or grandchildren
- Encourage open communication with the bereaved parents to discourage the grandparents from assuming what is best for the bereaved parents, e.g.,

funeral arrangements, care of surviving children, dismantling the infant's room, taking pictures down, or putting the infant's toys and supplies "away"
- Offer age-appropriate guidance regarding interactions with surviving children and other grandchildren
- Encourage the grandparents to offer help to the bereaved couple, but not to feel rejected if their offers are refused. Financial assistance, even if needed for funeral or cemetery expenses, may be viewed by the parents as their last responsibility to their deceased infant.

OTHER RELATIVES

Needs and Concerns

Siblings of the bereaved parents, the aunts and uncles of the dead infant, are also deeply affected. They may have children of the same age, be pregnant, or be contemplating future pregnancies. They may be teenagers who have provided care to the infant. Alternatively, although they may have had a close relationship with their sibling, they may live at a distance which prohibits them from attending the funeral or from maintaining frequent contact.

In the months after the SIDS death, relatives of the bereaved parents may feel that their visits for holidays or special events are "dampened" just by the presence of the bereaved parents (Schiff, 1986). They may be resentful or feel uncomfortable when the parents mention the deceased child or when they make an effort to share memories and pictures of the infant at events that are supposed to be "happy." Unwanted or unplanned pregnancies may also present conflicts for the extended family. Support to discontinue a pregnancy or expressed displeasure with a pregnancy may be met with disfavor from other family members who cannot separate the issue of the death of a wanted child from an unplanned pregnancy. Again, it will be important for the SIDS counselor or helper to gather as much relevant information as possible in order to provide appropriate suggestions.

Guidelines for Helping

A counselor or other person working in the field of SIDS might do some or all of the following to help other relatives in a family impacted by SIDS:

- Provide accurate information regarding SIDS
- Offer suggestions for being supportive, such as, phone calls, good listening skills, letters, offers to visit, or care for surviving children

- Refer to their medical care providers for infant care concerns and reassurance (and provide information to that person if appropriate)
- Provide age-appropriate counseling for their children regarding the cause of the death, the funeral, and questions related to grief and mourning
- Seek out individual concerns with which the other family members must deal and yet may feel they cannot share with anyone else.

Grandparents and other relatives within the extended family may find that they can have an important role in offering support to surviving siblings of the dead infant because the bereaved parents may be unable always to provide that support or to meet the care demands of the young sibling (Schiff, 1986).

DAY CARE PROVIDERS

Needs and Concerns

Day care providers who were caring for an infant at the time of death will be severely affected by the death of the infant for whom they had accepted responsibility. This may include staff members at a day care facility, volunteers at a day care center sponsored by a religious, civic, or other organization, and private individuals who operate day care programs in their own family homes on a formal or informal basis. Whatever the arrangement, it is not only the impact of the actual death event, but also the shattering of the bonding relationship that had formed between the day care provider and the now-dead infant which is affected.

When a SIDS death occurs, day care providers may experience intense feelings of guilt and failure. Their questions and concerns will be similar to those expressed by the parents: "What was missed?"; "Was anything done wrong?"; "Will someone blame me?" Of special concern to the individual proprietor is a fear of loss of income as he or she questions whether the parents of other children will continue with their day care arrangements. It is also possible that individual day care providers may worry whether they will lose their day care license.

Support to day care providers from their own customary or informal support networks may be short-lived as those close to them fail to recognize the bond that was formed between the provider and the now-dead infant. Spouses of the providers may complicate the grief by not understanding the depth of loss "when it wasn't even our child." Even in a large day care facility, staff may not be able to offer each other support, and outside resources for assistance may not be available.

In the private day care home setting, other families with young children who need day care may encourage the day care provider to continue in this role. They may not understand the individual's need to take a break from the daily routine in the aftermath of a SIDS death. Occasionally, because of their urgent need for day care, they may encourage the day care provider "to climb on the horse again" too rapidly. Or, in trying to demonstrate their faith in the day care provider, families may encourage the individual to continue too soon with their children. Also, day care providers may be hesitant to take leave time or time off "because the children need me," or, unfortunately, because of financial necessity.

It may be difficult for the day care provider to decide to continue to offer care for other infants who are the same age as the dead child or to accept new clients with infants. Fears that another death could occur may be overwhelming. Sometimes providers may decide to impose a limit on the youngest age child that they will accept for care. Day care providers should be encouraged to make decisions in their own best interests, as well as in the interests of the children for whom they are providing day care.

Day care providers frequently ask if they should inform current and/or new clients about the SIDS death. In general, it seems best to advise a direct, open, honest approach. Factual information should be available and clients can be referred to the appropriate people who can document the situation. (Day Care Licensing workers would usually be the primary contact. Although confidentiality requirements may limit the information they can provide, they can assure new or potential clients that the provider's record is clear of any infractions affecting his or her license.)

Not to be forgotten are day care providers for those infants who do not die in their care. Deaths that occur at home in the evening or over a weekend or holiday also affect day care providers. Even though they were not caring for the infant at the time of the death, they may question if they missed signs of illness or impending death when the infant was last in their care. They, too, will experience intense feelings of loss in the forced changes in their daily routines. Since the death did not occur in their facility or home, support regarding the loss may not be forthcoming from their family and friends who may not recognize the need for special attention to the loss.

Guidelines for Helping

A counselor or other person working in the field of SIDS might do some or all of the following to help day care providers who have been impacted by SIDS:

- Provide accurate information regarding SIDS
- Address concerns of the day care provider
- Provide reassurance regarding infant care practices
- Offer support regarding the impact of the loss

- Offer to speak with the other families utilizing the day care facility
- Encourage open communication with other families regarding the circumstances and the cause of the death
- Provide age-appropriate guidance for the day care provider's own children, as well as for the other children in the day care program.
- Suggest follow-up contact with first responders for children who were present during the emergency; they may need special attention to explain what happened and to confirm that the police or fire responders did not hurt the baby or take the baby away forever
- Refer to other day care providers who have experienced a death in their program and can provide support
- Contact the licensing worker to provide support
- Inform the day care provider of legal responsibilities and regulations for reporting the death to the proper licensing authorities; confirm with them that their license will not be revoked because of a SIDS death in their program
- Support decisions to take time off or to restrict ages of children accepted for day care
- Refer to resource people in the community, such as clergy, private counselors, or a regional SIDS resource center, to provide information and to address the impact of the loss
- Suggest that the day care provider ask the family for a photograph of the infant; this may help to replace the vivid memory of the infant when found dead.

BABYSITTERS AND OTHER TEMPORARY CARE PROVIDERS

Needs and Concerns

Although infrequent, deaths may occur while the infant is in the care of a babysitter or other temporary care provider, who may be an adult, a teenage neighbor, or a teen sibling. Feelings of guilt or fears about not having made an important observation may need to be addressed for these individuals, just as with the parents themselves or with a licensed day care provider. Counseling needs will vary depending on the relationship that the babysitter had with the family and the infant. Situations might include a neighbor who cares for the infant while the parent runs an errand, a teenage sitter who cares for the infant on a regularly scheduled basis, or a neighborhood acquaintance who participates in a "babysitting co-op" on an exchange basis.

The effect of the death may be especially difficult for teenage sitters who may not communicate well with their families and who may find it extremely difficult to identify for themselves an important linking person or resource, such as, a peer with a similar experience. Gordon (1986) describes the teenage environment which must be considered in providing support to the adolescent babysitter: "Nothing in previous experience has prepared the youth for the feelings of rage, loneliness, guilt, and disbelief that accompany a personal loss" (p. 22). Raphael (1983) notes uncertainty, gradual acceptance, and nonacceptance as common patterns with adolescents. Overt grief may be less intense or even suppressed because the adolescent may be uncertain of others' responses or fear loss of emotional control.

Certainly, in the context of a SIDS death and a teenage babysitter, the latter's school should be alerted to the situation so that counselors and teachers will be available to provide information and support. Adolescents who are reasonably secure and who can be comforted by an adult or older sibling will be able to mourn the lost relationship effectively.

Guidelines for Helping

A counselor or other person working in the field of SIDS might do some or all of the following to help babysitters and other temporary care providers who have been impacted by SIDS:

- Provide individual contact to the babysitter
- Offer information regarding SIDS and support literature to the babysitter
- In the case of a teenage babysitter, offer to contact the school counselor or social worker to provide SIDS information
- If possible, link with other teens with similar experiences
- Refer to a teen support group
- Provide an awareness of the lack of peer support and offer suggestions so the young adult can inform close friends of his or her needs
- Be aware of and inform the young adult (or his or her family) of funeral practices; prepare the teen for the funeral and the anticipated range of emotions that may be experienced
- Encourage participation in the viewing, funeral, and burial as helpful to the healing process.

FRIENDS OF THE FAMILY

Needs and Concerns

Friends of the family will be as deeply or even more affected than the relatives if they have developed close relationships with the parents. They will be stunned by the untimely death and may experience extreme grief based on their prior interactions with the infant and the family. Often, like the bereaved parents, they are young and have had little experience with death. They may have infants of their own for whom they are frightened of SIDS. Friends may hesitate to contact the bereaved parents, fearing that they are intruding during a private family time (Raphael, 1983). If they have an infant, they will be concerned as to whether the bereaved parents wish to see or hold their infant. Often, they will stay away rather than ask the family what is best for them. Lindemann (1944) documented the restlessness of bereaved parents and their inability to sit still, an inability to initiate and maintain organized patterns of activity, and withdrawn social behavior. Focusing on the lost relationship with the child may cause the parent to neglect other relationships, and the pain of seeing others with their loved ones encourages further withdrawal (Rando, 1986).

Guidelines for Helping

A counselor or other person working in the field of SIDS might do some or all of the following to help friends of the family who have been impacted by SIDS:

- Provide accurate information regarding SIDS
- Offer suggestions for being a good supportive friend and listener
- Offer age-appropriate guidance for the children of these friends of the family
- Provide a support to the friends when they have been the primary support to a bereaved family and need someone to listen to their own concerns
- Encourage the friends to maintain contact with the bereaved family, even if the family does not seem to want to receive calls or visits
- Suggest that friends remember anniversary dates with flowers, a card, a donation, lunch, or coffee.

COWORKERS

Needs and Concerns

Although most employers will initially be understanding of a bereaved family, and especially of a family whose infant has died from SIDS, eventually they are faced with a business or organization that must continue to operate and meet the demands of its customers or those whom it serves. Coworkers are also faced with these dual issues surrounding the aftermath of a SIDS death. Their compassion for the family may be complicated by the need for the bereaved coworker to carry his or her share of the work. Their expectations of their coworker may also be influenced by their own prior experiences with death and how they perceive their own adjustment and return to work. The comparison made will be unfair and aggravating to the bereaved parents because most of their coworkers' experiences will likely be with the death of a grandparent or parent, not with the death of their own child.

Uncomfortable times face coworkers during coffee break and on-the-job conversations that deal with topics which may seem trivial to a bereaved family member, such as, the weather, a child's poor grades, scratches on car doors, or lost keys. New pregnancies, holiday functions, and stress related to children's illnesses, grades, or poor behavior are common subjects in workplace conversation. These may not seem important compared to the issues surrounding the death of an infant. Behaviors which might be exhibited by a bereaved employee include difficulty in making decisions, inability to concentrate, disinterest in job-related details, frustration and irritability, depression and mood swings, or marital and family problems (The Compassionate Friends, 1985). In some cases, there may be a tendency to work constantly to avoid the home environment (Mandell, McAnulty, & Reece, 1980).

Guidelines for Helping

A counselor or other person working in the field of SIDS might do some or all of the following to help coworkers who have been impacted by SIDS:

- Provide accurate information regarding SIDS
- Send literature which can be shared with coworkers
- Offer to conduct an educational presentation for the coworkers in order to provide information about SIDS and suggestions for being supportive to the bereaved family
- Encourage coworkers to be comfortable with conversation related to the infant and the death
- Remind the coworkers to allow the family to make their own decisions to participate in work-related special functions, such as holiday parties or summer picnics
- Suggest that the coworker's desk and belongings be left as is; do not put away pictures or mementos of the infant unless specifically asked to do so
- Acknowledge the coworkers' own family problems which will still need supportive discussion at work, e.g., sick infants who have been up all night, behavior problems with older children, or poor grades, and the guilt they may feel in even mentioning such "trivial" problems
- Suggest that the employer inform business associates and coworkers who may not otherwise hear of the infant's death

- Encourage good communication which will allow the bereaved employee to make his or her own decisions; avoid one-sided decisions made "because I thought that would be best or easiest for you."

MEMBERS OF THE CLERGY

Needs and Concerns

Clergy, despite their religious belief systems and extensive experience with death and funerals, may find it difficult to cope with the death of an innocent infant from SIDS (Wolfelt, 1988). They may have poor information regarding SIDS, and they may feel inadequate as human beings in their reasoning about the death of an infant. Belief systems accepting a god who "causes" everything may inflict undue pain on the young couple. Within such systems, there may be a felt need by the parents themselves, by some members of the clergy, or by others to identify wrongdoing which could "explain" the cause of the death (Czillinger, 1986). In contrast, many churches have extensive support resources available through outreach groups, lay ministers, prayer "phone trees," and parishioners who will provide meals and child care to the family over an extended period of time.

Holidays associated with family gatherings, baptisms, and Mother's and Father's Days may be a source of conflict to the bereaved family, which is appreciative of the support received from the church, but cannot deal with the "happy" feelings expected for special religious celebrations. Consider the anguish of the mother whose only child has died who hears on Mother's Day, "Will all the mothers present please stand to be recognized." Does this woman stand with the others (she is a mother) and risk tears and comments, or does she sit quietly in her grief and sadness?

Guidelines for Helping

A counselor or other person working in the field of SIDS might do some or all of the following to help members of the clergy who have been impacted by SIDS:

- Clarify accurate information regarding SIDS
- Offer to meet with special church groups to which the bereaved parents belong to supply information and suggestions for providing support to the family

- Discourage comments which increase parents' guilt or imply opinions of "God's will" or "God's plan" (Czillinger, 1986)
- Encourage visits to be made to the home shortly after the death
- Encourage the clergy and church members to accept anger directed at the church or God (Czillinger, 1986)
- Foster acceptance of the family's timing regarding their return to active participation in church activities
- Assist the family in planning and participating in, if they wish, a funeral or memorial service for the dead infant which will be meaningful to them
- Where allowed, suggest music and/or liturgy that may be more familiar to the family, appropriate to the circumstances of an infant's death, and less oriented to traditional funeral practices (consider music from the hymnals or from children's services)
- Recommend a homily that speaks specifically to the infant and the family; refer to the infant by his or her full given name
- Inform the clergy of other resources available to the family for counseling and support.

HEALTH CARE PROVIDERS

Needs and Concerns

Health care providers, too, will be affected by SIDS deaths. Many will spend endless hours searching medical records for clues which they might have missed in evaluating the infant's medical care needs. Especially in small private practices, pediatricians and obstetricians are accustomed to life and the wonders of the developing fetus, infant, and child. Some may experience a sense of failure in not detecting an impending death. In addition, they may have a limited knowledge of SIDS and may be hesitant to acknowledge that to the family. Also, they may be reluctant to contact the family.

Bergman (1974, p. 115) noted that "few of us modern physicians tend to be very good at dealing with death . . . seldom do medical students have the opportunity to watch a senior physician serving as a model . . . managing a case of Sudden Infant Death Syndrome." Similarly, Schiff (1986) commented that the medical profession has much to learn about dealing with families. Apprentice physicians may still largely be taught by trial and error as they are directed as young residents to "tell the family of the death." Perhaps for this reason, Cornwell, Nurcombe, and Stevens (1977) found that more than half of the doctors felt themselves unable to handle the (SIDS) family. Nevertheless, because of their status in our health and social systems, health care providers fill roles of special importance to the family at the time of the infant's death, in its immediate aftermath, and in long-term contacts for the future.

Guidelines for Helping

Health care providers may have two areas in which they need assistance. First, in their roles as professionals offering help to the bereaved family; and, second, in terms of their own needs as persons who have themselves been affected by the death of an infant from SIDS. With regard to assisting the family, a counselor or other person working in the field of SIDS might suggest that health care providers:

- Contact the family to express condolences and offer information
- Make a home visit to the bereaved family
- Send a personal note to the family, attend the funeral or memorial service, or make a donation in memory of the baby
- Review medical records for family concerns and issues that may complicate their grief, e.g., an unplanned pregnancy, considerations about terminating the pregnancy, a desire for a child of the opposite sex, difficulty in adjusting to the new lifestyle demanded by the birth of the infant, or hesitancy to return to work after the birth of the infant
- Arrange an office visit shortly after the funeral and again when the autopsy report is available (usually six to eight weeks later)
- Assure that preliminary autopsy results are made available to the family (and day care providers, if appropriate) as soon as possible after the autopsy (usually within 24 hours of the death)
- Follow closely the adjustment of surviving siblings.

In response to their own needs as individuals who have been impacted by a SIDS death, a counselor or other person working in the field of SIDS might do some or all of the following to assist health care providers:

- Be a good listener while they share their feelings of frustration and failure
- Offer reassurance that signs of illness and/or disease were not missed, i.e., that SIDS could not have been detected in advance or prevented
- Review factual information and current research regarding SIDS
- Acknowledge their loss and grief
- Offer suggestions for what to say or do for the family
- Be available to offer resources for family counseling
- Send copies of literature which were sent to the family.

OTHERS

Many others beyond the immediate family and those who have been identified above will be affected by a SIDS death. These might include:

- Store clerks who may help with the purchase of a burial outfit or who assist with the return of items that are no longer needed
- Postal carriers who have delivered baby cards and now have a packet of literature from a SIDS program to deliver
- Secretaries at the diaper service who take calls to cancel the service, and the diaper service delivery person who picks up the service's items which had been left at the home
- Childbirth instructors and other members in the childbirth class
- Staff at restaurants which the family has visited regularly during the pregnancy and then accompanied by the baby
- Grocery clerks who last saw the infant sitting in the basket as the groceries were checked out
- And, the barber, the hairdresser, the manicurist, the bank clerk, etc. Grandparents, relatives, and friends also have multiple contacts with these same types of people. Caregivers will need to assess the meaning of the death for each of these individuals in order to know who may need assistance and how to be most supportive to them. Again, it should be stressed that the needs of each of these individuals will be unique and should be received in confidence.

GUIDELINES FOR HELPING THE BEREAVED FAMILY

The following are general suggestions which can be offered to grandparents, extended family members, and other significant persons who have been affected by a SIDS death as they attempt to provide support to a bereaved family.

The most important thing to do initially is to *acknowledge* the death. Call, visit the home (take food if you feel more comfortable if you have "done" something), or write a letter (a card will do, but a personal note should be added).

LISTEN. This is not the time to share your worst experiences or someone else's horror story. The bereaved family does not care about your worries. You are there to extend your condolences to them.

Allow the family to tell their story over and over and over. It helps to talk about the infant. Memories of the infant's life are important to the family. They need to be able to share the good as well as the bad times, and they will often find themselves laughing and crying at the same time as they remember special events. Add your memories, but do not bother to correct small details that you may remember differently. Accuracy is not the issue at this point. Offer your support of the positive interactions which you remember the family displaying. This can be especially important if the couple is expressing concerns about their abilities to be good parents. Reminders of the small details which you recall are very special. Be willing to look at pictures of the infant.

Do not try to think of things to say to make the family members feel "better," happier, or thankful for what they still have. The family is aware of their "blessings," but those factors are not central to their concerns right now. Comments of this sort only hurt and tend to discount the loss.

Keep your faith, beliefs, and clichés to yourself. If those beliefs help you, use them for your own comfort, but do not expect the family to appreciate or find solace in them.

Avoid trivial conversation; the weather, work, and gossip are of little interest to the bereaved family at this time. Remember that silence and mere presence can be helpful.

LEARN accurate information about Sudden Infant Death Syndrome. If you have questions or issues, ask an authority. Do not approach the family with your theories and research questions. In that way, you may unwittingly be implying that had they been aware of your information, their child might still be alive. When you hear or read of a new "breakthrough in the cause of SIDS," contact your local SIDS resource center for an accurate interpretation of the information *before* you call the family "to share the good news." Most often, these media announcements are misleading to the general public and devastating to the families who may assume they should have been more aware of research which could have prevented the death of their child.

OFFER advice only if you are asked. Frequently, requests for advice are requests for approval of what someone really wants to do, but is afraid to say. Before responding with your own suggestions, ask: "What do *you* want to do?" "What options do *you* have?" Focus more on the problem-solving process than on "answers," and help members of the bereaved family to work out their own individual solutions.

Offer to:

• Answer the phone, but allow the family to screen calls, decide to whom they wish to speak, and choose when to ask for a return call. Do not assume that you know with whom it is best or not best for them to speak.

• Try to think of details that will need attention. Make a list so that you can discuss these matters with the family when appropriate. Does clothing need to be taken to or picked up from the cleaners or laundry? Does everyone have something to wear to the funeral services? Does a paycheck need to be picked up and deposited? Does the family need cash for incidentals now?

- Call or write friends, especially those living at a distance from the family who may only communicate at special times, such as birthdays or holidays
- Cancel scheduled appointments or notify instructors of exercise classes or other programs in which the family may be participating
- Call the instructor of prenatal classes that the couple attended
- Arrange meals for the new few weeks and a weekly meal afterwards for the next few months
- Do the grocery shopping
- Notify the dentist, a favorite restaurant, or other service providers with whom the family has approaching or infrequent encounters
- Contact instructors and others involved with activities of the siblings, e.g., preschool, school, sports
- Transport or accompany surviving siblings to scheduled activities that they may wish to attend, e.g., preschool, birthday parties, gymnastics
- Pick up pictures that were left for developing. Call the photographer if the portraits were recently done and ask if the negatives might be given to the family. Offer to order an enlargement of a favorite picture of the baby. If portraits were done by a large company which specializes in inexpensive picture packages which are accompanied at the time of delivery with high pressure techniques to purchase the rest of the pictures, call ahead to explain the death. Ask the company to donate the picture set to the family.
- Accompany your friend to appointments, and offer to drive so that parking will not be a hassle
- If you have a baby, ask the family if they want your baby to be present or not at funeral services and other activities. Everyone is different in this respect and their desires may change from one visit to another. Do NOT assume that the presence of a baby "hurts too much" or that "they have to face it someday and the sooner the better."

There is no instant cure. Bereaved parents need comfort and kindness over many months. Thus, friends and helpers can do things like the following over the long term:

- Remember that the pain and hurt are present months later. Expect and accept bad days, crying jags, and anger. Do not ask: "Are you OK?" "Are you doing better?" "Have you gone to any of the meetings?" These imply that the bereaved person should be better or is not doing everything that you think they should be doing.

- Accept the anger, the comments of unfairness, the frustration expressed because of a lack of control
- Remember the holidays—all of them! Holidays which do not have much significance for some may be very difficult for families to face (Schiff, 1986). Shopping prior to these days may be especially difficult as the bereaved family views reminders of what they do not have and are not able or do not need to buy, such as a fancy red dress for Valentine's Day or a Halloween costume.
- Be aware of places with strollers when planning outings with the bereaved family. They are painful. In summer, it will seem like everyone is pregnant; there are no coats to cover maternity clothes, so the anticipation of new life becomes more visible.
- Visit the cemetery and accompany the bereaved parents on visits to the cemetery. Take flowers to the parents when they are taking flowers to the grave. Stop by the cemetery yourself and leave flowers or dust the marker. Tell the family that you were there.
- Offer to include the family in special parties, but allow them to decide if they wish to attend. Baby showers may be especially difficult for bereaved mothers to attend.
- Acknowledge anniversary dates, such as birthdays, the date of the infant's death, and, for the first year, the monthly date of the infant's death, as well as the date of his or her birth
- Acknowledge other "first" days as they occur, such as that time at which the child would have entered kindergarten, first grade, and high school. Peppers and Knapp (1980) recognize a "shadow grief" which may intrude on special occasions and may be present for the rest of the bereaved persons' lives—a reminder of the loss they experienced.
- Be aware of expressions of grief and of patterns in the mourning process. Accept mourning as a process which is highly individualized, takes time and energy, and will always be a part of the family's life. Rando (1986, p. xi) has stated that: "Parental loss of a child is unlike any other loss. The grief of parents is particularly severe, complicated, and long lasting, with major and unparalleled symptom fluctuations over time."
- If or when a future pregnancy is announced, do not assume that it will alleviate the family's grief. Do not be surprised if the grief seems magnified. Fears of another loss may overshadow the positive feelings, even though the pregnancy was planned. Do not focus solely on the new pregnancy. Remember the deceased infant. Allow the family to express their feelings, both positive and negative, without reproach. Be willing to listen to com-

parisons with the prior pregnancy, just as you would with anyone else com-
paring one pregnancy to another.

- With the arrival of a new baby, anticipate that the family will still need to
  speak of the deceased infant, will still need recognition of anniversary
  dates, will compare this infant to the one who died, and will still have some
  very sad times in their lives.
- And, when you do something wrong or not as well as you would have liked,
  share your feelings with the family. Ask what they need. Be prepared to
  help if you offer. Do not stay away!!

CONCLUSION

These tiny infants affected many people. In their death, there will also be a
lasting impact. Neither their lives, short as they may have been, nor their
deaths, should be discounted. Although the intensity of each individual's feelings will be affected by many factors, it is important to remember that the
family and friends of these infants will need a special understanding. Schiff
(1986, p. 255) stated that, "Although there are many supportive and caring
people out in the wide world, they need guidelines. They truly wish to help but
feel inept and overwhelmed when confronted with enormous grief." Many will
need assistance in understanding their own feelings, as well as suggestions for
maintaining a supportive relationship with the bereaved family. The value of
the SIDS counselor or others involved with the family in providing these resources cannot be underestimated.

Although the ideas and suggestions in this chapter may seem obvious to
skilled bereavement counselors, they are not always well addressed in professional education. In addition, collectively, they demonstrate the importance of
effective family interviewing and appropriate intervention in order to provide
maximum supportive resources to the families and others affected by the
death of an infant.

REFERENCES

Bergman, A. B. (1974). Psychological aspects of sudden unexpected death in infants and
    children: Review and commentary. *Pediatric Clinics of North America, 21*, 115–121.
Cornwell, J., Nurcombe, B., & Stevens, L. (1977). Family response to loss of a child by
    sudden infant death syndrome. *Medical Journal of Australia, 1*, 656–658.

Czillinger, K. J. (1986). Advice to clergy on counseling bereaved parents. In T. A. Rando (Ed.), *Parental loss of a child* (pp. 465–471). Champaign, IL: Research Press.

Gordon, A. (1986). The tattered cloak of immortality. In C. A. Corr & J. N. McNeil (Eds.), *Adolescence and death* (pp. 16–31). New York: Springer Publishing Co.

Kübler-Ross, E. (1969). *On death and dying.* New York: Macmillan.

Lindemann, E. (1944). Symptomatology and management of acute grief. *American Journal of Psychiatry, 101*, 141–148.

Mandell, F., McAnulty, E., & Reece, R. (1980). Observations of paternal response to sudden unanticipated infant death. *Pediatrics, 65*, 221–225.

Peppers, L. G., & Knapp, R. J. (1980). *Motherhood and mourning.* New York: Praeger.

Rando, T. A. (Ed.). (1986). *Parental loss of a child.* Champaign, IL: Research Press.

Raphael, B. (1983). *The anatomy of bereavement.* New York: Basic Books.

Resolve Through Sharing (1986). The grief of grandparents. La Crosse, WI: La Crosse Lutheran Hospital.

Schiff, H. S. (1986). *Living through mourning.* New York: Viking Penguin.

The Compassionate Friends (1985). When an employee is grieving. Oak Brook, IL: Author.

Wolfelt, A. (1988). *Death and grief: A guide for clergy.* Muncie, IN: Accelerated Development, Inc.

Worden, J. W. (1982). *Grief counseling and grief therapy: A handbook for the mental health practitioner.* New York: Springer Publishing Co.

Zebal, B. H., & Woolsey, S. F. (1984). SIDS and the family: The pediatrician's role. *Pediatric Annals, 13*, 237–261.

SUGGESTED READINGS

Jensen, A. H. (1985). Is there anything I can do to help? Suggestions for the friends and relatives of the grieving survivor. Redmond, WA: Medic Publishing Co.

Linn, E. (1986). *I know just how you feel . . . avoiding the cliches of grief.* Cary, IL : The Publishers Mark.

Miller, R. F. (1987). *What can I say? How to talk to people in grief.* St. Louis: CBP Press.

Parachin, V. M. (1988). How to help a friend through loss. *Bereavement, 2*(9), 9–10.

Schiff, H. S. (1977). *The bereaved parent.* New York: Penguin.

CHAPTER 7

Long-Term Impact on Family System Functioning

Barbara Y. Whitman and Pasquale J. Accardo

> All happy families resemble one another; every un-
> happy family is unhappy in its own way.
>
> Tolstoy (1898, p. 1)

There is no greater insult to a family than the death of a child, and loss of a child to Sudden Infant Death Syndrome (SIDS) appears to be particularly devastating. Conceptually, a SIDS death constitutes a crisis, yet crisis theory remains inadequate to explain the impact of SIDS on the family. Similarly, current conceptualizations of grief and bereavement appear to fall short when trying either to explain theoretically the experiences of SIDS families or to guide clinical work with them.

This chapter utilizes systems theory to explore the long-term functional impact of a SIDS death on individual family systems. In order to understand SIDS families more fully, we must first examine those unique properties that set the *family* system apart from other groups or collections of people. Once this framework is developed, we will look at the impact of SIDS on family units.

DEFINITION OF A FAMILY

A *family* is a small social system made up of individuals related to each other by means of strong reciprocal affections and loyalties, comprising a permanent household (or cluster of households) that persists over years and decades. Members enter by birth, adoption, or marriage, and leave only by death, if then (Terkleson, 1980).

It is worth noting that this definition allows for a variety of alternate family styles beyond the traditional two-parent family. Such styles include group marriage, polygamy, polyandry, communal arrangements, homosexual pairings, open marriage, unmarried coupling, and single-parent families. Research has not uncovered any significant differences among many of these family styles with respect to their long-term impact on early child development. Family "processes" are found to be more important than family "structure."

The most important feature of this definition is the way in which it highlights the properties that make a family unique and that distinguish it from other forms of social organization: a shared and predictable life cycle; membership permanence; and primacy of affectional ties. Each of these three definitional characteristics needs to be examined in somewhat more detail.

Families Have a Shared and Predictable Life Cycle

The shared and predictable life cycle of families is a repetitive, recycling set of configurations and issues through which the family passes. Unlike a human life, which begins with conception and ends with death, the life of the family does not have such clear markers but continues despite the death of some members and the birth of others (Combrinch-Graham, 1985). It remains possible to define common stages of the changing family relationship system over the course of the family life cycle (Carter & McGoldrick, 1988). These are: Leaving Home: Single Young Adults; the Joining of Families Through Marriage: The New Couple; Families with Young Children; Families with Adolescents; Launching Children and Moving On; Families in Later Life.

A pictorial representation of the interrelationships between these stages is presented in Figure 7.1. The passage from one stage to the next is not a single step in time; it is a transitional process that repeatedly (like the Roman god, Janus) looks both forward and backward.

Membership in a Family is Virtually Permanent

One enters a family only by marriage, birth, or adoption. Termination of family membership is virtually impossible. With other social structures, a person, on the one hand, may resign or quit, or, on the other hand, can be fired or voted out. While some organizations grant a type of permanent membership status (e.g., tenure for a university professor), most organizations have rules dictating routine termination procedures ("due process"), and organizations cannot permanently indenture persons.

In the life history of the family, however, there is nothing like being laid off or fired. Family members do not quit or drop their membership; there is no routine form of exit. In families, the emotional nature of the relationship is

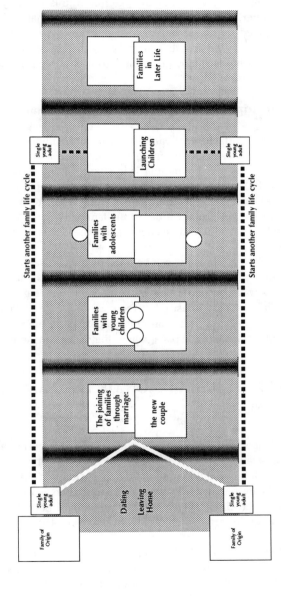

FIGURE 7.1 Common stages in the family life cycle.

such that one cannot leave. Physical absence does not terminate membership; the emotional ties remain. For example, a child may lose a father through death or divorce, but, whether or not the paternal role is filled by someone else (e.g., a stepfather, with new emotional attachments), that child remains emotionally influenced by his or her biological father. (A correlary to this quality of permanence is the fact that most family membership is not voluntary.) Family membership is simply not subject to expiration; it always carries a past and implies a future.

Family Relationships are Primarily Affectional in Nature

The emotional ties of attachment, caring, and loyalty within a family overshadow any successful or unsuccessful performance of roles and duties. Stereotypically, father earns a living, mother is in charge of housework, and children go to school. But father remains father and is loved even if he gets fired, mother retains her affectional position in the family even if the house is a mess, and children are not drummed out of the family if they bring home bad report cards. While value is placed on success, a higher value is placed on the affectional bond.

In the marketplace, a job opening can be filled by many different work units; employees are eminently replaceable. Not so in the family. Nonemotional functions can almost always be performed by another person (e.g., a maid can come in and clean the messy house), but the emotional role of "mother" can never be completely replaced. This non-utilitarian aspect of the family is highlighted in the motto, "Home is the place where they have to take you in."

THE SIDS EVENT: DISRUPTION OF THE FAMILY'S LIFE CYCLE

A SIDS death is a catastrophic interruption to the family life cycle. Infant mortality rates notwithstanding, it is a fundamental, although unconscious, psychological premise that our children do not die, particularly if they survive the neonatal period. Many parents who have lost a child, no matter the age of either the parent or the child, will say that, "It would have been easier to lose my spouse." In life cycle terms, a child's death is out of phase with expected life stages.

More importantly, however, SIDS deaths most frequently occur in young families whose life course together is just beginning. The average age of parents who have suffered a SIDS death is mid-twenties. Many of these parents, as individuals, are still negotiating the tasks of Leaving Home. Further, as couples they are likely to remain in the Joining Together phase of development, even while entering the Family with Young Children phase. For many of these couples, problem solving and negotiating common marital issues, such as budgeting, shared time together, affectional communication, and the like, are ongoing, not yet fully internalized processes. Patterned, predictable ways of moving together are still usually thought of in material terms (e.g., can we afford a new car; he wants to spend money on his hobbies, I want a new refrigerator). Typically, a smooth-running system that can withstand strain has not yet fully formed.

The SIDS event places emotional demands on an immature marital and family system of this sort that older, more seasoned, and well-adjusted families would have tremendous difficulty negotiating. These demands on the newly formed family are frequently not well handled. Even for those who subsequently remain married, the family system is forever altered.

SIDS families also illustrate the concept of membership permanence in several striking ways. Although physically dead, in most families the SIDS infant remains an active, ongoing member of the marital and family dynamics. Marital relationships survive or fail on the ability of each spouse to allow the other to grieve in his or her own way and to establish his or her post-death relationship with the SIDS infant. These might take the form of visits to the grave, open display and gazing at pictures, or simply talking about the lost child. In addition, relationships with future children are shaped in an immediate and ongoing manner by the way in which parents cope with the SIDS event and develop an ongoing relationship with the dead child.

Children who were present during the SIDS event must also absorb and cope with the loss of the child, the events surrounding the death, and the grief of their parents. Moreover, they face a sudden and brightening awareness of their own mortality that this event precipitates. The adjustment of such children both shapes and is shaped by the marital system, and by the resolutions that adults as individuals and as parents are able to achieve.

Finally, one has but to ask a SIDS parent to describe the occasion of the death and one is struck by the immediacy, clarity, and vividness of the description. However displaced by time, the memory of the event is fresh, real, alive, and intensely painful. In contrast, the events that followed—who called the police, who was at the funeral, where did your other children stay during this time—are frequently lost from memory. While there is psychological numbing or "shut down" for the subsequent time period, the discovery of the baby's death remains vivid.

That affectional and emotional ties are primary in families is most strikingly illustrated by children. In our culture, children are valued simply for "being," not for what they do, do not do, or will do. A sudden infant death occurs, by definition, at the time of most intense emotional bonding with one's child, when fantasies about the child and hopes for the child are untempered by the reality of this child's particular abilities and accomplishments or the family's capacity to provide future resources. This complete and unexpected disruption of the lives of all concerned, compounded by no logical explanation, remains one of the most devastating aspects to the remaining family members. Many families describe the loss created by the death of a child as leading to the "empty space phenomenon" (McClowry, et al., 1987). This space can never be filled, nor this loss compensated. Nor are the affectional ties to this child ever severed. In fact, for many these ties are intensified. Thus, the loss retains an ongoing and active impact on future family dynamics.

In all families, the fact that family relationships are virtually permanent, mostly nonvoluntary, and almost irreplaceable can be a source of both security and stress. Whether security or stress predominates will depend on two further characteristics of family systems: nonsummativity and circular causality.

Nonsummativity

A family is more than the sum of its parts. Modern family therapy takes its origin from General Systems Theory, a discipline that has had significant impact in biology and psychology. This theory postulates that the whole system is different from the sum total of its component parts, and that the relationships among the parts are the most important descriptors of the system. While this nonsummative property is fairly obvious in the life sciences (biologists and anatomists have long recognized the reductionist fallacy inherent in viewing living organisms as bags of chemicals), it was revolutionary to apply the same observation to nonliving systems such as families.

A common example of the family system as more than the sum of its parts occurs when someone has two close friends who get married. A new social unit is created: the married couple. It will subtly change its members and their relationships to their friends. The individual persons are not so much changed in themselves, but the successful prediction of their behavior requires taking into account the larger system they have created and to which they now belong. Old friends will need to discover new ways of relating to this third entity—the couple.

This principle can clearly be seen at work in SIDS families. One has only to relate to such a family for a short time to recognize that a major portion of the relational equation in this family is the deceased child. To relate to this family, one must also relate to this child and his or her impact. Even though one will never meet the dead child, the family's dynamics cannot be accounted for without this missing yet ever-present member.

Circular Causality

A correllary to the property of nonsummativity is that of circular causality (see Figure 7.2). In a family system, people relate in such a way that a change in any one member affects other members both as individuals and the group as a whole. For example, the first date of a 14-year-old young lady, the oldest child in the family, is an event whose impact is not restricted to that child. Mother and father now have to cope with a new set of anxieties and worries. Family activities and schedules now have to take into account whether or not daughter has a date. Other siblings are also implicated by this shift in organization. They must hope that this teenager behaves and does not break any family rules, so that when they begin to date, they will not have to live down or carry the negative burden of an older child who disappointed parental expectations.

Stresses created by such critical events or shifts in the life of one child (or family member) may lead to another child presenting in the health or mental health care delivery system with new health, behavior, or psychosomatic complaints, or for unexplained deterioration of previously controlled medical conditions, such as diabetes and asthma.

In SIDS families, this pattern is frequently illustrated by older siblings. While these children can demonstrate predictable fears for their own safety and immediate guilt over the baby's death, many will also demonstrate equally significant symptomatology on the occasion of subsequent sibling births, at times of hospitalization of other family members, and during other kinds of life changes. Clinical interviews can uncover the relationship of these symptomatologies to the SIDS event.

FIGURE 7.2 Circular causality.

By now it should be clear that a SIDS death is not a singular event from which a family simply picks up its shattered pieces and recovers. Neither is the outcome of this death on a family's functioning simple to understand in its psychological and dynamic impact. Nor is the ultimate recovery and adjustment of a family suffering a SIDS event a simple function of the family life cycle stage or family system properties alone. The next section details one context in which a family must be viewed in order to understand more fully and to intervene more effectively.

STRESSORS

Two distinct sets of influences on the family's response to a SIDS death can be identified (Carter & McGoldrick, 1980; see Figure 7.3). *Horizontal stressors* produce the anxiety a family routinely deals with as it moves forward in time, coping with changes and transitions in the family life cycle. These include both predictable developmental stresses and those unpredictable external events that may disrupt a family (e.g., loss of a job, birth of a handicapped child, illness, war, bankruptcy, or death of a member). Given enough stress on the horizontal axis, any family will appear dysfunctional.

The *vertical stressors* on the system are composed of patterns of relating and functioning that are transmitted through several family generations. These include family attitudes, taboos, expectations, labels, and loaded issues (for example, "family secrets") that everyone grows up with. These vertical stressors are "the hand one is dealt"; they are a family "given." And they are usually unspoken, unwritten operating principles that frame a family's approach to the world. Common examples of these types of stressors are: "Do not marry outside your religion/race/social class"; "Our family always attends Ivy League schools." Family secrets are often more toxic, such as "Aunt Jane killed herself"; "Uncle Joe was a womanizer." Some types of stressor messages may relate to the more mundane aspects of life, but carry enormous weight in determining a family's interaction pattern, such as, "Do not buy anything unless it is on sale"; "Stick to brand labels only."

When horizontal stressors intersect with vertical stressors, the resulting anxiety can become overwhelming. For example, the birth of a son with limited intelligence into a family where all the males go to Harvard can severely tax family coping abilities.

Clinicians dealing with families who have suffered a SIDS death are accustomed to dealing with horizontal stressors such as those expressed in the process of grief and mourning. What tends to be ignored, however, is locating this particular horizontal stressor within the perspective of existing family vertical

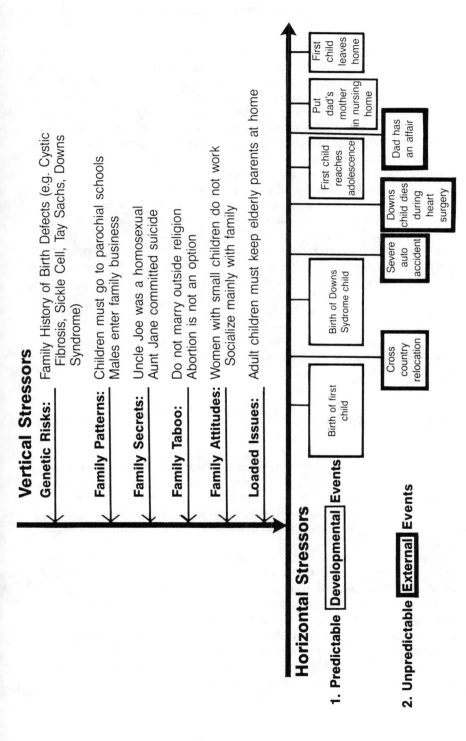

FIGURE 7.3 Family stressors—two conceptual sources.

stressors. Failure to do so can have major impact on the outcome of the mourning process and on subsequent family adjustment to the SIDS event.

Taking the definitional and supplementary properties discussed earlier, within the context of these vertical and horizontal stressors, will provide the foundation for current systems approaches to dealing with SIDS families. When families are viewed as systems with repetitious, patterned, and predictable behavior, it is clear that events which require adaptation for the system as a whole, or events which affect an individual family member, will have repercussions throughout the entire system. A SIDS death completely disrupts these repetitious, patterned ways of interacting. Coping mechanisms and behavior patterns previously relied upon are usually inadequate to deal with this event. Thus, a SIDS death throws the family into a crisis state. At the family level, this is often reflected in inability to complete ordinary activities of daily living, increased irritability with other family members, more fights and arguments, and a vague feeling of distancing between spouses that is counterbalanced by periods of intense closeness—a sort of exaggerated family mood swing cycle. Many emotionally traumatized families experience more colds and flu symptoms, car accidents become more likely, unusual impulsive spending may occur, and family decision making becomes sidetracked, perhaps ineffective, and often the occasion for an argument. A further complication in this disruptive state is the overlay of grief and mourning which may not coincide between a husband and wife.

THE AFTERMATH

After a period of time, most families begin to reorganize and cope. This reorganization can occur at three levels: (1) reorganization at the pre-crisis level of functioning; (2) reorganization at a higher level of functioning; and (3) deterioration from a previously more well-adjusted state (see Figure 7.4).

Two functional variables play a significant part in the family's post-death recovery and reorganization. These are: (1) the pre-death level of family cohesion; and (2) family adaptability (Olson, Russell, & Sprenkle, 1983; Olson, Sprenkle, & Russell, 1979). *Family cohesion* is the emotional bonding members have with one another and the degree of individual autonomy a person experiences within the family system. *Family adaptability* is the ability of the marital and family system to change its power structure, role relationships, and relationship rules in response to situational and developmental stresses. In current formulations, families at the extremes of either or both (see Figure 7.5) of these dimensions are at higher risk of deterioration or dysfunction as a result of a SIDS crisis than are those more balanced on one or both of these dimen-

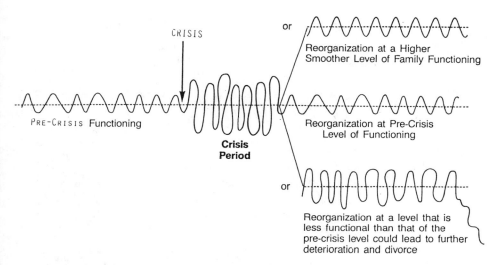

FIGURE 7.4 Crisis: its impact on family functioning.

sions. Thus, the more disengaged a family is prior to a SIDS death, the more they are at risk for complete disintegration and dissolution. The more enmeshed a family, the greater is the likelihood for long-term dysfunction. Similarly, in both very rigid and very chaotic families, family adaptation to the child's death is likely to be compromised.

A major factor in a functional recovery for a SIDS family is the availability of informal or formal support during the adjustment period. It is well documented that the outcomes of immediate and active intervention at this time are of greater efficacy than later therapeutic attempts. Using the systems perspective lets us look at a case example that illustrates a family with successful post-SIDS adjustment.

CASE STUDY #1: THE BAKERS

The Bakers were both 26 when they married. They are a middle class, college educated, dual-career family. The Bakers had one daughter after three years of marriage and a son, Tom, was born two years later. Although not financially necessary, both spouses continued to work while the children were cared for in a nearby day care center.

Tom had been napping when the day care staff determined it was time to awaken him to prepare for Mrs. Baker to pick up the children. Tom was non-

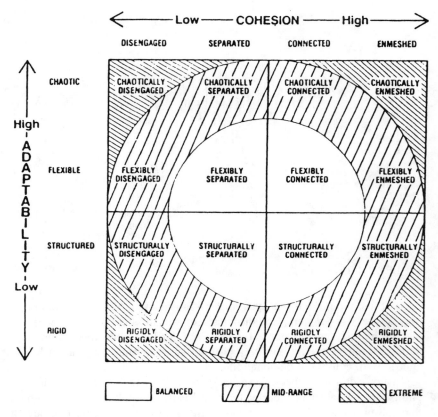

FIGURE 7.5 Two functional variables.

Source: From D. H. Olson, C. S. Russell, R. & D. H. Sprenkle (1983). Circumplex model of marital and family systems: VI. Theoretical update. *Family Process, 22,* 71. Reprinted by permission From Family Process. Inc.

responsive in the crib when the child care worker entered the room. She picked him up and rushed to the telephone to call for emergency help. Despite the typical heroic response by paramedical personnel, the child was pronounced dead at the local community hospital. Mrs. Baker arrived after the ambulance had left the day care center. A phone call had already been made to Mr. Baker, and he, Mrs. Baker, and his parents arrived at the hospital at about the same time. Despite some confusion, the parents were told that the baby was dead and ultimately were allowed to hold Tom and say goodbye.

Besides the grief issues inherent in the death, the first set of problematic feelings this family faced involved the day care center. Although neither parent felt any blame toward the center, when Mrs. Baker returned to work two weeks after her son's death, both parents had to confront the place where the death occurred, fear of leaving their other child in someone else's care, and ultimately the day care staff's own grief.

Second, the parents noted very different ways of grieving in each other—and accommodated accordingly. In addition, the parents faced the issue of further children and decided to have another child immediately.

Their daughter experienced many anxieties and fears associated with her own death. Each episode of these fears is still accompanied by acting out at school and nightmares at home.

Four years later, with two additional boys, this family can be described as well adjusted. Mother notes, however, that this adjustment involves a constant struggle both to face and resolve conflicting emotions, some of which remain unresolved. She adds that this process could have torn their marriage apart had she and her husband not been close prior to the SIDS death.

These parents have sought and used numerous support systems in their struggle. When asked what the most lasting impact of the death had been, mother reported a barely negotiated sense that "there is no control over life." A position of "never take anything for granted" attitude allows her to be more appreciative of small triumphs and to have a greater day-to-day appreciation and connection with her family.

This family had healthy levels of cohesion and adaptability prior to the death of their son. However, both parents note that these dimensions of family functioning are repeatedly tested and re-tested as they face the development of their children against the background of the SIDS death.

In addition, this family demonstrates the impact of vertical stressors on the system. One set of grandparents in this family had also had a child die many years before and had had no further children. They have had a difficult time accepting the subsequent two grandchildren, and this set of family relationships is compromised as a result of the SIDS death and the ensuing adaptational processes. Clearly, this is an ongoing source of pain for all concerned. Yet, it represents for us the altered life course, family dynamics, and daily impact that a SIDS event creates, even many years later.

Not all families recover in this way, however, and some develop long-term maladaptive patterns.

MALADAPTIVE PATTERNS

Maladaptive patterns represent a family's unsuccessful attempt to cope. Attempts should always be made to view the motivations behind these efforts in a positive light, since it is rare that they reflect any malicious intent. The four following maladaptive patterns were first described by Minuchin and his colleagues (1975) in their study of families with children with diabetes, asthma, and anorexia nervosa: enmeshment; overprotection; rigidity; and lack of conflict resolution. They represent disordered communication or dysfunctional feedback loops in the family system (Minuchin, Rosman, & Baker, 1978).

Enmeshment

Enmeshment refers to an extreme form of closeness and intensity in family interactions. A pathologically enmeshed family system is characterized by an excess of responsiveness and involvement. Subsystem boundaries are unclear, weak, or easily crossed; executive (parental) hierarchies are confused. The spouse relationship is subordinate to parenting functions. Parental control of children is usually ineffective. Spouse-child alliances against the other spouse are common. Children may act in an inappropriately parental manner toward their parents. Changes in one family member (or in the relationship between two members) reverberate throughout the system. Conversations between family members show extremes of interruptions, of speaking or answering for another and finishing another's sentences, and of intrusions by all members into two-person conversations.

A disagreement between two members in an enmeshed family may produce a chain reaction of changing alliances, allegiances, and responsiveness by all members. Individual autonomy is almost nonexistent. Individual efforts toward differentiation are met with a system response to bring the offender back into line. Excessive togetherness and sharing bring about a lack of privacy. Family members intrude on each other's thoughts and feelings. Frequently, these families will report that "bedroom doors are never closed." Children sleep in parents' beds far beyond the normal age that would be expected from frightened young children. All activities are family activities. Under the guise of "togetherness," family members are trapped together in a cage that has no room for individual interests or differentiation.

Overprotectiveness

This maladaptive characteristic becomes obvious in the extremely high degree of concern that family members show for each other's welfare. Nurturing and protective responses are constantly elicited as family members interact. A sneeze sets off a flurry of handkerchief offers. Complaints and questions about fatigue or discomfort punctuate the conversation. Critical remarks and demands are often accompanied by pacifying behaviors. Family members' perceptions of each other are centered around protective concerns.

Overprotectiveness is most pronounced when there is a sick child or one that is perceived to be vulnerable (whether that is really true or not). In these families, the parents' overprotectiveness retards the child's development of independence. A father tells his adolescent diabetic daughter, "If mommy and I could only take the needles for you, everything would be all right." A SIDS parent who is overprotective may not be able to separate from the next infant even to go to a movie for fear of another SIDS death. Similarly, when the child reaches adolescence, independence issues may be a source of overprotective responses, causing much family conflict. This overprotectiveness can become a heavy burden for the child to carry.

Rigidity

Pathologically enmeshed or overprotective families are heavily committed to maintaining the status quo. In periods when change and growth are necessary, they experience great difficulty. For example, when a child in an effectively functioning family reaches adolescence, the family will be able to adjust rules in ways that allow for age-appropriate steps toward independence. This can be accomplished while still preserving a degree of family continuity. However, the rigid family operates like a closed system. Issues that threaten change, such as negotiations over independence, are not allowed to surface to where they can be explored.

When events that require change (such as a first day at pre-school or a first date) occur, family members act swiftly to maintain and reinforce accustomed behavior patterns. Consequently, avoidance circuits must be developed. A symptom bearer is a particularly useful "detouring route." As a result, these families are in a chronic state of submerged stress. When coming to the attention of a professional, they typically represent themselves as "normal" and "untroubled"—except for one child's problem. They deny the need for change. Such families are extremely vulnerable to external events, such as change in employment or a death in the family. Almost any outside stress can overload their dysfunctional coping mechanisms and precipitate emotional illness.

The nature of SIDS predisposes already maladaptive families to develop further compensatory maladaptive patterns. However, even the most adaptive of SIDS families may experience some degree of what could be considered dysfunctional behaviors were they not seen in the context of an extreme situation. They are a system separately and collectively working to survive a devastating assault. Thus, their reactions may be extreme, but may also be situational and transitory responses to intense grief. For these reasons, in working with SIDS families it is important to distinguish transitory from long-term maladaptive systematic behaviors.

Lack of Conflict Resolution

Rigidity and overprotectiveness, combined with the constant invasiveness characteristic of pathologically enmeshed families, increase the likelihood of conflict. When a strong religious, ethical, or social code is used to rationalize avoiding conflict (e.g., "ladies and gentlemen don't argue"), there can be no negotiation of differences. Problems are left unresolved only to surface again and again.

Each maladaptive family's own particular communication pattern dictates its ways of avoiding conflict resolution. Often, while one spouse, the "non-avoider," brings up areas of difficulty, the other spouse, the "avoider," detours the conversation that would lead to acknowledgement of conflict and perhaps its negotiation. Or one spouse simply leaves the house when the other tries to discuss a problem. Some families deny the existence of any disagreement whatsoever; they see no need ever to disagree. Others openly disagree, but constant interruptions and subject changes submerge any conflictual issue before it is brought to resolution.

When such a family's low tolerance for conflict is approached, a child may exhibit behavioral or medical symptoms. These symptoms become both a mode of communication and a means to avoid communication. The family reinforces and rewards this deviance because of its usefulness in restoring and maintaining system equilibrium. Frequently, the original event that precipitated these maladaptive patterns has been lost to awareness as a dynamic force.

CASE STUDY #2: THE SMITHS

The Smiths are a SIDS family that demonstrate many of these maladaptive patterns. The Smiths lost their second child to SIDS. The infant was a daughter, named Grace. Mr. and Mrs. Smith both were in their late twenties and were college educated. Their professional positions gave them financial security, a socially advantaged position, and a home in a select neighborhood. Despite these external life advantages, the Smiths' marriage was very troubled even prior to their daughter's death.

Mr. Smith had been previously married and his two daughters from that marriage lived out-of-state with their mother. Mrs. Smith's first pregnancy had ended in a stillbirth. Neither spouse had dealt constructively with these earlier losses. After Grace died, they remained together, but became two socially isolated, marginally functional human beings clinging to each other out of fear of further loss.

Mr. Smith owned his own contracting business. Because of unpaid bills from subcontractors, his business went into bankruptcy two weeks before the baby was born. His efforts to rebuild the business in the three years since their daughter's death have been only moderately successful.

In the time since Grace's death, an interactive cycle of dwindling financial resources, intensely enmeshed family interaction patterns, and completely ineffective problem-solving skills has left this family rigidly trapped in their own isolated space.

Over time, this family has become so dysfunctional that the original insult has become submerged in a pile of unresolved issues, hurts, and problem situations. Resentments between members are collected like badges of honor, and a laundry list of reasons for family dissolution is openly and frequently aired, even as the parents still cling closely to each other for protection from further hurts and losses. One can predict very poor outcomes for all of the members of this family.

The parental and family environment for the child born subsequent to the SIDS death requires this child to use his psychological resources for daily survival, leaving little to invest in his own growth and development. Individuation and autonomy from this environment will be obtained only at great expense. Neither their family nor the outside world is perceived as safe. We can predict a very troubled adult who will carry to his own family the impact of an event now generationally interwoven into the family's maladaptive coping patterns.

CONCLUSION

The two families described in the case studies in this chapter represent polar and extreme ends of an adjustment continuum. Yet, in each we can recognize the intense, severe, and forever-present impact of a SIDS death on family dynamics and functioning, and, conversely, the impact of pre-existing functioning on the family. We have come full circle and return to the statement that there is no greater or more irremediable insult to a family than the loss of a child. And of all the ways that a child can die, SIDS appears to be particularly devastating in its impact.

Yet, this devastation need not lead to permanent dysfunction. Immediate and intense family-focused crisis intervention services can serve a critical support function for these families. In addition, these services need to lead to a continuum of support services that are available to a SIDS family for a period of three-to-five years. Parent support groups, sibling intervention, and extended family and other caretaker support efforts are vital components of such a coordinated program. Ideally, area emergency personnel will provide immediate linkage to and mobilization of these services. Model programs do exist. Until they become more widely available, we stand to see many more unnecessary difficulties in families arising from the insult that is SIDS.

REFERENCES

Brown, F. (1988). The impact of death and serious illness on the family life cycle. In E. Carter & M. McGoldrick (Eds.), *The changing family life cycle: A framework for family therapy* (2nd ed.; pp. 457–482). New York: Gardner.

Combrinch-Graham, L. (1985). A developmental model for family system. *Family Process, 24,* 139–150.

Carter, E., & McGoldrick, M. (1980). The family life cycle and family therapy: An overview. In E. Carter & M. McGoldrick (Eds.), *The family life cycle: A framework for family therapy* (pp. 3–20). New York: Gardner.

Carter, E., & McGoldrick, M. (1988). Overview of the changing family life cycle: A framework for family therapy. In E. Carter & M. McGoldrick (Eds.), *The changing family life cycle: A framework for family therapy* (2nd ed.; pp. 3–28). New York: Gardner.

McClowry, S. G., Davies, E. B., May, K. A., Kulenkamp, E. J., & Martinson, I. M. (1987). The empty space phenomenon: The process of grief in the bereaved family. *Death Studies, 11,* 361–374.

Minuchin, S., Baker, L., Rosman, B., Liebman, R., Milman, L., & Todd, T. (1975). A conceptual model of psychosomatic illness in children: Family organization and family therapy. *Archives of General Psychiatry, 32,* 1031–1038.

Minuchin, S., Rosman, B. L., & Baker, L. (1978). *Psychosomatic families.* Cambridge, MA: Harvard University Press.

Olson, D. H., Sprenkle, D. H., & Russell, C. S. (1979). Circumplex model of mental and family systems: 1. Cohesion and adaptability dimensions, family types and clinical applications. *Family Process, 18,* 3–28.

Olson, D. H., Russell, C. S., & Sprenkle, D. H. (1983). Circumplex model of marital and family systems: VI. Theoretical update. *Family Process, 22,* 69–83.

Terkleson, K. (1980). Toward a theory of the family life cycle. In E. Carter & M. McGoldrick (Eds.), *The family life cycle: A framework for family therapy* (pp. 21–52). New York: Gardner.

Tolstoy, L. (1898). *Anna Karenina.* In Vol. 10 of *The complete works of Lyof N. Tolstoi* (12 vols.). New York: Thomas Y. Crowell Co.

PART III

SIDS—Guidelines for Helping

Helping those who have been affected by a SIDS death depends upon the timing in relationship to the death; the resources that are available to be mobilized; and a determination as to the appropriateness of various possible forms of intervention. Chapter 8 sets forth guidelines for emergency responders in the very first moments following the death. These guidelines are distinguished by the way in which their exposition maintains a shifting balance over time among clinical, legal, and human tasks.

Chapters 9 and 10 consider guidelines for individual and family counseling, on the one hand, and for group work, on the other hand. Each approach has its own value. They may be employed together or independently for different sorts of people and needs. What is most notable here are the ways in which these complementary approaches are related closely to characteristic features of the SIDS experience. Much has been written previously about counseling and group work modalities, but very little of that literature has been informed by the specific situations of those who are involved with SIDS.

Chapter 11 brings all of these guidelines together in the more general, interrelated concepts of advocacy and networking. Helping individuals throughout the aftermath of a SIDS experience is an interactive process involving various forms of advocacy and several kinds of networks. Much of this occurs outside the framework of formal counseling and/or group situations. Typically, it brings together those who need help, those who want to help, and those whose help is needed (whether or not they might have previously intended or planned to be helpers). That is, the concepts of advocacy and networking synthesize efforts of those mentioned in previous chapters of Part III through the mobilization or re-creation of a caring community.

CHAPTER 8

Guidelines for Emergency Responders

Connie Guist and Judy E. Larsen

EMERGENCY RESPONDERS AND THEIR RESPONSIBILITIES

The support and care offered to surviving family members immediately following the sudden, unexpected death of an infant or young child greatly impact on how they cope with this tragedy long after the immediate crisis is over. No one can prevent the pain a family will feel or protect them from experiencing grief following a sudden infant death. However, if the professionals who help with the infant and interact with the infant's family immediately following the death are compassionate and knowledgeable, they can facilitate a more healthful recovery of the surviving family members from this devastating life event.

Providing sensitive care to families immediately following a sudden, unexpected infant death requires the involvement and cooperation of professionals from various specialty areas. Examples of people who have immediate contact with the family are: (1) the emergency medical dispatcher, usually the first person to hear a parent's plea for help; (2) the first professional arriving at the scene of a death; (3) the health care provider who confirms what family members fear but do not want to believe; and (4) the funeral director and the clergy who help the family with possibly their first experience with death. What is said and done (and *not* said and done) by these people will play an important role in determining how the death of the infant is viewed and interpreted by those most deeply touched by this tragic event.

It is important to provide intervention guidelines to the professionals who are often involved immediately following a sudden, unexpected infant death. This assures that families experiencing this crisis will be cared for in an effective manner. Those who respond to a sudden death of any nature represent a multilevel network of support personnel and are referred to by various titles from first responders to paramedics. Each represents a different level of knowledge and responsibility. To facilitate discussion in this chapter, the phrase "emergency medical (EM) personnel" refers to any medical personnel responding to a medical emergency in the community. Therefore, no distinction is made here between first responders, emergency medical technicians (EMTs), and paramedics. Further, there is no distinction here between volunteers and paid professional emergency service providers.

Because of the unanticipated nature of the death, other persons commonly involved immediately after a sudden infant death include representatives of the medical and legal system, such as the police, the medical examiner or coroner, emergency department staff, and pathologists. In this chapter, the phrase "emergency responders" refers to anyone responding to a citizen's call for help at the time of a sudden, unexpected death.

Many of the contacts families have with EM personnel may be brief. During the initial crisis, events often are blurred and specific details may be forgotten by the infant's family. However, grieving parents tend to remember those who were particularly helpful, as well as those who were perceived as not supportive or who made the situation more painful. It is important for emergency responders to provide a smooth transition from their care to other caregivers who will have more long-term contact with the infant's family. If the infant is transported to an emergency facility, the hospital emergency department staff and, frequently, clergy may be the next support people available to the family. After death has been confirmed, no matter where the infant's body is, contact with funeral service personnel generally occurs within a few hours of the death.

Three areas of responsibility are associated with the care initially provided following an infant's sudden death: clinical tasks; legal tasks; and human tasks. The clinical tasks relate to the practical, intervention, action-oriented activities of the emergency response. These include (but are not limited to) physical assessment of the infant, initiating basic life support measures, obtaining a history of events leading to the call for help, and determining what may be the best plan of intervention.

The legal tasks relate to protecting the rights of all persons involved, including the rights of the infant, the parent(s) and other family members, and the caretaker at the time of the death. Emergency responders are responsible for following the policies and procedures of their organization, collecting data about the events surrounding the crisis, and contacting the appropriate authorities. All EM personnel must be aware of legal mandates of their community and state related to sudden, unexpected infant death.

The third aspect, the human tasks are perhaps the most intangible and yet the most challenging care responsibilities to address. Knowing what clinical care to provide while considering the legal constraints is only part of knowledgeable, compassionate care. The important aspect is *how* that care is provided. The people providing support must be caring individuals who have come to terms with their own feelings about death, are aware of normal grieving responses, and are able to avoid projecting onto a family what they *think* the family should be feeling (Smialek, 1978). All those who come in contact with sudden infant death, in essence, become victims. Acknowledging how the sudden death of an infant affects the professionals involved at the time of the death, as well as the family members, is essential to assure effective intervention. In order for caregivers to be effective, they must be aware of their own feelings before attempting to help others deal with their feelings.

These three areas of responsibility are interwoven. In the first moments of an emergency, clinical tasks tend to take priority without totally displacing legal and human concerns. After the initial crisis, the situation changes and other responsibilities may assume greater prominence. Thus, the order in which these tasks are addressed will vary in the discussion that follows.

THE CRISIS

No matter how much one attempts to prepare for responding to the sudden, unexpected death of an infant, it is impossible to anticipate fully each situation. For the most part, many aspects of any suspected instance of Sudden Infant Death Syndrome (SIDS) will seem familiar to the seasoned emergency responder, yet very few of the deaths can be considered ordinary or *typical.* Parents often have commented that their experience with a SIDS death was not typical. There was something out of the ordinary, something that made their situation unique. A parent may have been in the same room as the infant for some time before discovering its lifeless body. The person who found the child may have been an older sibling, another relative, or a day care provider. The mother may be a single parent who feels very much alone. The infant may have been riding in a car seat or sleeping in a camper. The body may have been found in an unusual or peculiar position, or in bed with the parents. The death of the infant may have been obvious to the parent(s), but they called the emergency number because they did not know what else to do. There are many circumstances which make each suspected SIDS death different from the typically described SIDS death. Therefore, the best approach to the sudden, unexpected death of an infant is to expect the unexpected.

It is difficult to outline a standard response to a sudden infant death. Who is called upon for intervention and who responds depends on the local emergency response network. The protocol may require that the body be transported to a local hospital emergency room or that the medical examiner or coroner be called to the scene. Law enforcement personnel could be the county sheriff or the neighborhood police officer in a metropolitan community. Clergy from the family's church or synagogue may be the source of spiritual comforting or the pastoral care department at the hospital might be the family's first source of consolation. The body could be taken to the local hospital or morgue or it might be sent to a university-based or statewide laboratory for autopsy. There is no universal scenario for all circumstances.

At the moment a call for help is initiated, it is known only that there is a crisis which may involve the death of an infant and the cause of death is unknown. Only an autopsy can determine the actual cause of death. Therefore, it is best to make no assumptions about why the infant died. The general appearance of the infant may be misleading and it is imperative that emergency responders are knowledgeable about distinguishing between SIDS and child abuse or neglect. Since approximately 85% of such sudden, unexpected deaths are later confirmed to be SIDS, emergency responders are encouraged to give the parents the benefit of the doubt until an autopsy proves otherwise (Bureau of Community Health Services [BCHS], 1979).

Knowledge of the major causes of infant death also will guide the emergency responder's assessment of the crisis and facilitate accurate determination of the cause of death by the medical examiner or coroner. Although it is not the responsibility of emergency responders (apart from medical examiners or coroners) to determine the diagnosis or cause of death, Table 8.1 may be useful as a guide to differences between SIDS and child abuse or neglect. Other causes of sudden death in infants and young children include congenital birth defects, injury, and overwhelming infection (Jones & Weston, 1976).

GUIDELINES FOR RESPONSE

Before the Crisis Occurs

EM personnel have a responsibility to be prepared for the possibility of responding to a sudden, unexpected infant death at any time. Although this type of crisis may not occur frequently in any given area, it is essential that all components of the emergency medical system be ready to provide comprehensive, compassionate care. By following some basic guidelines, EM personnel can insure that everything possible has been done for the infant and family.

TABLE 8.1 How to Distinguish Between SIDS and Child Abuse and Neglect

Sudden Infant Death Syndrome	versus	Child Abuse and Neglect

Sudden Infant Death Syndrome versus **Child Abuse and Neglect**

Incidence:
Deaths: 7,000/year
Highest: 2 to 4 months of age
When: More frequent in winter months

Incidence:
Deaths: 1,000 to 4,000/year
Deaths in infants: 300/year
When: No seasonal difference

Physical Appearance:
• Exhibits no external signs of injury.
• Exhibits "natural" appearance of deceased baby:
   —Lividity—settling of blood; frothy drainage from nose/mouth
   —Small marks (e.g., diaper rash) look more severe
   —Cooling/rigor mortis—takes place quickly in infants (about 3 hours)
• Purple mottled markings on head and facial area.
• Appears to be well-developed baby, though may be small for age.
• Other siblings appear to be normal and healthy.

Physical Appearance:
• Distinguishable and visible signs of injury:

   —Broken bone(s)
   —Bruises
   —Burns
   —Cuts
   —Head trauma (e.g., black eye)
   —Scars
   —Welts
   —Wounds

• May be obviously malnourished.
• Other siblings may show patterns of injuries commonly seen in child abuse and neglect.

May Initially Suspect SIDS When:
• All of the above characteristics appear to be accurate

PLUS

• Parents say that infant was well and healthy when put to sleep (last time seen alive).

May Initially Suspect Child Abuse/Neglect When:
• All of the above characteristics appear to be accurate

PLUS

• Parents' story does not "sound right" or cannot account for all injuries on infant.

Note: The determination of whether the child is or is not a SIDS victim is the responsibility of the medical examiner or medical coroner. It is **NOT** the responsibility of the Emergency Medical Technician.
Source: Produced by the Department of Health, Education and Welfare (now the DHHS), office of Maternal and Child Health (Title V, Social Security Act), Contract HSH 240-7701.

These guidelines include anticipating the event and being prepared for the situation; assessing the situation; identifying what is needed in a particular situation; and being sensitive to the needs of the family.

Clinical Tasks

For emergency responders, continuing education is a vital part of obtaining current information about low-occurrence, high-impact situations like sudden infant death. Demonstrating competency in basic life support and advanced life support techniques for children also is essential. Refresher courses on the use of equipment and technical skills that may be used infrequently are required to have competent practitioners in the field. The immediate need of the family at the time of a medical emergency is for efficient action when EM personnel arrive.

Legal Tasks

Many EM systems have established policies regarding the care and transportation of victims of sudden infant death and their family members. Written policies and procedures should include guidelines about: (1) who responds to a pediatric medical emergency in the community; (2) what is the extent of on-the-scene treatment; (3) who will transport the infant; (4) how and where will the infant be transported; (5) who may or should accompany the infant during transport; (6) who is contacted to investigate the death; and (7) who is responsible for the pronouncement of death. Coordination among the various levels of the EM system is necessary in order to assure appropriate intervention at the time of a crisis. In other words, law enforcement agencies, fire departments, ambulance services, area hospitals, and the medical examiner or coroner's office must all determine the policies and procedures related to sudden infant death to assure that legal mandates are carried out.

Human Tasks

Knowing the community resources before the time a crisis occurs is also necessary to provide comprehensive support to families experiencing sudden infant death. It is essential that periodic review includes information on the emotional and psychological impact of sudden infant death, as well as technical skills. Are there local support groups for bereaved parents? Is there a professional SIDS network available not only for the family, but to help emergency responders deal with their feelings following an infant death?

How individuals respond to death may depend on their religious or cultural background. It is important to be aware of various religious practices and ethnically diverse groups in the community, and to know how different religions and cultures treat an infant's death. Failure to appreciate these influences on a person's grief response may lead to misunderstanding the response and inaccurately assessing the grief response itself (Rando, 1984).

Continuing education of emergency responders must include information about how to cope with their own feelings about childhood death. Contact with death may heighten awareness of past personal losses or fear of future personal loss (Worden, 1982). It is important to acknowledge that "helping" professionals often have difficulty seeking support for themselves. The culture of many EM organizations historically discourages admission of a need to express feelings or to acknowledge that individuals are somehow affected by what they experience in their job. More and more organizations are setting up ongoing encounter or support groups for emergency responders to provide a forum for open discussion (Hansen & Frantz, 1984).

Responding to the Call for Help

Perhaps no call provokes a greater emotional reaction for an emergency responder than "baby pulseless and not breathing." Travelling to the scene, one begins to prepare physically and mentally for what may lie ahead. Assignments are made so that personnel are clear on their roles. Once at the scene, each emergency responder must proceed in a calm and deliberate manner. Remember that no assumptions should be made about what is wrong with the infant or why the infant may have died. The only fact that is known is that the infant is dead or has experienced an unexplained life-threatening event. Support of the family begins when the care providers project an attitude of confidence in a calm, efficient manner and exhibit concern.

Clinical Tasks

The first person responding to a call involving a life-threatening event or suspected death of an infant assesses the situation and makes decisions about the best way to proceed. The assessment includes the status of the infant, the physical environment, who else is present, and if cardiopulmonary resuscitation (CPR) has been started. Once started, CPR should be continued until the proper authority pronounces the infant dead.

There are several factors that will determine what occurs next. These include the policies and procedures of the EM system organization, what is observed at the scene of the death, and the wishes of the parent(s). In many instances, it is customary for the emergency responders to transport the infant immediately to a hospital emergency department. If this is the case, parents must be informed of the destination and, if permitted, at least one parent is encouraged to accompany the infant in the ambulance. A neighbor, relative, or other emergency responder may assist with the transport of the parent(s) to the hospital. Allowing a distraught parent to drive from the scene to the hospital alone is not considered a safe practice. If other children are in the home, arrangements must be made so they are not left unattended. A brief explanation of the situation should be provided to the children in an age-appropriate manner.

In other situations, the infant remains at the scene and an attempt at resuscitation occurs there. If this is the case, it is essential to keep the parent(s) informed and to continue resuscitation efforts until the appropriate authority pronounces death. Convey to the family that everything that can be done is being done.

Often there is little that can be done for the infant. The infant obviously is dead, resuscitation is not needed, and it is the family members who require attention. Extreme care must be taken by the emergency responders not to suggest by word, facial expression, tone of voice, or nonverbal actions that any blame or suspicion is being attached to any individual. The family may misinterpret the slightest gesture or casual comment. Again, sensitive support at this time helps to alleviate future emotional burdens for family members (BCHS, 1979).

Human Tasks

To repeat, it is often the family members who will need support. Emergency responders must be prepared to deal with a wide range of responses from hysteria and anger to withdrawal and denial. Each person is unique and will respond differently to the crisis of sudden infant death. Some factors which may affect the grief reaction are:

1. The personality and level of maturity of the person;
2. The situation surrounding the death;
3. Interpersonal family relationships;
4. The meaning of the child to the person;
5. Sociocultural and ethnic background;
6. The parent's religious convictions;
7. Other concurrent family stresses; and
8. Previous experiences with death and how the individual dealt with those experiences.

Asking questions about the infant and what happened is never easy. It is even more difficult with young parents, a single parent, a babysitter, a day care provider, or another relative, especially at the time immediately after finding the infant. It is important to obtain essential information with minimal trauma to the parent or guardian.

Keep in mind that the purpose of an investigation is to determine what happened to the infant, *not* what the parents or caretaker did or failed to do. The family has the right to a presumption of parental innocence unless the postmortem examination reveals evidence to the contrary. When obtaining information from the parent(s), avoid using the phrase "did you" when asking questions. In this way, the parents will feel less threatened and their almost inevitable feelings of guilt will not be reinforced by the way in which the question is phrased. Examples of how questions can be asked to avoid the use of "did you" are as follows (Guist, 1988).

Ask: What time was the baby (use name when possible) put to bed?
NOT: When did you put the baby to bed?

Ask: When did the physician last see the baby?
NOT: When was the last time you took the baby to the doctor?

Ask: What time was the baby last fed? Seen alive?
NOT: What time did you feed the baby? Check the baby?

Ask: How was the baby found? And by whom?
NOT: Did you find the baby? How did you find the baby?

In addition, open-ended questions will provide more accurate information than will leading questions. A leading question is one in which the answer is contained in the question. Even if not intended, leading questions are often perceived as a form of implied accusation. For example, "You did cover the baby when you put him down, didn't you?" Open-ended questions cannot be answered with a "yes" or "no." *What, when, tell me, how,* and *which,* are good ways to begin questions that will elicit the most information.

Allowing the parent(s) to talk and actively listening to them will provide much of the information needed. Statements such as, "It's my fault, I should have checked her earlier," are responses to the situation and not an admission of responsibility. Avoiding comments like, "I know how you feel," is important to maintaining open communication. No one can actually know how another person is feeling in this type of situation. A statement such as, "I can't imagine what you are going through," is a far better way of encouraging the family to talk. Simply saying nothing may have the same effect. Again, the importance of understanding common reactions to sudden infant death cannot be overemphasized.

Legal Tasks

In a majority of communities in the United States, all instances of sudden, unexpected death are, by law, reported to the legal authorities, usually the medical examiner or coroner, who have the responsibility of determining the cause of death. An investigation is conducted which includes information obtained from the parents about the infant's medical history and events occurring prior to the death. Observation of the scene is another essential part of this investigation and is conducted according to routine investigation protocol (BCHS, 1979). In addition, there are several things to look for and note.

- Physical appearance of the infant
- Position of the infant at the time of death (this may account for marks found on the infant)
- Physical appearance of the place in which the infant was found and the presence of objects in the area
- General appearance of the room or house
- Unusual items or medications in the area where death occurred.

There may be little time to assess the scene and gather data. Remember that in many instances, the infant has been turned over or moved from the original position when discovered. Parents may have difficulty recalling the specific order of events, and the investigator will have to rely on observation skills to aid in data collection. All types of information (verbal, nonverbal, observed) will be helpful in determining the cause of death. Any investigation must be thorough and yet done as discreetly as possible. In the long run, a well-managed investigation not only allows for an accurate determination of the cause of death, but also reassures parents that all possible theories were researched and that they are not responsible for the death of their infant. If appropriately conducted, the investigation is another way of providing support to the surviving victims.

Follow-Up

Whether the infant is transported to a hospital emergency unit and pronounced dead or the body remains in the home until released to the funeral home or the place where the autopsy will be performed, the support offered to the surviving victims at this time is critical. Transferring responsibility for the infant's care is vital. Letting the family know when the emergency responders are leaving and who will be available to provide continued support to them insures continuity of care and shows compassionate concern for the family. Assuring that the family remains informed and knows how to get information about their infant is also important. The most critical role for the emergency responders at this time is to be available to the family, to answer questions tactfully, and to LISTEN. If one or both parents are not present, vigorous attempts to contact them should be made.

Usually, at this point in the crisis, clergy, funeral directors, and other counseling personnel have initiated contact with the family and have created at least the foundation for a bridge between crisis intervention and long-term support. Their contacts with the family continue long after the infant is pronounced dead and the EM providers have completed their tasks. The guidelines in this section relate not only to emergency responders who initially may be on the scene of a sudden, unexpected infant death, but also to those persons involved in this transitional period of support.

Human Tasks

Although an emergency responder may have some previous experience with infant death, probably the family does not. Most parents do not know what they can do or cannot do. For example, the mother may wish to wash the body of her infant and prepare it for transport. However, fearing that someone might consider her odd or her wish unusual, she may suppress her desire. Similarly, the family may wish to spend time just being with and holding their infant. Unless the parents are given permission to do what *they* need to do, many opportunities to aid in the grief and mourning process will be missed. Some general guidelines to follow include:

• Provide a quiet, private place for the parents to express their grief, be with other loved ones, and be with their infant. If possible, a caregiver should stay with the family. It can be uncomfortable and awkward standing by and observing a family in grief and it is difficult to know what to say. Often, it is not the words that parents will remember, but the gentle touch, a hug, or just the presence of a caring person.

• Allow and encourage an opportunity for the parent(s), siblings, and other family members to see and hold the infant after the infant is declared dead. Parents may wish to see and hold their infant several times between the time of death and the funeral, including after the autopsy has been completed (Schofield, 1987). This provides an opportunity to acknowledge the reality of the death and to say goodbye. Have the infant clothed and made as presentable as possible. The parent's wishes are the most important consideration in determining what occurs shortly after the infant's death. Basically, anything parents wish to do that will help with the grieving process should be encouraged. In other words, anything goes unless it inflicts emotional or physical harm on themselves or others. The effective caregiver will be able to respect the family's desires even if they are radically different from those of the caregiver.

• It is important to handle the infant as an infant. Parents have commented about the devastation they felt seeing their infant's body placed in the back seat of the coroner's car, on a high, narrow ledge in the emergency room, or on a table without any attendant or supervision. Even though the infant is dead, the need to care for and protect the infant still exists for the parent. Many emergency department staff have found that wrapping the infant in a blanket and carrying the infant to the parents rather than taking the parents to the infant is an effective way of handling the body. Some hospitals even use an infant crib from the nursery to move the body. The family will long remember the respect shown for the infant's body.

• Legitimize the family's feelings. Say, for example, "It's okay to be mad, sad, afraid—even to feel guilty." Some professionals suggest that parents should not *feel* guilt, saying "Don't feel guilty, it's not your fault." It is more supportive to acknowledge the feeling of the parent with a comment like, "It is common to feel a sense of guilt, even though the death is not your fault." Avoid using "Don't" when attempting to support the bereaved. In spite of such requests on the part of caregivers, parents will continue to feel the way they do. Even though it is known that the death was not their fault, they also need to know that their feelings, including guilt, are common responses often experienced by other parents in similar situations. If they repeatedly hear "don't cry" or "don't feel guilty," they likely will begin to feel guilty about the feelings they are having, which, in turn, can interfere with healthy grieving.

Another feeling that may be felt by a parent, but very rarely expressed, is one of relief, or calm. The feeling may be fleeting in nature and may be an attempt to make some sense of the death. This can cause parents to feel confused or add to their sense of guilt. They wonder how they can be experiencing such a feeling while struggling with all the other emotions caused by their infant's death. Casual comments by parents about not having to worry about nighttime feedings anymore, or not needing a babysitter next weekend, may be perceived as flippant, callous, or unfeeling by an observer. Such comments usually are no more than attempts to put some order into a chaotic situation. Parents need to be reassured that experiencing such a feeling does not mean that they did not love their infant or that they are uncaring parents. It is only another emotional response that they may experience in response to this tragedy.

The simplest of words can have heightened significance to a newly bereaved person. For example, it may be more helpful for parents to know that what they are experiencing is "okay" or "common," but not as helpful for their feelings to be considered "normal." Normal refers to conforming to an accepted norm or standard, anything normal, natural, or usual. There is probably very little, if anything, about a sudden infant death that feels normal, natural, or usual. By contrast, "common" is defined as belonging or shared by each or all, general, or widespread (Arnold & Gemma, 1983; Guralnik, 1984). It is helpful for family members to feel that they are not alone, that others have had similar reactions, and that they are not "going mad" or losing their minds.

• Keep the family informed. Most imperative is the prompt notification of the cause of death. Historically, a large number of parents had not been given an adequate explanation of the cause of death or were told that death was caused by something other than the cause listed on the death certificate (Bergman, 1973). Know who is responsible for informing the family of the autopsy findings and let the family know who they can call with questions about the cause of death. Providing informational brochures about Sudden Infant Death Syndrome may answer the family's basic questions. Such brochures can be given to others or can be taken home and read later. However, this does not replace the need for parents and family members to know the specific cause of death for their infant.

• Offer spiritual support. Offer to call other family members, the hospital chaplain, or their own spiritual advisor. The parent(s) may also request that the child be baptized. Again, the more responsive caregivers can be to the family's needs, the more support the family will receive. Avoid saying things like, "It was God's will," or "You have an angel in heaven," unless these are first said by the parent(s). These ideas may be comforting to some people, but they are very upsetting to others. Listen for terms or words that the parent(s) use and repeat those terms to express concern. This will aid in assessing the family's religious convictions.

• Offer basic assistance. Offering a cup of coffee, calling the funeral home, arranging transportation back home for the family, or calling other family members to come to the hospital or to the home are thoughtful responses that provide comfort. The simplest tasks may become burdensome to the parents and they may not even think of practical tasks at this time. Suggesting that a call be made to the parents' places of employment if they will not be going to work, or to the siblings' schools may be very helpful.

• Make appropriate referrals for follow-up. Contact the local SIDS support network. Even if someone else has contacted them, it is better to err on the side of too many referrals than to have no referrals made on behalf of the family. Provide written information to the family about the emergency personnel who cared for their infant and how to contact them if there are questions in the future. It is often helpful to identify one person at the hospital who knows the family and who the family may feel comfortable contacting in the future.

Remember the individuality of responses that may be encountered. One parent may be reassured by seeing resuscitation equipment or physical evidence that the emergency department staff did everything possible to revive the infant. Another parent may want to cut a lock of the infant's hair or have the infant's blanket. The key is to give the family permission to do what they need to do and to facilitate the realization of their wishes. It is important that families are told that there are no rules, no right or wrong way to grieve or to deal with their infant's death.

Most parents benefit greatly from seeing and holding their infant after death and may later regret the decision not to see the infant. Therefore, it may be difficult to support the decision of parents who choose not to do this. All one can do is to identify the options available and respect the individual parent's choice. Some hospital staff routinely take a picture of the infant and place it in the infant's medical record so that it may be available to the family at a future time. This is especially helpful if the parents choose not to see the infant at the time of death. After all is said and done, one must accept that the parents made the right decision for themselves at the time.

Acknowledging one's own responses to a sudden infant death is an important aspect of the human tasks at this time. Emergency responders have a responsibility to themselves to assess how they feel about the death, to identify their reactions to the death, and to determine if they need support in coping with their feelings. No one benefits from hiding behind a mask or projecting an unaffected facade. Society as a whole does not wish to observe public displays of grieving, but caregivers must allow themselves to feel, express, cry, and talk about the effect this experience has had on them (Schneider, 1984). Seeking help or talking about one's feelings in a group that has had similar experiences can reinforce that the response is not uncommon and the responder is not alone.

Clinical Tasks

It is very difficult to separate the human tasks from the clinical tasks at this point. It has been determined that the infant is dead and attention turns to providing support to the surviving family members. Except for one major clinically related concern, intervention revolves around assessing the needs of the family and responding accordingly. The one exception is securing permission (if needed) for an autopsy, completing the autopsy, and informing the parents of the preliminary cause of death. Accurate diagnosis is more than a medical necessity. It is an essential component in helping the parents cope with their infant's death. An accurate diagnosis relies on a thorough postmortem examination. Without an autopsy, other identifiable causes of death may be overlooked, and the diagnosis of SIDS is not used appropriately (Krous, 1984). Even though it may take several weeks or months to obtain all laboratory results, it is imperative that the family is informed of the preliminary cause of death in a timely manner, if possible within 24 hours of the death. The final postmortem report can then be forwarded to them when it is available.

Legal Tasks

In this situation, it is not a matter of whether or not the infant's death is reported, but rather, to whom is the death reported. Accurate documentation of the EM personnel response efforts, as well as the cause of death, is imperative. Appropriate use of the medical diagnosis of "Sudden Infant Death Syndrome" on the death certificate, rather than non-committal phrases like "cardiorespiratory arrest" or "undetermined cause" is encouraged. Emergency responders also are encouraged to review the response routinely in order to learn from the experience and improve future responses to this type of emergency. Case study conferences and record reviews can insure the deliverance of sensitive, quality care to the victim and to the victim's family and loved ones.

NEXT STEPS: THE FUNERAL AND BEYOND

Rando (1984) stated that "A rite of passage is necessary after the death of a loved one, for the passing of that person must be recognized, his survivors must be supported as they start a new life without him, and they must be reintegrated into the community . . ." (p. 190). Hence, a funeral is a vital part of the mourning process and acts as a vehicle for expressing and acknowledging grief. Often, the funeral director has more contact with the whole family shortly after the death than any other caregiver. How the family perceives the support received at this time will impact greatly on their ability to cope with this crisis and future losses. Research has shown that many families have been grateful for the assistance which they received from thoughtful funeral directors (Center for Death Education and Research, 1971; Cook, 1983).

A funeral is ". . . an organized, purposeful, time-limited, flexible, group-centered response to death, involving rites and ceremonies during some or all of which the body of the deceased is present" (Raether & Slater, 1983, p. II-72). Critical psychological, spiritual, and social needs are fulfilled through the rituals of a funeral. Since the family experiencing a sudden infant death is usually young, it is likely that they have not had previous experience planning a funeral and may never have attended a funeral before.

The role of the funeral director is to be a skilled and compassionate guide and facilitator. As previously mentioned, caregivers, especially the funeral director, must understand the customs, religious and cultural values, and norms of the society in which they provide service. By following the guidelines related to *human tasks* that are set forth in this chapter and by responding to the individual needs of each family, funeral directors can insure that their services are delivered in an effective manner. Often, it is difficult to address differing needs of the various individuals within a family. By facilitating open communication among the family members, it is more likely that all of the needs of each person will be met (Rando, 1984).

The funeral director who is sensitive to the family's unspoken and spoken needs and who explains that there is no right or wrong way to arrange for a funeral (or to grieve) will assure a meaningful experience for the bereaved

(Horan & Jensen, 1985). Above all, families have indicated that what they needed the most was someone willing to sit down with them and listen, to reassure them that there was nothing they could have done to prevent their infant's death, and to confirm that what they are feeling is both common and healthy (Schofield, 1987).

How involved the family is with the actual planning of the funeral service often depends on the funeral director giving the family permission to make the service as personal as possible. Again, families usually do not know what options are available to them. Opportunities to hold the infant again, to cut a lock of hair, to take pictures, or to put mementos in the casket can be very comforting to the family members. Also, the use of colored helium-filled balloons, stuffed animals or toys, and/or children's songs instead of funeral hymns during the service, may be appreciated by the parents. But the opportunity to do any of these things must be presented to the parents in order for them to know that such options exist.

Anticipatory guidance about what the parents may experience in the near future is also helpful. Thinking that they hear the infant crying or finding themselves fixing the infant's formula or both, even after the funeral, can be very frightening for parents unless they are told this may occur. Anger at God, the medical personnel, the funeral director, or even at their infant who died is often immobilizing to parents and needs to be validated as a common reaction to the death of a loved one. Referrals to the local SIDS support network, including bereaved parent support groups, will provide the family with resources long after the initial contact with the funeral director ends.

CONCLUSION

No one can prevent the pain a family will feel or protect them from experiencing grief following the sudden, unexpected death of an infant. If professionals who assist with the infant and interact with the infant's family are compassionate and knowledgeable, there is potential for the surviving family to achieve a more healthful outcome from this difficult experience.

Those persons most likely to be involved at the time of an infant's death and immediately following the crisis include: (1) emergency medical personnel, such as paramedics, emergency medical technicians, and first responders; (2) law enforcement personnel; (3) the medical examiner or coroner; (4) hospital emergency room staff; (5) clergy; and (6) funeral service personnel. All personnel responding to this medical emergency and human tragedy must be prepared to respond in an effective and caring manner.

The tasks related to the care initially provided following an infant's sudden death can be viewed from three perspectives: clinical, legal, and human. Clinical tasks relate to the practical, intervention, action-oriented aspect of the emergency response. Legal tasks relate to protecting the rights of all persons involved. Human tasks, perhaps the most important aspect, relate to *how* the clinical and legal tasks of the care are provided. Each situation is unique and by learning to expect the unexpected, emergency responders can respond to each situation in a compassionate and caring way.

In reality, all those who come in contact with sudden infant death are victims. Acknowledging how sudden infant death affects the professionals involved at the time of the death, as well as the family members, is essential to assure effective intervention and a healthful outcome. Guidelines for meeting the needs of the infant, the family, and themselves have been suggested for emergency responders involved immediately following the discovery of a "baby pulseless and not breathing."

REFERENCES

Arnold, J. H., & Gemma, P. B. (1983). *A child dies: A portrait of family grief.* Rockville, MD: Aspen Systems.

Bergman, A. B. (1973). *A study in the management of sudden infant death syndrome in the United States.* Baltimore: Central Maryland SIDS Center.

Bureau of Community Health Services (HSA/PHS). (1979). *Training emergency responders: Sudden infant death syndrome. An instructor's manual.* DHEW Publication, No. (HSA) 79-5253. Rockville, MD: Author.

Center for Death Education and Research. (1971). *A compilation of studies of attitudes toward death, funerals and funeral directors.* Minneapolis: University of Minnesota.

Cook, J. A. (1983). A death in the family: Parental bereavement in the first year. *Suicide and Life-Threatening Behavior, 13,* 42–61.

Guist, C. (1988). Responding to an unexpected infant death. *Information Exchange,* June, pp. 1–3. McLean, VA: National Sudden Infant Death Syndrome Clearinghouse.

Guralnik, D. B. (Ed.). (1984). *Webster's new world dictionary of the American language.* New York: Warner Books.

Hansen, J. C., & Frantz, T. T. (Eds.). (1984). *Death and grief in the family.* Rockville, MD: Aspen Systems.

Horan, J. J., & Jensen, J. P. (1985). Sudden infant death syndrome: The funeral home experience. *Forum Newsletter, 8*(7), p. 7. Lakewood, OH: Forum for Death Education and Counseling.

Jones, A. M., & Weston, J. T. (1976). The examination of the sudden infant death syndrome infant: Investigative and autopsy protocols. *Journal of Forensic Sciences, 21,* 833–841.

Krous, H. (1984). Diseases masquerading as SIDS—The need for autopsy in sudden unexpected infant deaths. *Oklahoma SIDS Newsletter.*

Raether, H. C., & Slater, R. C. (Eds.). (1983). *Advocating understanding: A manual for funeral directors to care-giving organizations.* Milwaukee, WI: National Funeral Directors Association.

Rando, T. A. (1984). *Grief, dying, and death: Clinical interventions for caregivers.* Champaign, IL: Research Press.

Schneider, J. (1984). *Stress, loss and grief.* Baltimore, MD: University Park Press.

Schofield, P. M. (1987). Sudden infant death: Parents' views of professional help. *Health Visitor, 60*, 109.

Smialek, Z. (1978). Observations on immediate reactions of families to sudden infant death. *Pediatrics 62*, 160–165.

Worden, J. W. (1982). *Grief counseling and grief therapy: A handbook for the mental health practitioner.* New York: Springer Publishing Co.

CHAPTER 9

Guidelines for Counseling

Helen Fuller, Carol Ann Barnickol, and Teresa Roberson Mullins

> Once you face and understand your limitations, you can work *with* them instead of having them work against you and get in your way, which is what they do when you ignore them, whether you realize it or not. And then you will find that, in many cases, your limitations can be your strengths.
>
> (Hoff, 1982, pp. 48–49)

APPROACHES TO COUNSELING PERSONS WHO HAVE BEEN IMPACTED BY SIDS

This chapter offers an approach to counseling individuals and families who have been impacted by Sudden Infant Death Syndrome. This approach is intended for those who have professional training which enables them to function as counselors in connection with their vocation—whether they be psychologists, social workers, members of the clergy, health care workers, funeral directors, or other types of counselors. The contents of this chapter are also intended to be of assistance to lay persons who act as helpers and friends of SIDS victims. In short, this chapter is concerned both with formal and with informal counseling or helping relationships.

In view of the nature of the SIDS experience, counseling relationships may be very short term; for example, they may only occur immediately after the death of the infant. Alternatively, counseling may involve a long-term process and it may begin long after the SIDS event or even be superimposed upon another counseling process. Despite all of this diversity, SIDS-related counseling shares some common ground and is distinctive in its own right.

In the first place, it is important to note that the academic and professional preparation of most counselors, social workers, and public health nurses may not provide them with an adequate background or appropriate perspective that is essential for working with families who have been assaulted by Sudden Infant Death Syndrome. If this is true for professionals, it applies with even more force for most lay helpers who, in cases of the sudden, unexplained death of an infant, find themselves faced with one of the most difficult death-related experiences in our society.

Most professional counselors approach individuals or families with a view toward assessing dysfunction, both in individual coping skills and in interpersonal relationships. Clinical experience usually reinforces this perspective. Only infrequently does clinical experience require counselors to look through the opposite end of the telescope, that is, to look *first* at an outside event and its impact upon an individual or group.

In fact, however, those who are impacted by SIDS are a population which can be depicted by the same bell-shaped curve that describes the population in any society as a whole. Most SIDS parents, for example, fall in the middle of the distributional curve describing the general population. That is, they are typical of people who make their way through the child bearing and child raising years. They experience the usual ups and downs, along with some unique individual responses to particular situations. They are, in short, just like anyone else who functions in a relatively normal manner, until their sense of control and stability is suddenly assaulted by some overwhelming external event.

To pursue this analogy: at either end of the distributional curve, both in the population as a whole and among those who have been impacted by SIDS, one will find "tail end populations," or individuals and families who are truly dysfunctional. These extreme individuals will require all of the professional skill, preparation, and experience that can be brought to bear in counseling interactions. However, such persons are atypical, both in the population as a whole and among those who have been impacted by SIDS. More is said about dysfunctional individuals and reactions later in this chapter.

Most individuals who have been impacted by SIDS are relatively normal people navigating the usual challenges of life with reasonable success, who suddenly find themselves in the midst of an unanticipated and very difficult situation (Markusen, et al., 1978). From counselors and helpers of all sorts, they require patience, knowledge about SIDS, and an appreciation for the havoc created in their lives by SIDS (Bergman, 1974; Mandell & Belk, 1977). That is to say, they call upon us to return to the most fundamental aspects of any counseling relationship: the provision of a safe environment wherein one can address the situation in which one finds one's self; and clarification or assistance with the problem-solving process (Calvin & Smith, 1986).

We provide a safe environment when we value these people as individuals and when we actively listen to their concerns. This does not imply that we "solve" problems of persons impacted by SIDS—indeed, how could one ever "solve" the problem of a dead baby. Instead, counselors and other helpers can assist with the problem-solving process by validating feelings, providing accurate information, identifying resources, and suggesting options which those impacted by SIDS can pursue at their own initiative (Mandell, 1988; Mandell & McClain, 1988).

What is most needed by individuals who have been impacted by SIDS is not "therapy" in the clinical sense so often associated with other counseling relationships, but constant and appropriate validation of their experiences and of the small, but terribly difficult steps that must be taken in order to re-empower them again as individuals, parents, and family members. Counseling SIDS parents is *working* with *them*. It is the hardest *work* they and the counselor are ever likely to do. And it is a *joint effort* (Robinson, 1989).

A point to keep in mind is that some people will not desire or be able to undertake the required effort. For the time being, the death and accompanying grief journey will be put on hold. The "work" will, however, be waiting for those individuals and families. For counselors, it may be difficult to accept that everyone who turns to them cannot immediately start down the long road to gradually empowering themselves again. But to think that everyone can do that is unrealistic and inconsistent with the experience of SIDS counselors.

For the individuals whom we are discussing, the counselor's fund of knowledge about SIDS is a matter of great importance (Taylor, DeFrain, & Ernst, 1986). In the first place, this means that the counselor must know that SIDS is not an experience for which individuals can be held at fault and that there is nothing that anyone could have done to prevent a SIDS death. But those most intimately involved are likely already to have been told that in the first moments after the death. So an effective counselor must be prepared to go further.

The next step to consider involves awareness of the counselor's resources for medical expertise and consultation. Again, the needs of individuals and families will vary. For most, it is sufficient to be made aware that such resources are available should they be required. For some, access to such expertise is essential. For example, parents who themselves are health care professionals may need the "last word" in medical expertise. Also, individuals and families with special medical circumstances will be greatly limited in their ability to move forward with their own grief and mourning when they are unable to draw upon the most complete and current knowledge available. As a result, their confidence in and ability to work with the counselor or other helper will also be limited.

It is also important to have a working knowledge of theories, models, and literature that relate to grief and mourning (Osterweis, Solomon, & Green, 1984; Worden, 1982). That knowledge is a basic framework which can be called upon to validate the experiences of those impacted by SIDS. General or abstract theories and models are most useful when they serve to illuminate the experiences of concrete individuals. At the same time, such theories and models can also be misused. Few people are textbook cases, but many have been stereotyped in harmful ways through the prism of a simplistic theory or a rigid theoretical understanding. Thus, there is great wisdom in Jung's caution: "Learn your theories as well as you can, but put them aside when you touch the miracle of the living soul" (Jung, 1954, p. 7).

Grief is one of life's most powerful and consuming experiences. It has physical, emotional, cognitive, behavioral, and spiritual dimensions. Individuals react to loss according to who they are and where the shattering experience of a death finds them. Thus, grief is fluid, evolving, and unique in each individual situation, but those who have been impacted by SIDS rightly testify to the difficult qualities of a grief that arises from a sudden, unexpected, and untimely death (Krein, 1979; Smialek, 1978).

One of the hardest issues for many counselors and helpers to overcome is their sense of personal inadequacy if they are not SIDS parents or because they may not even have children of their own. Many feel a need to apologize for these perceived limitations. Once, a new SIDS parent asked, "Have you, too, lost a baby?" The response was a standard, guilt-laden, "No, I have not." The mother quickly retorted with an emphatic, "Thank goodness! I would never want anybody to feel as bad as I do right now!"

What this mother needed was validation of her experiences, access to medical resources, and introduction to other SIDS parents. In short, she needed a means to start working through a lifelong process. This mother needed her counselor not to be as disabled as she was at that point in her life. No disparagement is intended or implied with regard to experienced SIDS parents who themselves, at an appropriate time in their lives, function as counselors or helpers for the newly bereaved. Such parent-to-parent supportive relationships can be extremely effective. But certain essential elements in the counseling relationship must be kept in mind.

Individuals who are involved in a counseling relationship with those who have been impacted by SIDS need to be prepared for how much it will change their own view of life. To share in the situation of people so cheated by life and so robbed of all of their natural defense mechanisms is a wrenching experience. One cannot be the same once touched by such intense pain. As one is profoundly changed by the life and death of an infant one has never met, one tries to imagine the effect upon individuals who invested themselves in that baby. In fact, one cannot really enter into the depth of what others are feeling. The wise counselor or helper is one who can say with Thurman:

I know I cannot enter all you feel nor bear with you the burden of your pain.

I can but offer what my love does give: the strength of caring, the warmth of one who seeks to understand the silent storm-swept barrenness of so great a loss.

This I do in quiet ways, that on your lonely path you may not walk alone. (Thurman, 1953, pp. 211–212)

ISSUES IN COUNSELING PERSONS WHO HAVE BEEN IMPACTED BY SIDS

Matching People and Resources

The optimal situation for all counseling relations is to have sufficient information and resources to match each individual and family with a support system that is part of their own existing or natural system of care, or that is congruent with their particular needs. This is especially important in short-term counseling relationships with individuals impacted by SIDS. Also, as a practical matter, few counselors, even staff members in SIDS organizations, are in a position to counsel large numbers of such individuals. Thus, experience has demonstrated that the most beneficial services offered to such individuals may be delivered by a well-informed network of professionals or lay helpers who already were connected with a particular family or who had intense involvement around the time of the death (Mandell & McClain, 1988). The ability of the SIDS staff to educate and work effectively with members of these helping networks who provide direct services is a necessary and functional aspect of their counseling role.

In the early days of SIDS program evolution, approaches that seemed to be more formula-based were utilized. Public health nurses were the first, and often only, available bastion of service for SIDS families. These nurses deserve much credit for the key roles they have played in establishing SIDS services in the United States. Such nurses were well trained with information about SIDS and likely were one of the most enlightened resources about SIDS to which a family had access. Families received public health nurse visits regardless of whether or not they had a private physician or used a neighborhood health center as their primary source of health care. SIDS parent contacts or support groups were often used as ancillary support for the public health nursing visit. In some areas of the United States, this approach continues to be employed.

In areas where SIDS organizations have had the opportunity to develop their service networks and to learn from the growing number of families whom they have served, a differentiated approach to matching a family with a system of support is now commonly used (e.g., Lowman, 1979). The increasing sophistication of these direct service programs reflects the developing expectations of people in general about the needs of SIDS families. Here the lay press (and an occasional professional journal), despite its imperfections, has helped to create a much greater awareness of the problem. We owe the media a great debt in this regard from a community awareness point of view.

There is a lot of street knowledge about "crib death" even among poorly educated mothers and on up the social scale to the highly sophisticated interest in research among some parents who themselves are health professionals. To fail to match very diverse SIDS families and individuals with systems of support to which they can relate reflects a lack either of resources or of understanding about how to build continuity of services into the lives of these individuals and families.

In some communities, both rural and urban, a SIDS family will have a pre-established and strong relationship with a county health clinic or with a neighborhood health center. Not infrequently, the parents will call their nurse or other center staff to tell them of the baby's death before the reporting systems of a SIDS organization have come into play. The family may need people in existing relationships to help with the funeral or with the disarray that the death has created. Continuity of follow-up support for that family is already present. When such existing networks can be utilized, the people already involved with a given family will use the resources available that are SIDS-related, will see themselves as the family's advocates in yet one more capacity, and will be quite prepared to indicate when they need something more for one of "their own" families (Collins & Pancoast, 1976).

In some communities, the public health nurse or other helping person is such an integral part of that town's life, that whether or not the SIDS family uses the clinic or has a private pediatrician is of no consequence. The family's relationship is with that individual and with the supportive and caring role that he or she had previously established in that community. One is fortunate to have such a person—nurse, minister, funeral director, or social worker—in one's inventory of resources.

For families with private systems of health care, we have found that introduction of a public health nurse can lead to a lack of continuity of services. Neither is a natural fit with the other. If the resources are available, direct contact by SIDS professionals is more effective in determining what will be most helpful to the family in the long run.

SIDS parents who have found ways to cope effectively with their own losses (a matter more of qualitative achievement, than mere quantity of time) are an invaluable resource (Lord, 1987). As a group, they would be the strongest voice in asserting that not all SIDS parents could or should be parent contacts for the newly bereaved. When, after careful preparation and assessment, it is established that a parent contact is appropriate, the benefit for everyone involved can be tremendous. SIDS parent contacts are at a serious disadvantage, as is the newly bereaved family, if no "pre-screening"and "matching" has been done by the helping counselor.

There are occasions when an unofficial network of SIDS parents can work effectively with no professional intervention, but there can also be difficulties in this approach. Above all, SIDS parents do not need to face any additional problems in a time of great pain and vulnerability.

Parent support groups are an important option for some parents (see Chapter 10). There is no substitute for the validation that mutual experience provides. Far exceeding this seems to be a less definable quality that can be felt in a cohesive support group: it is the quality of the spirit and love which members have for each other. That quality, from which they all draw, is found in no other quarter.

Those who serve urban areas are accustomed to the problems faced by inner city, poor families, and our own limitations in trying to create systems of services that address needs arising from the death of their babies. However, none of us were prepared for the absolute frustration of dealing with SIDS among the homeless. Not only are there next to no existing systems of support available to such families or single parents, but also once they leave a shelter (which is usually right after the baby's death), there is seldom an address or telephone number through which they can be located.

The single most important service one may be able to provide for the homeless in relation to SIDS is the ability of first responders and the shelter staff to work well together and to give appropriate information about SIDS. If the family appears again in another shelter or in a public health center, there may be one more opportunity to fill in any missing pieces of information surrounding the baby's death. If that does not occur, then the best and only services are provided through the effectiveness of the emergency responders and the medical examiner system in providing prompt and accurate information, as well as through the shelter staff's ability to handle the crisis in the best way that it can. These may be the only sources from which the homeless receive informed and humane assistance regarding a SIDS death.

Time Framing and Establishing Expectations

Matching follow-up services to the family's natural system of support is part of the initial effort to provide continuity of care and to remobilize shattered coping mechanisms (Mandell, 1988). Individuals impacted by SIDS do not know what to expect from themselves; much less do they know what to expect from friends, co-workers, and family members. They want to know when they can count on not hurting so much any more. Or can they ever count on any relief from this pain, if life has suddenly become so unreliable? Their sense of self-confidence and ability to control their own lives are shattered. They feel powerless because so much that was taken for granted has gone awry.

Assisting these individuals to establish realistic expectations as soon as possible can be extremely helpful to everyone involved. Although each family and its circumstances are unique, there are some basic guidelines that have been useful in setting the stage for the work that is to come.

- The parents or other individuals should expect nothing from themselves other than what they feel at that moment. Their feelings are most likely to be appropriate and to be expected.
- Things may seem to be getting worse. When the initial protective layer of shock and numbness starts to wear off (that thawing-out process can happen in a week, a month, or longer), instead of feeling better one usually feels worse. That, too, is to be expected.
- If family and friends are exerting pressure to get into a support group or to "talk to someone right away," it should be made clear that such suggestions are options, not mandates. Only those involved will know what is right for them. What is helpful to one person is not necessarily useful for another. Each individual will have to determine which approaches work best for that particular person.
- People may not know what to say to individuals impacted by SIDS when they go back to work. Inappropriate or hurtful comments may be made. Co-workers may also be unsure of themselves. Remember that survivors are not themselves and are likely to be on a short fuse. Little things that would not have bothered them before the baby's death may now incense them. If it is possible, get information about SIDS into the work place before impacted individuals return to work. This will help co-workers ask fewer questions about what happened to the baby. We are just beginning to grapple with how best to educate colleagues, not only about SIDS but also about what to expect from survivors and how to give support while still getting the necessary work done.
- Determine who in the family was a talker before the baby died and who was not. It is usually at this point that both ways of coping should be validated and supported. To expect a quiet person who in the past has worked out problems in other ways to suddenly start talking his or her heart out is unrealistic. It is not going to happen. In actuality, individuals and family systems often become more rigid in their coping mechanisms when they find themselves under stress. This is not the time to tamper with old coping mechanisms. New ones may need to gradually replace old, ineffective habits that cannot function effectively under the new stress. However,

newly bereaved persons may need to be supported even in "doing it their own way" (barring outrageous conduct or behavior that is harmful to themselves or others, of course). It is not helpful to dictate the way in which they must cope.

- Although it should be emphasized that each person will deal with grief in his or her own unique way, it should also be made clear that it is a mistake not to work at mourning. Putting off the pain does not necessarily diminish it. Because of the magnitude of grief, the energy required to avoid it may be greater than working through it.

- "Will I lose my marriage, too?!" Individuals may not say this directly, but they often inquire about rumors of high divorce rates among bereaved parents, and they deserve reassurance that there is no reliable basis for expecting more marital disruption here than in the general population. SIDS catches a marriage where it was already, with existing communication abilities and disabilities. If a relatively stable relationship exists beforehand, and if a couple has access to reasonable external support, it is likely that the marriage will remain intact. If the relationship was under stress prior to the SIDS experience, special care, patience, and sensitivity will be needed in order to insure that each partner is allowed to grieve in his or her own way, while at the same time maintaining the marital relationship. This balance between each partner's individuality and the preservation of marital unity will be necessary for coping with day-to-day living situations, as well as for long-term acknowledgement of and accommodation to the child's death. It should also be recognized that unmarried parents will grapple with these issues within their relationships in similar ways.

- Time and the future are sometimes seen as the great enemy. People ask: How will we get through the months or years until we feel better? This can be an unbearable prospect. Concentrating on getting through one day, or sometimes just one hour, at a time is all that should be attempted or expected. That is sufficient and can be a victory at the end of a bad day. Life should be approached in small, manageable chunks and tasks. Those are achievable expectations that do not add unnecessarily to the pervasive sense of being overwhelmed or defeated.

- For individuals who have read about the "grief process" or who start reading about parental bereavement after the death of their own baby, time frames can be a trap. One must carefully put into perspective that the validation and comfort people can receive from such reading is extremely important. However, they must be careful not to accept a given author's perspective as a yardstick for their own experience. Reading is an important source of reassurance and information. It is not an infallible guide on how to get through grief and mourning.

In the first weeks following the death of a baby, some people exhibit a great need to gather information about SIDS. For parents accustomed to using their intellects to solve problems, this search is extremely important. While aiding them in this effort, we are careful to make clear that some of the answers they seek may not be in the literature, even as the most crucial questions may remain unanswered.

There are subtle differences in the reactions of individuals who were present when the death occurred and those who were not present. The differences among people in this respect are hard to define, but are immediately evident to a counselor who has experience with SIDS families. One SIDS parent who is a nurse and paramedic offered the following analysis. She believes that the parent who is present or the caregiver who finds the dead baby must work through the trauma of the appearance of the death, as well as all that is said and done to them by others in the immediacy of the crisis.

Individuals who were not present usually need to know exactly what happened in the brief period of their absence. For example, details of the circumstances and all that transpired seem to be extremely important for parents whose child was in the care of a sitter or a day care center when the death occurred. For many, there is also a kind of gratitude that they were not the ones who found the baby. The face of death adds an undeniable and long-lasting dimension to the grief of those who were present at the time of death.

When one is assisting persons impacted by SIDS to establish realistic expectations for themselves and to prepare for the work ahead, it is sometimes important also to introduce the concept of "closing doors." Helping individuals to search out relevant literature, to seek medical consultation for lingering questions, and to talk to those who were present at the time the death occurred are all steps to "closing those doors in the mind" on issues that are amenable to such closure. It is a necessary exercise for some as a means to enable them to move forward with the experience and to balance the bigger questions which for now remain unanswered by research. This early and concrete process that counselors and other helpers go through with many families is determined by the needs of each individual, and by the responsiveness of the counselor to those needs; it is not an approach related to socioeconomic status.

Nothing Is Easy or Simple Any More

Much of what is discussed in the previous section is focused on the first weeks and months following the baby's death. But perhaps the full weight of the baby's death and all of its ripple effects are only felt when the "long haul" effect begins to settle in. The first effect that is often observed is that family and friends have gotten back to the business of their own lives. It is not that they no longer care; it is just that the timing is all off from the point of view of those most severely impacted by SIDS. Everyone else is getting better when they are getting worse! This is common and many people find it helpful if they are prepared before such experiences actually occur. Such preparation may take a bit of the edge off when surrounding people get on with life and when one still does not know where to start. This is not surprising when those most severely impacted have been knocked off a hitherto hard-won and previously safe plateau.

What to Do with Important Dates and Which Ones Will Be Difficult?

One can expect that the first year of holidays, birthdays, anniversary of the baby's death, and many other smaller, special, personal milestones will be difficult (Zebal & Woolsey, 1984). Personal contact with other survivors or reading about their experiences can greatly aid recently bereaved persons to struggle through these times. One cannot always anticipate and plan for every seemingly innocuous date or holiday that will trigger a "really bad day." Thus, permission and validation must be given to each individual to find ways to get through such days in the best possible way that he or she can.

This may sometimes require that those impacted by SIDS declare their independence from their own parents or family members. "No! We will be gone that weekend! All the babies that will be there will make us feel terrible. We don't want to ruin everyone's day or ours. There will be other times!" One young couple rehearsed this statement at a support group meeting and then, much to everyone's surprise, used it successfully with their families.

Please note that when discussing the first year of milestones, the word "survive" is used. It is survival; each individual challenge must be worked through somehow. Very important precedents will be established during this critical time period. Parents will have to make their own individual decisions, anticipate tough times, and then find ways to get through them. They will need this preparation to pave the way for all that follows. The ensuing years will not become simpler, though they usually are less painful. There are still all of those other important dates "that should have been" in the life of a child which remain as hurdles.

One mother commented on this subject in the following way: "I was in the store buying Valentine's Day cards, when a "Happy Birthday Eight-Year-Old" card caught my eye. I walked over, took it out of the rack, and bought it. Had my daughter not died, she would have been eight years old that month. When I arrived home, I signed the card that I couldn't mail anywhere. For days it sat on my piano, a symbol of my unresolved emotions every February when I had nowhere to mail the birthday card, no one to buy a gift for."

Various families have celebrated or memorialized some of these special dates in different ways. One person chose to use the birthday card to mail to a SIDS organization a donation that would have been used to buy a birthday gift. One father buys a rose for every birthday that his daughter would have celebrated so far, and the family keeps them in a special place at home. Some grandparents contribute to their favorite charity on Christmas and the baby's birthday. One man said that he goes out every year and buys the football or baseball bat and glove that he dreamed of buying for his son, and gives them to a little boy in the neighborhood whose family cannot afford such items.

One father marked the first anniversary date of his baby's death by organizing a clothing drive through their church to take to an inner city parish. The other children in the family helped, as did their friends and others in the church. This reminds us that an important part of the "celebrating" or remembering is including the siblings, those who remember the baby and those who wish they could.

The Next Baby

Friends and relatives frequently have a great deal of advice to offer on the subject of "the next baby" (Mandell & Wolfe, 1975; Szybist, 1976). Parents are told: "If you have another child right away, you are trying to replace the one you lost." Or, "have another baby right away; that will be the best thing for you." No matter what parents decide to do, someone will always have a different opinion to voice. The decision of when and if to have another baby will not be made with the same priorities in mind. Somehow, whether or not it is a convenient time to have the baby does not seem as important as whether or not the next baby will live! Typically, when a pregnancy is planned it relates more to career, spacing with other children, family finances, and other more routine questions. Suddenly, those things do not seem quite so important. It can be more a matter of, "Oh my God, I'm not pregnant yet!", and then, "Oh my God, I'm pregnant!"

Pregnancy is a time of some physical discomfort, emotional ups and downs, and the gradual (for some, immediate) attachment to the child who will soon be the focal point of the family. For parents who have previously lost a baby to SIDS, it is also a time of cold sweat and fear: "How will we get through the first year?"; "Do I want a monitor if it's not a guarantee?"; "If I love this baby, does that mean I don't love the baby I lost?" Some parents worry that the memory of their prior child will fade. The wise counselor will use the time of the pregnancy to examine and clarify how the parents feel and what options they have to supplement their own sense of control.

One option is *home monitoring*. There are occasional instances when use of a home monitor for the next baby will be medically indicated by conditions completely separate from the issue of SIDS (SIDS Resources, Inc., n.d.; Slovik &

Kelly, 1988). However, placing an infant on a home monitoring device specifically because of a prior SIDS death provides neither a predictor nor a prevention for SIDS. Nevertheless, the monitor can, when used in a properly informed context, provide some parents with the minimum assurance that "blinking lights" and silence mean all is, for the moment, well. Very few SIDS parents with asymptomatic next babies, when asked directly, believe that a modest piece of machinery is a guarantee against the syndrome that continues to frustrate researchers. But many state that use of a monitor lessened their anxiety somewhat during the next baby's first few months of life. Still other families feel that use of a home monitor will only increase their anxiety, and, since no one can guarantee its use as a prevention, they choose not to monitor the subsequent infant.

A subsequent pregnancy is also a time to put into perspective that as things are different for the parents and family with this pregnancy, they will be different throughout the childhood. As every step of the pregnancy has been questioned, so will everything be questioned after the baby is born. Prior decisions that were made about other babies (e.g., sitters, day care centers, going back to work, and runny noses) will not be made so matter-of-factly. All sides of each subject will be considered and rarely will any decision appear to be clear cut.

Though the next baby brings great joy to the parents and family, it is not the same joyful experience that it was prior to the death. The new baby is "bittersweet." Where there is one child, there should be two. When this baby begins to crawl, his sister or brother never had that chance. And so it goes on through the age at which the dead child should have started school and passed all of those other milestones out there lurking in the future.

Things also are no longer easy or simple for those parents who choose not to have more children. Not all SIDS deaths occur to parents in their middle or late twenties just starting their families. In families where there are several older siblings, the dead infant may have represented the last attempt at childbearing. Such families may choose not to have additional children. As time passes for some families who have other children, demands on parental time and energies increase tremendously. Some parents come to a point in their lives when they ask: "Do I want to go back to changing diapers and losing sleep?" Or: "Do I want to drag a baby and a stroller everywhere with me again?" When added to all of the other questions that are related to SIDS, the answer can sometimes appropriately be: "No."

How Many Children Do You Have?

Without belaboring the complexities of raising children after losing a baby to SIDS, this question poses familiar difficulties for bereaved parents (Klass, 1988). After discovering that they share the common bond of parenthood, people routinely ask how many children one has. That raises issues of self-identity and communication for SIDS parents. Some simply tell the truth: "I had two children, but one died from SIDS." Sometimes, they simply give the number of children who are still living. Other people say, "I had a little girl, but she died." There are many other possible answers. How the question is answered depends on what mood the bereaved parent is in or who has asked the question. That is completely appropriate. Parents should be encouraged to make a quick assessment of how they feel at that moment, what an honest answer might possibly elicit as a response, and what their relationship is with the person who asked. After some practice, this method of fielding a common and potentially difficult question can be handled with only a short pause.

Tying Things Up for Now

If parents have learned to close some of those invisible doors in their minds and have worked themselves through many of the obstacles posed by the first few years following the death of their child, they will usually reach a plateau where they have regained some happiness and sense of control over their own lives. It is important to help individuals and families understand that this may change for reasons that sometimes cannot be anticipated.

Some of those unanticipated reasons relate to the changing developmental levels of other children in the family. As they grow older, their questions and perceptions about their missing sibling will also change—and usually arise when parents are completely unprepared to deal with them. One mother reported that one afternoon as she pulled frozen fish out of the freezer for dinner, her seven-year-old son blurted out, "Disgusting! Lisa would hate that if she were here!" His mother looked at him in disbelief and then burst into tears. In her mind, she thought that Lisa should be here to hate the fish as much as her brother. This family had carefully created a place for their missing daughter. Thus, the little boy was free to work with the fantasy of what she would be like if she were still here and able to join him in the "no" vote about what was planned for dinner.

Another mother stated that her oldest son kept a treasured picture of himself holding his baby sister because it helped him remember what she was like. The younger sister, a subsequent sibling who never knew her sister, burst into uncontrollable tears one day. Everyone else had known the baby except her, and now they were making her feel left out! By the time the child's tears were dried and a picture obtained for her room, too, the mother was in tears herself. The baby who had been real for the parents and son had just been an abstraction for her "subsequent sibling." It took the picture to give the child a sense of connectedness with her sister.

Inanimate objects can also upset the balance. On a trip to a cemetery to place flowers on the grave of his son, one father became unexpectedly angry. The marker he had looked at for years now suddenly incensed him. "It was too small! It looked tacky! Why couldn't we have bought something better when our son died?" The honest answer to that angry question was that they bought what they could afford at the time. So now that a different headstone was so important to the father, a new one was purchased.

Each of these parents was knocked off balance by the unexpected, but each took action in his or her own way. Two parents had created a loving and honest atmosphere for their other children to cope with the death of their sibling, thereby propelling themselves to a different plateau with the death. The other parent did not berate himself for getting angry about nothing. He affirmed his feelings by getting a different gravestone. Individuals impacted by SIDS work to achieve a peace within themselves; at some point this may no longer be a daily undertaking, but nevertheless it requires an ongoing effort.

COMPLICATED GRIEF REACTIONS

In this chapter, considerable time and attention have been devoted to normal and expected responses to the irrational event of a SIDS death. In our experience, the great majority of grief reactions are not pathological. But some may be less healthy, and they deserve attention here also.

Worden (1982) has identified four general categories of abnormal, pathological, or what he prefers to call "complicated" grief reactions. These are: chronic grief reactions, marked by prolonged duration which never comes to a satisfactory outcome; delayed grief reactions, those which have been inhibited, suppressed, or postponed, and which may only surface when activated by some subsequent loss; exaggerated grief reactions, characterized by their excessive and disabling qualities; and masked grief reactions, which usually involve unmanifested grief and may be expressed as physical symptoms or some type of aberrant or maladaptive behavior. In relationship to SIDS, the following sorts of reactions attract particular concern.

Cosmic Anger, Hostility, and Exploitation

Some situational reactions give pause due to their severity. For example, a couple might present themselves in counseling, and use their SIDS-related resources (e.g., parent contacts or a support group) well and appropriately. They have loving families and friends. Quickly, one partner emerges as the "primary griever" and more vocal parent. Both parents are dependent on their support systems in their devastation. The "primary griever" in the family becomes hostile when the pain becomes more intense and no one is able to relieve its intensity.

All SIDS parents are entitled to be angry that life has cheated them of their child and of any opportunity to fight for that child. "Cosmic anger" seems to be an all-consuming anger; the death is everyone's fault and, worst of all, it is no one's fault. No one can bring back the baby, no one has suffered as they have suffered, and no one can take away the awful pain! How could this have happened to them? Behavior reflecting what we term "cosmic anger" is disconcerting in its intensity, especially when it is definitely out of character from all that we have learned about the client's personality prior to the baby's death.

It is this "out of character" response which may indicate a situational reaction rather than a pathological one. "Cosmic anger" cannot be interrupted with any rational approach. It drives away the people that are most needed by the grieving person at this time. It is unfortunately necessary for many individuals experiencing this kind of anger to find the bottom of the angry hole they have dug for themselves before they can climb back out again. It can only be hoped that they will reach out once again to the very people they drove away in their all-consuming anger.

Some individuals who can best be described as cosmically angry were going through life as essentially intense, hostile people. The baby's death fuels the fire of their nonspecific anger. These people become what is called in the vernacular "loose cannons." They are not infrequently articulate and professionally ambitious, successful people. Often, they express their desire to work for the "cause" immediately after their baby's death, and, in fact, will want to take on a leadership responsibility. This is usually premature.

The efforts of vocal, committed SIDS parents are critical to the advance of research and services, but not until they have worked at their grief or at least begun a process of "self-care." Some may have learned to set no limits on their high energy level, nor have they learned through a counseling relationship to structure realistically the expectations for what they believe they can accomplish. When people who fit this description become advocates without first beginning their own grief work and learning to practice some basic self care, they are likely to burn out from their own scattered intensity. In the process, they may have hurt as much as they have helped the cause to which they have with all good intention dedicated themselves. Unfortunately, many of these individuals either do not participate in counseling or only enter it after the "fall."

Within this same group of cosmically angry individuals, there can be found another subgroup loosely described as "users" or people who engage in exploitative behavior. Immediately following the death of their baby, these persons will seem to make prompt and appropriate use of all of the resources available to them. They often will express their feelings quite articulately and share issues common to all SIDS parents. Soon, it seems that they have accumulated many helpers. Friends and helping professionals often go far beyond the boundaries of what could reasonably be expected from them in terms of support. The first warning signs may be the counselor's own quiet, but growing annoyance with such individuals.

No effort on their behalf is acknowledged or appreciated. No thanks are expressed. Often, in fact, these persons are angry about what was not or is not being done for them. No One Can Do Anything Right! Nothing short of returning their missing child will in reality suffice. The "user" phenomenon can be quite subtle and not all helpers involved will be alert to it. Such clients often do not stay in counseling, as the professional is just one more person who falls "short" of what should be provided in the relationship. If they continue, one must engage in an ongoing process of turning responsibility for their own lives and future happiness back over to them. Needless to say, there will be resistance.

Anger is an important and powerful emotion in the grief work of some parents. In general, we are not taught to handle our anger in a constructive manner. Anger is negative. Society says we should not get angry or express our feelings when we are angry. In fact, it is not constructive never to allow oneself to become angry or always to engage in the unrestrained anger of a small child who has never had appropriate limits set on his or her behavior. In an adult, such inability to control oneself is both inappropriate and counterproductive. All parents who lose children to SIDS can and should be angry. But individuals who have never learned how to be angry in an appropriate and focused manner will either be greatly impeded by their anger or entirely overwhelmed by it.

Exaggerated Control

Many counselors do not meet parents who exercise "iron control" over their grief until many years after the death of the baby (if they meet them at all). "Iron control" is seen in those parents who for their own reasons simply refuse to confront the death. Parents fall into this group for a variety of reasons or life experience. For some, as small children they learned to overcome their circumstances or troubled family of origin not by processed problem solving, but rather by taking charge of their environment. Such coping skills no doubt helped them acquire academic and professional success. For persons who have believed themselves always to be in control of everything, the loss of a child goes beyond shattering. They may appear to cope well with their grief when indeed they have blocked it. They want to hear nothing and see nothing related to SIDS. There are, of course, variations on this theme.

Blocking sometimes is related to the meaning that the pregnancy and life of the baby did or did not have for one or both parents. For such individuals, to confront the death fully means that they must confront themselves and the meaning the baby had for them. Some people can maintain this balance for many years. It takes a great deal of energy and singlemindedness of purpose. When the effort becomes too great or when a shift in the family balance regarding the death takes place, these individuals may then end up in counseling.

Again, it is worth reiterating a word of caution regarding "red flag" grief reactions. People do not exhibit extreme, prolonged reactions solely as the result of their grief. They respond according to who they are and what their coping methods were prior to the death.

Sadness and Depression

Sadness, depression, and a sense of hopelessness are consuming emotions that are familiar to persons who have been impacted by SIDS and that were explored by Freud (1957) in an essay on the differences between mourning and "melancholia" (his term for depression). In order for a counselor or helper to enable such individuals to work effectively with (some would say, to combat) these feelings, it is important to assess each person's prior coping skills and to evaluate their personal histories in terms of possible pre-existing depression.

When a medical history reveals serious periods of depression, the emotional upheaval following a baby's death is likely to be particularly frightening. Such individuals will have reason to be afraid of what this catastrophe might trigger within themselves. Each person in this situation will need help to assess whether or not their depression goes beyond that appropriate to their bereavement. It is critical that such individuals be helped immediately with concrete tasks for hourly or daily coping. Counselors must be sensitive to each effort that a person makes to pull out of a "bad day" and must validate that effort.

Individuals who were in a state of depression at the time of the baby's death will bring that to the bereavement, just as everyone brings pre-existing functional or dysfunctional qualities to their grief. Sadness and a depressed mood, for example, are certainly appropriate following the death of a child (Knapp, 1986). But severe clinical depression is a more serious, difficult, and even dangerous condition. Active suicidal gestures (going beyond a passive mood of "no desire to go on living," which is sometimes expressed) or prolonged alcohol or substance abuse often indicate an underlying state of depression.

Even for those individuals who have experienced no pathological behavior related to depression, their feelings for a period of time may be both frightening and immobilizing. Validation of the appropriateness of the depth of their feelings is essential, as is attention to its implications. Most often, they are not losing their minds, their ability to make decisions, or their capacity to think. They are simply responding to one of the worst assaults on themselves that they will ever face.

Psychotic Behavior

Individuals who present themselves with lengthy psychiatric histories are probably the most obvious foci of concern among a complex client population. If the counseling relationship antedated the death of the baby, the loss will be interwoven into the treatment regime. Alternatively, the death may be the event that initiates counseling. Here the question may be whether or not it is desirable to enter into larger underlying issues. In any event, the tremendous stress that grief introduces will be present at all times, making each pre-existing problem that much more onerous.

Psychotic clients who appear in a crisis, often around an anniversary date related to the baby's death, are most troublesome. They have often worked hard at defeating their therapists and proudly display their victories like trophies. Experience has demonstrated that these clients can exhibit truly bizarre and sometimes potentially dangerous grief reactions. One memorable client believed that her baby was not dead, but held captive at the medical examiner's office and was now three years old. This same client also had experienced violent outbursts most of her adult life and was calmly entertaining the idea of a hostage situation with a co-worker she considered to have been unsympathetic at the time of the baby's death. She had gone so far as to warn her employer of this and to recommend therapy for herself. She carefully defeated each counseling relationship she entered (thereby defeating herself also), and regularly flushed her medication down the toilet. There is little that can be done in such a situation except to provide whatever structure and limit-setting possible when called during a crisis, and either to make a referral when appropriate or to work as a team with existing psychiatric resources already involved.

In all of these circumstances, counselors and families need to use all of the appropriate SIDS-related resources that are available to them. Families and individuals who are able to enter into or continue in a therapeutic relationship under such stress should be viewed as "cautiously encouraging." People who are able to use the structure in their lives that is provided in an ongoing treatment relationship may make modest progress and not present themselves in the same kind of crisis situations as those individuals who are not able to connect with and utilize counseling.

SELF CARE FOR COUNSELORS

Johnson (1987) has discussed self-care in a realistic and practical way, both for clients and for counselors after the death of a child. Her advice about good nutrition, exercise, and giving oneself permission to find distraction in an outside interest even for a short period of time is very helpful. The most constructive method is common sense coupled with an honest appraisal of one's own stress and coping levels.

We are aware that working with bereaved parents is exhausting for many counselors. It is draining emotionally, and sometimes the reality of these losses is not tolerable. However, if the counseling relationship continues over a long period of time, there are rewards. People laugh again, they find a "new normal" in their lives, and often counselors can share in the bittersweet experience of the next baby. For some counselors who lead support groups, it can be a restoring experience to watch parents give to each other and move each other along one step at a time. Support groups are hard work and someone invariably needs to have limits set on their attempts to sidetrack the work of the group. But we are constantly in awe of the strength which group members exhibit as individuals and which they draw from each other.

It is unfortunate that many counselors do not have opportunities to see the more representative group of SIDS parents, those who do not experience profound variations in coping with their grief. They are the people who struggle and overcome. They would be surprised that their efforts are seen by others as inspiring. At one point or another, they have simply made the choice to go on living. In making that choice, they set off down a long and unpredictable road.

Experience with burnout among helping professionals involved with bereaved persons seems to vary. Rather than the extremes so often cited, such as, short-tempered outbursts, inability to concentrate, drinking too much, or being angry at your spouse all the time, it would appear that chronic fatigue and feeling "numb" are the more day-to-day problems of burnout. Short of career change, the self-care methods remain the same: Know yourself, be aware, and then do something about it.

CONCLUSION

The grief of parents, family members, and other individuals who have been impacted by the sudden and unexpected death of a child bears some similarities to the abrupt amputation of a limb. First, there is an intense, physical pain surrounding the loss, a pain that grows and deepens as the implications of the death gradually penetrate the barriers of shock and numbness. Typically, that searing, initial pain subsides after a while—at least in some degree. One parent said that no one could go on living if the intensity and omnipresence of the pain did not somehow diminish. Nevertheless, the rest of one's life is spent compensating for and adjusting to the loss of the child.

The principal task of counselors—whether trained professionals or lay helpers, in formal or informal counseling relationships, through short or long-term contacts—is to validate the horrendous experiences of those who have been impacted by SIDS, as well as to re-empower them both as human beings and in their specific roles as parents, siblings, grandparents, etc. Inherent in this process is helping such individuals to make good use of already existing coping skills or to learn new ones which are necessary for the work at hand. Another responsibility is to provide these persons with appropriate information, to link them with useful resources, and to draw upon the support of formal and informal networks that are available to them.

In the end, however, it is important for counselors to recognize that the journey to be undertaken must be navigated by the bereaved persons themselves. It waits for them and is pursued in their ways. We can walk alongside, as Thurman (1953) has said, so that those who have been impacted by SIDS do not walk alone. But we cannot walk in their place, much as we might wish to do so. Along the way, we can offer the strengths of our own experience, skills, limitations, and vulnerabilities. We cannot choose the timing or the place, but we can contribute as opportunities are presented to us. SIDS is an awful tragedy; renewed living in its aftermath is an awesome achievement. As a counselor, it is a privilege to be permitted to contribute to the process of renewal in any way.

REFERENCES

Bergman, A. B. (1974). Psychological aspects of sudden unexpected death in infants and children: Review and commentary. *Pediatric Clinics of North America, 21*, 115–121.

Calvin, S., & Smith, I. M. (1986). Counseling adolescents in death-related situations. In C. A. Corr & J. N. McNeil (Eds.), *Adolescence and death* (pp. 215–230). New York: Springer Publishing Co.

Collins, A. H., & Pancoast, D. L. (1974). *Natural helping networks: A strategy for prevention.* Washington, DC: National Association of Social Workers.

Freud, S. (1957). Mourning and melancholia. In J. Strachey (Ed.), *The standard edition of the complete psychological works of Sigmund Freud* (Vol. 14, pp. 243–258). London: Hogarth Press.

Hoff, B. (1982). *The Tao of Pooh.* New York: E. P. Dutton.

Johnson, S. E. (1987). *After a child dies: Counseling bereaved families.* New York: Springer Publishing Co.

Jung, C. G. (1954). *The development of personality.* Vol. 17 in H. Read, et al. (Eds.), *The collected works of C. G. Jung.* Princeton, NJ: Princeton University Press.

Klass, D. (1988). *Parental grief: Solace and resolution.* New York: Springer Publishing Co.

Knapp, R. J. (1986). *Beyond endurance: When a child dies.* New York: Schocken.

Krein, N. (1979). Sudden infant death syndrome: Acute loss and grief reactions. *Clinical Pediatrics, 18*, 414–423.

Lord, J. D. (1987). *When a baby suddenly dies: Cot death—the impact and effects.* Melbourne: Hill of Content.

Lowman, J. (1979). Grief intervention and sudden infant death syndrome. *American Journal of Community Psychology, 7*, 665–677.

Mandell, F. (1988). The family and sudden infant death syndrome. In J. L. Culbertson, H. F. Krous, & R. D. Bendell (Eds.), *Sudden infant death syndrome: Medical aspects and psychological management* (pp. 182–197). Baltimore: The Johns Hopkins University Press.

Mandell, F., & Belk, B. (1977). Sudden infant death syndrome: The disease and its survivors. *Postgraduate medicine, 62*(4), 193–197.

Mandell, F., & McClain, M. (1988). Supporting the SIDS family. *Pediatrician, 15*, 179–182.

Mandell, F., & Wolfe, L. C. (1975). Sudden infant death syndrome and subsequent pregnancy. *Pediatrics, 56*, 774–776.

Markusen, E., Owen, G., Fulton, R., & Bendiksen, R. (1978). SIDS: The survivor as victim. *Omega, 8*, 277–284.

Osterweis, M., Solomon, F., & Green, M. (1984). *Bereavement: Reactions, consequences, and care.* Washington, DC: National Academy Press.

Robinson, R. (1989). Working through grief. Paper presented at the First SIDS Family International Conference, London, England, April 5th.

SIDS Resources, Inc. (n.d.). Home monitoring facts for families. St. Louis, MO: Author.

Slovik, L. S., & Kelly, D. H. (1988). Family reactions to home monitoring. In J. L. Culbertson, H. F. Krous, & R. D. Bendell (Eds.), *Sudden infant death syndrome: Medical aspects and psychological management* (pp. 198–226). Baltimore: The Johns Hopkins University Press.

Smialek, Z. (1978). Observations on immediate reactions of families to sudden infant death. *Pediatrics, 62*, 160–165.

Szybist, C. (1976). *The subsequent child.* Rockville, MD: U.S. Department of Health, Education, and Welfare, Public Health Service, (HSA) 76-5145.

Taylor, J., DeFrain, J., & Ernst, L. (1986). Sudden infant death syndrome. In T. A. Rando (Ed.), *Parental loss of a child* (pp. 159–180). Champaign, IL: Research Press.

Thurman, H. (1953). *Meditations of the heart.* New York: Harper & Row.

Worden, J. W. (1982). *Grief counseling and grief therapy: A handbook for the mental health practitioner.* New York: Springer Publishing Co.

Zebal, B. H., & Woolsey, S. F. (1984). SIDS and the family: The pediatrician's role. *Pediatric Annals, 13*, 237–261.

CHAPTER 10

Guidelines for Group Work

Marion McNurlen

The death of a family member is a difficult, chaotic, and often very vulnerable time for anyone. When death occurs suddenly, without warning, without time to prepare or say goodbye, people find themselves in what seems like a nightmare of pain. With the death of a child, our sense of safety and order is thrown asunder. So it is that SIDS (Sudden Infant Death Syndrome), the sudden, unexpected death of a seemingly healthy infant, brings those involved into a previously unimagined realm of pain, confusion, and panic.

Regardless of an individual's coping skills or the strength of one's support system, a sense of almost total disequilibrium will still be experienced. Those with strong internal resources and good community supports may gain some balance in a short period of time, but the long process of mourning a SIDS death is often beyond the scope of normal internal and external resources. Few people have within them the knowledge and strength to "go it alone." The aid of others is important, perhaps even essential. The others who are needed must provide a comforting presence for a long time (Bowlby, 1980). They must also be knowledgeable about SIDS, understand the experience of a child's death, and believe in the healing processes of grief and mourning. Many natural support systems will have some of these needed resources; few will have them all.

Support groups for people experiencing the grief of a SIDS death can provide needed assistance that is not available in the natural helping environment (Wasserman & Danforth, 1988). This chapter will offer an understanding of why and how support groups (sometimes called self-help or mutual-help groups) assist people, the issues involved in developing and leading a support group, and the ongoing issues of self care for leaders and participants. Even though support groups may not be suitable for everyone, it is clear that they are very valuable for many.

WHY AND HOW SUPPORT GROUPS WORK TO HELP THE BEREAVED

Basically, there are two types of support groups: those that effect change in their members, such as Alcoholics Anonymous or Weight Watchers; and those that enable members to cope with life change (Wasserman & Danforth, 1988). SIDS groups are of the latter type. Their aims are highlighted by Silverman (1980) in her description of a mutual-help support group:

> The essential purpose of this group is to provide people in similar circum-stances with an opportunity to share their experiences and to help teach one another how to cope with their problems. . . . In this situation the professional is not concerned with factors in the participants' pasts which may have led them to act in one way or another, but rather with the com-monality of their present experiences and their approaches to them. (p. 40)

Two areas of knowledge are useful in understanding the workings of support groups: social support theory provides insight into general issues of support in the lives of individuals; and literature on psychotherapy groups gives an un-derstanding of general group processes. Combining these areas results in a clearer understanding of the work of support groups.

Social Support

The following comments by group participants clearly reflect their experience of the support provided by a SIDS parent group: "The group was the only place I could go through the details of finding my baby dead without people thinking I was morbid"; "Seeing other people whose baby died who are 'making it' gives me hope I will make it too"; "I need to hear that I won't go crazy"; "Having many people who know about SIDS tell me I couldn't have saved my baby helps me forgive myself." In short, "for all bereaved, the central issue in any helping encounter is to learn to build a life without the deceased" (Silverman, 1978, p. 40).

Thus, the work of a SIDS parent group is to assist parents whose child has died in their process of coming to terms with the death. They must make a life for themselves without their child being alive. This work happens as members are supported in a number of specific ways by other group members. The term "mutual support" is particularly appropriate because each participant may be a receiver and a giver of support at the same time and certainly during the same meeting. "Sharing of experience is the fundamental concept that distinguishes the mutual help experience from other helping exchanges. . . . The essence of the process is mutuality and reciprocity" (Silverman, 1980, p. 10). Research on the specific functions of social support has shown that those types of support which are most necessary for the bereaved are: (1) presence; (2) expression; (3) evaluation; (4) esteem; and (5) fun.

Presence

Support in the form of presence refers to a simple but essential need—someone "being there" for you. Grieving parents often speak of feeling absolutely alone in the world. When both spouses are actively grieving, often they not only cut themselves off from outsiders, but also from each other. The group provides a place where people can come individually or as a couple and experience a sense of community. There is often an intense feeling of connectedness in the group, a sense of *not* being alone.

Expression

The presence in a person's life "of a confiding relationship (i.e., a relationship in which a person can talk about the things that are troubling him/her with the other person) is critical" (Mueller, 1980, p. 152). After the sudden, unexpected death of a baby, parents are overwhelmed with feelings and thoughts. Often they are fearful of expressing their true feelings because the intensity and kinds of feelings are so foreign to their normal experiences. There is an almost insatiable need for many SIDS parents to express feelings, and the group is a place for them to be assured of confiding relationships. "There is something about sharing experiences or feelings with a body of like-minded others that reduces anxiety and promotes more constructive behavior" (Antze, 1979, p. 273).

Evaluation

As this relates to SIDS support groups, evaluative support has two main facets. The first is providing *accurate information* about SIDS. In order to absolve themselves of responsibility for the death, SIDS parents must be given, over and over, accurate information about SIDS and the inability of anyone to prevent the death of the child. Through receiving information about SIDS in small amounts over a long time, they come to accept the facts. The second area of evaluation for SIDS survivors concerns *how they are grieving*. Most have never experienced anything as emotionally difficult as this death and need repeated reassurance that they are grieving "as they should." They need to know that they will eventually feel better and it is especially helpful to hear this from other bereaved parents (Klass, 1988).

Esteem

"In a child's death, there is a possibility that everything in our lives we have ever deemed a failure will be brought up to add to the current experience, we will be certain we have failed" (Bordow, 1982, p. 55). When parents come to a support group, they have experienced, in their eyes, an ultimate sense of failure: they have failed to protect their precious infant from death. One of the most moving experience in a SIDS group is when parents gain back their self-esteem and can say with certainty that they are good people and were good parents to their baby. This is a slow healing process which occurs as parents hear from other members that they are valued, that they are normal, that they are grieving as they should, and that they could not have prevented their baby's death. Parents may hear these comments from friends and family, too, but they believe them more fully when the comments come from others in similar situations.

Fun

Although not generally mentioned in social support theory, the element of fun is an important one in some support groups. Through spending time with others coping with a similar tragedy, group members may be able to find relief from their pain long enough to laugh at a situation and, even at times, at themselves. Group members grow to trust each other enough to share their blunders and uncertainties. Laughter can come as a mutual recognition of shared experiences. Members may also connect with each other at times outside the group and find that they have shared so much pain together that they can also share fun as a release from the pain.

Curative Factors in Support Groups

In addition to providing social support to group members, mutual-help support groups also assist people by providing a group experience. There is a "magic" that can occur in groups which makes the group experience much greater than anticipated or imagined. The group is more than a collection of individuals supporting each other. Drawing on work related to psychotherapy groups (Yalom, 1975), one can identify a number of ways that SIDS groups can help their members. At different stages in the history of the group, the importance of specific factors may vary among individuals at any given time. But all come into play at some time. Discussion of ways that the most prominent of these curative factors operate in SIDS groups will help to explain how the group works (Lieberman, 1979a).

Identification

While this factor is of little significance in therapy groups, it is of prime importance in SIDS groups. Members often feel that no one in their normal support system really understands, but they identify immediately with a group of fellow SIDS survivors. An almost instantaneous bond is created for many. Members also gain by coming to know people who currently are further along in the grief process and who continue to manage their grief successfully. Senior members serve as role models for new members.

Universality

This is the experience of knowing you are not alone, that others share your experience. Many people barely know that SIDS exists before they are told by police or the coroner that it is the cause of their baby's death. Because co-workers and neighbors may not know how to respond to this death, parents may feel like outsiders at work and in their neighborhoods. In the group they have a feeling that they are no longer alone with their sorrow.

Catharsis

The group is a safe place to release long-pent-up feelings and emotions. Normal support systems often put pressure on SIDS parents to "get yourself together" after a few months. In the group it is safe to let out feelings for as long as necessary. Some members may attend the group regularly for a year or two and return to the group for a number of years on significant dates, such as birthdays and death anniversaries.

Guidance

Parents need to be told over and over that there is nothing they could have done to prevent their baby's death. Relating SIDS information and providing repeated reassurance help fill this need. Also, some teaching about normal feelings after a loss and the normal processes of mourning provides a normalizing experience. The group "can serve the function of displaying for the mourner just what is the average range of emotions for a given period of time" (Sarnoff-Schiff, 1986, p. 235).

Instillation of Hope

Grieving parents face an intensity of emotion and hopelessness that can make life nearly intolerable. Newly bereaved parents think they will never get over the pain. Hearing from a professional leader who has worked with many families, and knowing parents further along in the grief process, helps members realize that they will get better. They come to know that there is hope for a meaningful life again.

Existential Issues

Among the existential issues that SIDS parents raise are: life is not fair; there is no escape from death and pain; I could not prevent the death of my child; God has abandoned me. At times, people are not able to raise these questions in any other setting. Their church may attempt to give pat answers. Their friends may not understand. But there are others in the group struggling with similar questions. When these existential questions are raised, answers are not found, but there is healing in the asking of them.

Cohesiveness

The group works best when there is cohesiveness among members. Such cohesiveness is assured when a safe, caring environment is established and when members have shared a similar life experience. With a feeling of cohesiveness in the group, the other curative factors can take effect.

Altruism

Discovering that when you feel at your lowest you can still help someone else is a very healing experience. Members have an opportunity to tell what they are going through and by doing that, help others. Also, when people stay in the group for a long time, and when group members move to a leadership role in the group, they are able to give back to others what they gained from their earlier membership. A group member who returned to be a facilitator stated: "When I first came to the group, I was certain I could never find a way out of the pain of losing John. Over time, with the support of group members, I have resolved most of my grief and moved on. If I can come back and help others see there is hope, then it adds a great deal of meaning to John's life and his death."

HOW SUPPORT GROUPS DIFFER FROM THERAPY GROUPS

In groups, as in life, there are few, if any, absolutely clear divisions. This is certainly true when looking at the differences between support and therapy groups. Some characteristics clearly pertain to "support"; others are unique to "therapy"; and many are evident in both types of groups (Wasserman & Danforth, 1988). Differences may be very subtle or not discernible at all. Because bereaved parents are in an extremely chaotic and vulnerable time in their lives, these distinctions may be further blurred. For example, if a group member displays suicidal tendencies in a meeting, the leader must act in a forceful, therapeutic way to intervene on the member's behalf. The focus here on characteristic differences between support groups and therapy groups is intended to suggest a *sense* of the differences between therapy groups and support groups for grieving parents and families. These differences fall into two primary categories: issues related to membership; and those relating to the content of group meetings.

Membership Issues

The essential characteristic of a support group is that its members come together because they share some *similar life experience* which is causing them
difficulty. The more similar the shared experience, the more useful the group
for the members and the easier the job of facilitation. Members wish to attend
support groups because they have experienced something that is out of the
ordinary, out of sync, beyond their understanding. They come as generally
well-functioning individuals who face a life crisis. They seldom are people who
have found need of therapy to cope with life's struggles; they can usually be
seen as "together" people. However, their normal support systems and their
coping abilities are seriously taxed by the SIDS death. This situation—plus a
need for information to really understand what happened—brings people to a
support group. Issues such as age, educational level, or even intellectual ability, are much less important than the shared experience.

Criteria for membership in a therapy group may be very different. A careful
screening process occurs with consideration of issues such as ego strength,
internal conflict areas, and motivation for change (Yalom, 1975). Therapy assumes that people enter the group because there is a deficit in some aspect of
their psychological make-up and/or the existence of some interpersonal pathology. A psychiatric diagnosis recognizing some maladaptation is a prerequisite in many therapy groups, but may be a cause for concern and a potential
reason for referral out of a support group. Members of therapy groups highly
desire personal change in some aspect of themselves. Broadly speaking, the
work of a therapy group focuses on the internal composition of members and
their relationships to others in the group.

A second issue is the group's shared view of expertise. A therapy group
assumes that the therapist has knowledge and skills that group members do
not possess. The therapist is given (or takes) the responsibility of evaluating
the work of each member in the group based on some goals mutually agreed
upon with the members individually. The therapist has an "expert" role which
sets him or her above the members. In a SIDS group, members themselves are
the experts on the content, feelings, and issues of coping with loss. They share
gifts of experience, knowledge, and understanding with the group. The leader
contributes expertise on group process and facilitation skills. But the professional leader and the group members must work together as an equal team
with shared responsibility for the group and its achievements.

Any professional working with a mutual-help support group must have a
deep respect for the knowledge and expertise of the members. Members themselves are the givers of support to one another. Members can relax about issues of group process, trusting in the skills of the professional. It is not a
hierarchical system in the way a therapy group inherently is.

A final membership issue is that support group members are encouraged to become involved with each other outside the group. Members often find other bereaved parents are the ones they turn to between meetings for support and encouragement. The professional staff person is available for crisis intervention, but opportunities for support from members continue beyond meeting time. Out-of-group socializing is generally discouraged in therapy settings and seen as counterproductive to the process of therapy.

Focus of Meetings

Major differences in focus exist between support groups and therapy groups. Support groups deal with issues that members bring to the group. A topic of discussion may have been decided on by the members in advance or as the meeting progresses. Members know they may choose to participate and share as they wish. Only that which individuals wish to share is expected. A sense of gentleness and a respect for each person permeates the group as each takes responsibility for sharing. No one searches for hidden meanings. By contrast, in therapy groups much more emphasis is put on finding the underlying causes and interpretations of issues. Work focuses on the underlying implications of statements, the covert as well as the overt messages, and the emphasis is on the actual interactions of members during group meetings.

Many support groups have a rule regarding advice giving: it is discouraged. The group's task is to explore situations and to talk about problems. No pressure exists to *solve* problems. Members are encouraged to share their ways of handling situations without "telling" others what they should do. It is assumed that members can and will make good choices when they feel ready. Conversely, giving and seeking of advice is a characteristic activity in therapy groups, which attempt as a whole to provide practical solutions to members' problems (Yalom, 1975). Therapy groups also place great emphasis on analysis of behavior and on finding blocks to implementing change.

Conflict and the resolution of intra-group conflict are primary areas of work in traditional psychotherapy groups. It is assumed that people enter these groups because of some unresolved and/or unmanageable interpersonal conflict in their lives. Consequently, confrontation and movement toward insight and interpersonal conflict resolution are goals for many clients seeking therapy. Almost the opposite scenario would describe a SIDS support group. When participating in the group, members feel a deep sense of respect and acceptance from others. Members are encouraged to accept that they are grieving as they need to and to learn to be more patient and gentle with themselves. Rather than pushing toward change, the SIDS support group moves toward acceptance and patience about the personal grief of its members. Each person is encouraged to do what he or she needs to do to cope with the impact of loss. There is respect for a variety of different solutions.

PROCESSES OF GRIEF AND MOURNING IN THE GROUP

Most of the actual content of a support group meeting focuses on issues about grief and mourning. Profoundly hurting people come for understanding about SIDS and for assistance through the maze of feelings and problems brought on by their sudden loss. Sherman (1979) noted that bereaved parents often have problems in the areas of: (1) personal adjustment; (2) family relationships; and (3) social reintegration, specifically in dealing with others in their environment who are not willing or able to communicate about the loss. It is clear that the total life of each bereaved person is affected by the loss. Support groups enable members to gain some mastery over affected aspects of their lives by assisting them to understand and accept their own grief.

There are many theories about processes of grief and mourning. One that has been most useful to members and leaders of SIDS support groups is Worden's "tasks of mourning" (1982). These tasks clearly reflect the work done by group members. Worden's theory is particularly helpful because SIDS survivors deal with some significantly different issues depending upon which of the tasks they are addressing. The tasks also serve as a useful way for determining what issues might be of relevance for discussion in the group. As Worden (1982, p. 10) has said: "It is essential that the grieving person accomplish these tasks before mourning can be completed. Incompleted grief tasks can impair further growth and development. Although the tasks do not necessarily follow a specific order, there is some ordering suggested in the definitions." After a brief overview of Worden's theory, topics that commonly arise in SIDS groups will be reviewed. The point is not to give details on each of these topics, but to convey a sense of the types of topics discussed and a feeling as to how topics change as individuals complete specific tasks of mourning.

Four Tasks of Mourning

1. *To Accept the Reality of the Loss.* After a death, there often is a period of denial. Statements such as, "This can't be happening to me," and "I don't believe it," are common. Parents may hear their dead baby crying or may buy diapers at the store. They are not able to let in the reality all at one time. They just want their baby back at all costs. For some, intense searching for their child is present (Parkes, 1970). For SIDS survivors, this searching is evident in their quest for answers and their need to identify the cause of their baby's death. If there is no clear diagnosis of SIDS immediately, the search must continue until a cause of death is confirmed. Once the cause is certain, the search switches to understanding SIDS and how it happens. Issues of responsibility and what could have been done to save the child are prominent throughout this quest. In fact, of course, nothing could have been done; survivors need to hear this over and over again. They also need *facts* about SIDS to back up their emotional questioning.

2. *To Experience the Pain of Grief.* Families that have a SIDS death are dealing with pain from the instant the child is found dead. Pain is ever present for most people while they are accepting the reality of the loss. But when the reality is fully accepted, the pain moves in on a new level, in a different way.

The Minnesota SIDS Center offers two SIDS support groups. One, the New Parent Group, meets twice monthly. The majority of those who attend are parents, although there are a few grandparents, relatives, and day care providers. Most of these people first attend the group within one month after the death, with some coming during the first week. Therefore, all are working on issues of accepting the loss.

At some point, which is wholly determined by individual members themselves, people move to the Ongoing Support Group which meets monthly. There are reasons commonly given for the change, reflecting a change in the subjective experience of members. For example, parents state: "The New Parent Group deals a lot with details of death, funerals, and immediate events. As you get further along in the grief cycle, new issues such as subsequent children come up." Or: "I got depressed hearing about people finding their dead babies. I realized I had to get beyond that."

From a theoretical standpoint, what has happened is that those in the Ongoing Support Group have moved more fully into the second task of mourning. Once they have accepted the reality of their baby's death, they no longer feel helped by hearing "dead baby stories." One mother described this change in her feelings in the following way:

> I really felt the pain fully after we had the headstone in place. There was nothing in the world I could do for my son ever again. He was totally dead. At the same time, the cards and phone calls stopped. I felt completely alone in my loss, so I relied even more on the group and friends made there. They were the only ones who understood.

Society encourages people to move away from pain; yet, to do so results in complicated bereavement. So, group members encourage each other to face the pain head on and to trust that it will end. Long-time members for whom the pain has subsided greatly facilitate this work in the group.

3. *To Adjust to an Environment in Which the Deceased is Missing.* Each large loss is made up of many small losses. For bereaved parents, each realization of their losses moves them closer to resolution of their grief. SIDS survivors face issues such as: never seeing their child learn to walk; never hearing the child talk; always having an empty space in their family. (This last is particularly difficult for parents whose only child has died. They are still parents, yet they have no one to parent.) Eventually, through facing each of these issues, members gain a sense of mastery. They come to be able to think about each of these issues without *intense* pain. There may still be some pain, but as it diminishes, they move on to the final task.

4. *To Withdraw Emotional Energy and Reinvest It in Another Relationship.* This can be a difficult task for parents to complete. Often, "moving on" is equated with "forgetting," but parents never want to forget their baby. Yet, they need and are ready to move on from the pain. This task often works itself out for SIDS parents as they find a way for the child to live on in their lives. It is common for parents to do some of this work of making meaning of their child's life by giving back to a SIDS program. Rather than be a group participant, they become outreach volunteers, fund raisers, speakers, and group leaders.

Group Topics

Any of the common and possible topics for group discussion could occur at any time in coping with grief. However, there are familiar themes when parents are completing the four tasks of mourning. Presentation of these topics is divided into three sections. The "New Parent Issues" are generally dealt with while working to accept the reality of the loss and when the members begin to feel the full pain of the loss. When the pain is fully felt and people are coping with adjusting to the world without their baby, the "Later Issues" are more common. Finally, there are "Ongoing Issues" that may arise at any time and are often dealt with repeatedly throughout the healing process.

New Parent Issues

- Telling the story of finding their dead baby needs to occur over and over. Details of each story are repeatedly recounted, as are interactions with police, the coroner, day care staff, and family.
- Families talk about the funeral, picking a cemetery plot, and decisions about cremation versus burial. They share cards and memorials they received. They also talk about those people who did not send cards or acknowledge their loss.

- There are repeated expressions of shock, along with questions about why this death happened to me and why my baby is dead. Many express anger at God, the doctors, hospital staff, etc.
- A major part of the work for new parents is searching for the cause of death. "Finding a cause is seen as a way of protecting against such trauma in the future, of gaining some control to negate the powerlessness that is otherwise felt" (Raphael, 1983, p. 256).
- Talking about guilt and the inability to save their baby from death is a prominent factor in SIDS bereavement. Clear, factual information helps eventually to relieve the guilt.
- There is sharing of concerns and practical ideas regarding what to do about such things as the baby's clothes, toys, crib, and pictures. Often pictures of babies are shared for group members to see.
- Parents share stories of their visits to the cemetery and discuss their decisions about headstones. Because the headstone is a final acknowledgement of the death, it is a very difficult issue for most parents. They often express a strong sense of relief when decisions regarding the headstone are made and it is in place.
- Recurring discussion occurs regarding how to handle situations such as encountering an old friend who does not know of the death, or what to do when you start crying at work.

Later Issues

- People have a need to discuss coping tactics and making plans for birthdays, holidays, and death anniversaries. They often share ideas and things that helped them through similar events. A long discussion can be involved in holiday plans. Some of the issues are: "Do I put my baby's name on the Christmas cards—he *is* still part of our family?"; "Do I hang up her Christmas stocking?"; "Other family members won't mention my child when we're together for the holidays—should I bring her name up?"
- It is difficult when the cards and phone calls have stopped. Many expect the grief of survivors to subside in four to six months, yet that is often the time when people are most intensely feeling the pain of the loss. Members share their need to get support for a long time and their ways of finding support. Parents who experience the death of a child do not feel their pre-death level of happiness for about three years (DeFrain, Taylor, & Earnst, 1982). Support needs continue for much longer than most support systems can respond.
- A major topic for parents who stay in the group past their initial grief has to do with having subsequent children. They ask: "Are we ready to have another child?" "Are we just trying to escape from the pain?" "Should we put the new child on an apnea monitor?" "Will this baby live?"

- When parents do have subsequent pregnancies, there are surprises for them which they share with others. Particularly, many have intense feelings of grief as they relive the pregnancy, birth, and early months of the baby who died. Each new phase of the pregnancy brings up grief issues. They feel very attached to their new baby, yet sad about what they do not have. The most difficult of these feelings often subside when the subsequent child passes the age of the one who died.

Ongoing Issues.

- Throughout membership in the group, participants seek understanding about normal processes of grief and mourning, and match that information with their own personal experiences.
- Many members have surviving children and want to learn how to help them.
- There are discussions about how to respond when someone asks how many children you have.
- There is an on-going (probably life-long) search for meaning that is shared by group members.
- At times, people share the effects of this loss on relationships, especially their marriage. There appears to be a high rate of marital problems following the death of a child. Many couples face difficulties and are concerned with different ways in which men and women grieve.

Each bereavement program has a unique character and set of situations. Some may deal with this entire range of topics; some may focus only on a few of them. Topics generally arise from within the group with little guidance from the leaders. Participants more often than not know just what they need to talk about. If there is an open, caring, respectful feeling in the group, any discussion topic is acceptable.

ISSUES IN DEVELOPING A SUPPORT GROUP

The primary issues to consider when developing a support group concern what will be most helpful in creating an atmosphere in which members feel safe to share. There are other factors to consider, too, especially those involving the level of resources, both human and financial, that is available to the group. Even with very limited resources, a support group can still provide a place for people to open up and to move through their grief. Once the general group development issues have been decided, attention needs to be paid to the format of individual meetings.

Support Group Safety Issues

SIDS parents and family members have experienced horrible trauma and pain prior to coming to the group. Pain is what brings them to the group. Often they may say, "I came to see if I could find a way out of my pain." They come to the group already deeply hurt, and have a strong need for a gentle and safe environment. People who attend SIDS support groups differ somewhat from first-time attenders at other types of support groups. They have seldom spent a great deal of time deciding whether or not they need the group, whether or not the group might be of help to them. Rather, in the midst of their recent loss, they come trustingly, groping for anything offering a promise of help with their pain. Also, many participants have little other support group experience; hence, they are very openminded to this experience.

Ground Rules and Group Norms

People in great pain are very vulnerable. Such people often feel safer if they have a good idea of what is expected of them and what the rules are. When these ground rules are clearly laid out, it is easier for members to relax and gain optimum benefit from the group.

Ground Rules

Explicit ground rules govern the operation of a group. They can be given to the group verbally at the start of meetings and/or can be available on a handout for members. Generally, a combination of verbal and written rules works best. For example, at the start of a meeting, the leader might mention a few of the most important rules (such as confidentiality and the right to pass) and then give a list of the rules to new members.

Aside from creating a safe environment, ground rules serve to assist leaders in directing the group interaction. If a group meeting is dominated by one or two members, the rule about allowing time for each member to share can be brought up. This reminder may be all that is needed to assist members in sharing time more equitably.

If a new group is forming, the members themselves, with some guidance from the leaders, may decide which rules to adopt. Among those of value are:

- Confidentiality and respect for the privacy of others. What people say in the group stays in the group.
- Non-judgmentalness and acceptance of others' feelings. Feelings are neither right nor wrong.

- Only one conversation occurs in the group at a time. The energy in a group comes in part because everyone's attention is focused on the one person speaking. Side conversations disrupt this energy.
- No advice giving. It is much more helpful to share with others examples of what things have worked than it is to "tell" others what to do.
- People have the right to pass, that is, to be silent during the group if they choose.
- Time should be shared among members, with an opportunity given for each person to speak.
- Each person is expected to speak for themselves, not for others.
- Members are to listen carefully and respectfully to others.

It is important to adopt rules that fit the particular circumstances of the group. For example, in a short-term group a rule about making a commitment to come to all meetings might be adopted.

Group Norms

Group norms are the unwritten rules of the group. These need to be on a conscious level for the group leaders, but generally are passed on by actions to the group members. If one thinks about the family in which one grew up, it is generally easy to identify a few rules that were never talked about but everyone knew. (Some examples are: Mom is really the boss; don't change TV channels during a football game; if you need money, talk to Dad.)

Group norms can be developed which make the group a caring, respectful place. When these norms have been initially instilled by leaders, the energy of the group carries them on. Because of the way that group norms develop a "life of their own," attention must be paid to their development. Examples of group norms and their implementation or modeling are:

- Each member is valuable. (A call or note can be sent to someone who has missed meetings; a warm welcome is offered to each person upon arrival.)
- The group is a safe place to share thoughts and feelings. (Vigorous intervention by leaders occurs if one person puts down another.)
- The group is self-monitoring. (One decides how well the group is doing primarily by how well the members are getting their needs met.)
- There is respect for each person's unique experience. (No value judgments are allowed; there are no right or wrong ways to grieve.)
- All members are equal. (Time for each person is assured; no one is allowed to dominate a meeting.)
- Members' time is valuable. (Meetings start and end on time.)
- Members are the source of help to other members. (Leaders do not take a hierarchical stance; members are regarded as the experts on grief.)

Designing a Support Group

Ground rules and group norms are the underlying structure upon which a group is built. In addition, some specific design factors need to be considered. Most often for SIDS support groups, these design factors depend upon available resources and demographics. Almost any combination of these factors can work to provide help for SIDS families.

Time-Limited vs. Ongoing

A time-limited group is set up to meet for a specific number of times, with a set beginning and end. Generally, members enter into the group together and end at the same time. Ongoing groups meet at a regular time; monthly, bimonthly, or weekly. Both new and older members are present at each meeting of an ongoing group. The advantage to a time-limited group is that there is a clear amount of leadership time and financial resources devoted to the group. Both members and the group leader make commitments for a set amount of time. By contrast, ongoing groups require an open-ended commitment of time and resources. Advertising the group, notification of meetings, and planning must be continuous. The positive aspect of an ongoing group is that grief lasts a long time, so the group can be available to people as long as they need it.

Open vs. Closed Membership

Open membership means people may enter the group at any time. Some groups request people to come three or four times before deciding if the group fits for them, but there is generally no specific time commitment required of members. In a closed group everyone starts and ends together. No members are added after the first or second week, and each member makes a commitment to attend all meetings. Usually, open membership fits most easily with ongoing groups and closed membership is used for time-limited groups.

General Bereavement vs. Specifically SIDS

In a large metropolitan area, the number of SIDS deaths will be great enough to permit a group devoted specifically to survivors of SIDS. A medium-sized community might have enough childhood deaths to have members for a parental bereavement group, but not exclusively for SIDS. Less populated areas might support a general grief group with no specific populations in mind.

A grief group of any kind is better than no grief group. If one can choose, however, the more similar the shared experiences of members, the more helpful is the group. (And the easier it is to facilitate!) An elderly widow and a SIDS parent have only a few similarities, such as, they both face the tasks of mourning and must learn to make adjustments in their lives. However, the adjustments they must make are very different. In a general group, the main focus will be on processes of grief and mourning. Education about SIDS may need to be made available to parents separately from the formal group time.

Group Formats

Finally, one should consider the format of the group. Some general pattern or format is helpful for leaders and works to create a safe environment. If everyone has some idea of what will happen in the group, even though there is minimal structure, anxiety will be relieved. Formats depend upon issues about group content and issues regarding group opening and closing rituals.

Group Content

Some groups have formal content input at each meeting and then provide open discussion time. This is generally done in time-limited groups where leaders feel a need to introduce as much content as possible in a short period of time. In this way, leaders can be certain they will cover important information and outside experts can be used to share their knowledge. For less experienced leaders, having a set focus for each meeting is helpful. Drawbacks to having presentations at each meeting are that it can be more difficult for members to attach in a warm way to the group and to each other when much of the focus of the meeting is on information-gathering and not on the members. Also, this can set up a hierarchical model that goes against support group development because the leader is put into the role of expert. Finally, if members come to the group each week in a "listener" mode, it may be difficult to move them to a "sharer" mode. Sometimes a presentation can bring deep discussion, but that is uncommon unless the members have a history of sharing personal thoughts and feelings prior to hearing the presentations.

At the other end of this continuum are groups with no content structure. These groups have no topical input; they deal at each meeting with whatever members bring to the group. All the group time is open for members to share their experiences and feelings with one another. The group leader simply facilitates the process. This style works well for developing a sense of community among participants. While this time to talk and share is very important, some content is very helpful to SIDS survivors.

The format used by the Minnesota SIDS Center groups combines the two preceding models. Primary emphasis is on the open discussion model, with most group meeting time mainly used for sharing. Out of this sharing come expressions of need for information. If that information is immediately available, it is provided by the professional leader at that time or during a subsequent meeting. For example, information about SIDS and grief is offered during many of the meetings. Also, each year the SIDS Center medical director is brought in for a comprehensive update on SIDS research. If a presentation is needed, it is scheduled for a future meeting and notices are sent out. Thus, topics arise from the group and occasional presentations simply add to the richness of the group, while the major emphasis remains on personal interactions.

Opening and Closing Customs

Having a clear beginning and end to meetings is important. Exactly what the opening and closing rituals are matters less than the fact that they exist. Some groups call these their "check-in" and "check-out" times. The purpose of a check-in is to acknowledge the start of the group and to get each member fully present. It provides time to welcome people to the group, to go over some group rules, and then to hear at least an introduction from each person. Usually members give their name and some information about their baby and the death. In addition to this basic information, an open-ended question can be added to arrive at some sense of how members are doing and what some major issues might be. This also allows leaders and members to know if someone is having a particularly difficult time. If there is a presentation, the check-in can occur either before or after the presentation.

It is also good to have a tradition about how the group ends its meetings as a way to give members a chance to finish up their time in the group and begin to disengage. There are a number of ways a group can end. Some groups have each member say how the meeting was for them. A group leader can summarize some of the themes that were talked about during the meeting and mention some topics that need to be discussed further. Announcements and information about following events can also be given. The leader or a member can read something that has been found helpful. There is no single right way, but it is important for the formal meeting time to come to a distinct end. After the formal portion of the meeting, it is common for members to sit and talk for a long time. Encourage this, since it is a vital part of building informal support networks among members.

LEADERSHIP OF SUPPORT GROUPS

"Mutual help . . . stresses experiential knowledge" (Silverman, 1980, p. 21). The members of a SIDS support group are the experts in the SIDS experience. Newly-bereaved parents are usually "looking for comfort, support, and advice" (Lieberman, 1979b, p. 119). While they have a great deal to offer each other, the amount of energy they have and their ability to focus on others is often quite limited. Because of this, the leadership functions in a SIDS parent group cannot follow a pure self-help model. Professionals take on many of the leadership tasks while allowing the group to form its own "distinctive culture" (Klass & Shinners, 1983, p. 363). As group participants move along in their grief process, they may wish to become involved in group leadership (Klass, 1988). These participant leaders provide an excellent link from professional to group members.

Professional Leadership and Roles

A mental health professional working with a mutual-help support group can fill a number of essential roles. The generally accepted view is that "the professional always works at the direction of the group, and all the professional's activities are subordinate to the group's own process" (Klass & Shinners, 1983, p. 366). In other words, the professional fosters and maintains a supportive environment, while the participants are the actual support givers. Professional roles in support group leadership might include:

Helping to Develop New Groups

Often an organization or agency providing services of any kind to bereaved parents may recognize the need for a support group. There may be a cluster of families with similar loss experiences who could benefit from the knowledge and support of others, or the families themselves may request such a group. Professionals may help with organizational or logistical issues, or show how to address emotional topics.

Acting as an Intermediary Between the Group and the Professional Community

SIDS professional staff are generally notified soon after a death. The ongoing contacts that they maintain with such agencies as police, emergency room personnel, and coroners' offices make it easy for new SIDS families to get information about the availability of SIDS groups. Also, contacts between SIDS leadership and community mental health professionals, such as clergy, counselors, and physicians, allow the group to be presented to community professionals and mutual referrals are made as needed.

Facilitating the Group Process

As mentioned above, any professional working with a support group must have a clear understanding of group processes and a belief in the value of mutual help. Professionals do not take over support groups; rather their role is to provide expertise on group processes so that members are freed to focus on content.

Serving as a Resource Person

Ideally, professional leaders will have knowledge which will assist group members in some content areas. In addition to this expertise, leaders can help the group identify areas of knowledge which they wish to acquire and then find appropriate community resources.

Acting as a Referral Source

There is disagreement in self-help literature on the role of the professional in making referrals (Klass & Shinners, 1983; Silverman, 1980). Personal experience has shown that there is a need to make referrals occasionally. The following are instances in which a referral might be necessary:

1. Assisting a group member experiencing multiple stresses to find help outside the SIDS group. Support group meetings are focused on a single topic. Therefore, a person needing help with an unemployment situation or a marital problem, for example, will not be able to find it within the SIDS group. If requested by the member, a referral to appropriate services should be made.

2. People who are using alcohol or other nonprescription drugs to block their pain cannot be helped by a grief support group until the drug problem is dealt with. A referral away from the SIDS group is essential. Returning to the group when drugfree is encouraged.

3. A person determined by the professional to be mentally ill may not be able to benefit from the group. Also, the individual may be so disruptive that the group does not function while he or she is present. Fortunately, this is a very rare occurrence, but the presence of a psychotic person, for example, would be unmanageable for most support groups. A referral is needed to meet the individual's needs and to keep the group functioning well. In addition, any member showing suicidal tendencies must be referred to appropriate resources when this situation arises (Hatton & Valente, 1984).

4. Since newly-bereaved parents often want and need very specific information about their child's death, referrals to a pathologist or pediatrician knowledgeable about SIDS are common and appropriate. Parents can discuss the autopsy report with such a physician. This physician must be selected with particular attention to his or her ability to relate to the emotional and intellectual needs of SIDS survivors.

Participant Leaders

A participant leader (sometimes called a parent or lay leader) is a former member of a support group who has had some group leadership training. This person would work with the professional leader in group facilitation. For members who no longer need the group for their own grief issues, co-leading the group can be very meaningful. Thus, the Minnesota SIDS Center has parents who are three to seven years beyond the death of their child co-leading a group. Participant leaders find that they can give back to the group in this way some of the energy and help which they received from it.

The primary gift from participant leaders to the group is hope—they personify hope to newly bereaved members. Participant leaders also have a wealth of personal experience which they can share. In fact, when a discussion is lagging or when a group seems to be having a hard time moving to a deeper level of understanding, a participant leader can be invaluable. A comment, such as "My wife and I felt very distant and isolated from each other after our son died," can quickly move the group to discussion. If a question probing that feeling was asked by the professional leader, members might feel it was intrusive. But given as a personal experience, it is heard.

Some training is necessary for participant leaders prior to assuming leadership responsibilities. The Minnesota SIDS Center has recently developed a training program consisting of three sessions of three hours each plus ongoing training and supervision. This training emphasizes: (1) general listening skills; (2) understanding normal feelings of grief and tasks of mourning; (3) support group theory and the leader's role in the group; and (4) personal self-care needs. Because participant leaders have extensive group experience, the focus is mainly on their new role in the group. It is important for participant leaders to have regular group processing time with a professional (perhaps after each meeting) and to get feedback about how they are doing. This role meets some altruistic needs of former participants while helping both the group and the professional leader. A team of professional and participant leaders is ideal for a SIDS support group.

Self Care for Group Leaders

Work with the bereaved is interesting and challenging. Providing assistance to bereaved parents offers particular challenges because a person's sense of order and safety inevitably gets shaken. We each want to believe that horrible things such as SIDS happen in other communities, to other people. But as we work with a SIDS parent group, as professionals we cannot keep our own denial of death at bay (Yalom, 1980). It is no longer "they" to whom death happens, but now "we." The group has strong feelings of "we-ness," as opposed to the rest of society which has not experienced such a death (Lieberman, 1979a). It would be difficult for professionals to do this work well without being personally affected and changed. Even while maintaining a professional stance, we repeatedly face our own death issues.

It is therefore essential that professionals working with grief issues should take care of themselves. Each individual must develop the skills to identify his or her own needs and to evaluate the particular stressors being experienced. There must be a support system available to assist in coping with the grief-specific aspects of this work. In a sort of never-ending cycle of support, group leaders must themselves also get regular support.

Two particular aspects of support needs exist for the grief professional: supervision and limit setting. Because group participants are very needy and vulnerable, leaders may want to meet needs which are beyond the scope of the group and outside the leader's area of expertise. Good supervision can assist a leader to: determine appropriate limits to set; monitor involvement with the group; identify vulnerable personal areas; and obtain regular support.

The actual work of assisting the bereaved is not inherently stressful (Vachon, 1987). The major stressors are organizational and environmental. Role ambiguity, not knowing clearly what is expected, is far more stressful than the actual work. Clear goals for the group and the leader, plus organizational support, make the work of leading grief support groups manageable and reduce staff burnout. With adequate self care, SIDS support group leadership provides important opportunities for professional and personal growth.

REFERENCES

Antze, P. (1979). Role of ideologies in peer psychotherapy groups. In M. A. Lieberman, L. D. Borman, & Associates (Eds.), *Self-help groups for coping with crisis: Origins, members, processes, and impact* (pp. 272–304). San Francisco: Jossey-Bass.
Bordow, J. (1982). *The ultimate loss: Coping with the death of a child.* New York: Beaufort Press.
Bowlby, J. (1980). *Loss, sadness, and depression,* Vol. III in *Attachment and loss.* New York: Basic Books.
DeFrain, J., Taylor, J., & Ernst, L. (1982). *Coping with sudden infant death.* Lexington, MA: Lexington Books.
Hatton, C. L., & Valente, S. M. (1984). *Suicide: Assessment and intervention* (2nd ed.). Norwalk, CT: Appleton-Century-Crofts.
Klass, D. (1988). *Parental grief: Solace and resolution.* New York: Springer Publishing Co.
Klass, D., & Shinners, B. (1983). Professional roles in a self-help group for the bereaved. *Omega, 13,* 361–375.
Lieberman, M. A. (1979a). Analyzing change mechanisms in groups. In M. A. Lieberman, L. D. Borman, & Associates (Eds.), *Self-help groups for coping with crisis: Origins, members, processes, and impact* (pp. 194–233). San Francisco: Jossey-Bass.
Lieberman, M. A. (1979b). Help seeking and self-help groups. In M. A. Lieberman, L. D. Borman, & Associates (Eds.), *Self-help groups for coping with crisis: Origins, members, processes, and impact* (pp. 116–149). San Francisco: Jossey-Bass.
Mueller, D. P. (1980). Social networks: A promising direction for research on the relationship of the social environment to psychiatric disorder. *Social Science and Medicine, 14A,* 147–161.
Parkes, C. M. (1970). "Seeking" and "finding" a lost object: Evidence from recent studies of reaction to bereavement. *Social Science and Medicine, 4,* 187–201.
Raphael, B. (1983). *The anatomy of bereavement.* New York: Basic Books.

Sarnoff-Schiff, H. (1986). *Living through mourning: Finding comfort and hope when a loved one has died.* New York: Viking-Penguin.

Sherman, B. (1979). Emergence of ideology in a bereaved parents group. In M. A. Lieberman, L. D. Borman, & Associates (Eds.), *Self-help groups for coping with crisis: Origins, members, processes, and impact* (pp. 305–322). San Francisco: Jossey-Bass.

Silverman, P. R. (1978). *Mutual help groups: A guide for mental health workers.* Rockville, MD: National Institute of Mental Health.

Silverman, P. R. (1980). *Mutual help groups: Organization and development.* Beverly Hills, CA: Sage.

Vachon, M. L. S. (1987). *Occupational stress in the care of the critically ill, the dying, and the bereaved.* New York: Hemisphere.

Wasserman, H., & Danforth, H. E. (1988). *The human bond: Support groups and mutual aid.* New York: Springer Publishing Co.

Worden, J. W. (1982). *Grief counseling and grief therapy: A handbook for the mental health practitioner.* New York: Springer Publishing Co.

Yalom, I. (1975). *Theory and practice of group psychotherapy.* New York: Basic Books.

Yalom, I. (1980). *Existential psychotherapy.* New York: Basic Books.

CHAPTER 11

Advocacy and Networking

Carol Ann Barnickol, Helen Fuller, and
Connie Cunningham

$\mathbf{A}$ny helping effort, professional or voluntary, is necessarily defined by the cause served and the inherent needs of the client population. In the case of Sudden Infant Death Syndrome (SIDS), the unique characteristics of the experience have influenced the service systems which have evolved to assist those who are affected. Thus, the sudden and as yet unexplainable nature of SIDS, in conjunction with the vulnerability inherent in the process of coping with any death experience, make this a prime situation for the application of *advocacy* principles. It is apparent that families, professionals, and volunteers affected by SIDS are all potential beneficiaries of advocacy, as well as potential advocates themselves.

Further, a SIDS death occurs unexpectedly, in the home or with a child care provider. Thus, it involves emergency responders, such as police, fire, ambulance, and hospital emergency department staffs. Any death requires the services of a funeral director, and the sudden nature of the SIDS death makes it the province of medical examiners, coroners, and pathologists, as well. Physicians and nurses may have been involved in well baby care and often continue to provide pediatric treatment for other children in the family. Members of the clergy are important to many families. In addition to this list of professionals, a vast number of extended family members, friends, neighbors, co-workers, and acquaintances are affected by the sudden, unexpected, and unexplained nature of the death, as well as the far-reaching ramifications of *infant* death. In this context, it is easy to understand why a *network* approach, involving both formal and informal systems of support, has evolved as not only the most effective helping format for SIDS services, but the only practical approach.

SIDS service systems in the United States had their origin in the early 1960s in the advocacy efforts of many parents who had suffered the loss of a baby to SIDS. They understood through their grief—which was frequently compounded by uninformed mistreatment—that there was a critical need for consistent information and support for families who experience a SIDS death. In addition, services which have been designed and implemented in the intervening years have gone beyond advocacy to capitalize upon methods of formal and informal networking to meet the needs of both families and professionals. This chapter discusses advocacy and networking as they are related to SIDS, utilizing in each case a brief sketch of theory to illuminate practical applications. Throughout, it is important to recognize that advocacy and networking efforts intertwine. In principle, therefore, either could precede the other; in this chapter, however, we begin with advocacy and then turn to networking.

ADVOCACY

Advocacy has many faces. Every action taken in behalf of a cause is an advocate action. In the United States, early social workers, such as Jane Addams and her colleagues in the settlement houses, pioneered actions to achieve better lives for families. Accordingly, Briar (1967, p. 28) suggested that an advocate is "his client's supporter, his adviser, his champion and, if need be, his representative in his dealings with the court, the police, the social agency, and other organizations that affect his well-being." Brager (1968, pp. 12–13) conceptualized advocates as having relationships to three systems: (1) *client*, defined as "those whose interests are served—those who benefit from the worker's activity"; (2) *action*, defined as "those who are engaged in the planned action"; and (3) *target*, defined as "groups, programs, or institutions that are strategic to the change attempts and that need to be modified if the objective of the process is to be attained." Advocates facilitate and guide interactions among persons or mediate between persons and institutions. Thus, advocacy may be found in any interaction in which a client's interest is opposed by some other person or institution.

Briar (1967, 1968) emphasized that the advocate has a choice between direct intercession and mobilization of clients on their own behalf. Regardless of the type of advocacy in which a practitioner engages, knowledge of the relevant service delivery system, institutional dynamics, and institutional change strategies is crucial.

ADVOCACY FOR SIDS

As stated at the outset of this chapter, the cause of SIDS had its birth in the advocacy efforts of those parents who undertook to sensitize others to the needs of SIDS families, and to the equally critical need for ongoing, dedicated research efforts to solve the mystery of SIDS. Nearly three decades after these beginnings, we are at a point where many of the needs of families are being met, to a greater or lesser degree, in various parts of the United States and in many other countries around the world. Research continues, providing us with greater understanding of what is normal and abnormal about the period of infancy, but cannot as yet offer predictive or preventive measures.

Those who have been involved in furthering the cause of SIDS year after year realize all too well that we have made no more than a credible start. Our efforts might be described as having grown from their "infancy" into "childhood" or "adolescence." This has occurred even though national leadership in the United States and in other countries has been fragmented, roles and goals have been unclear, and funding has been limited for both family services and research. In renewed advocacy lies the potential coming of age or maturation of the SIDS movement which has as its goal the eradication of the need for all the services which we have worked to provide.

Those Who are Served by Advocacy

In any discussion of advocacy, the fundamental unit of concern is always the affected person or family. The SIDS organization becomes the central focal point for individuals, families, professionals, and the community working together toward a resolution of the multifaceted problem of SIDS. A circular or synergistic effect develops in which network and family members evolve into advocates for all those affected by SIDS, and likewise help such people advocate for themselves.

The nature of SIDS involves the family immediately with the medical-legal system. When the system works effectively, a family receives consistent information and support from each member with whom they come into contact. In situations where some part of the system fails to provide this help, the SIDS organization may have to intervene on behalf of the family. This may mean providing information to police officers or child protective workers who lack the experience and knowledge to offer needed help to a family. In some cases, this lack of understanding leads to accusations of abuse or neglect. Advocacy efforts may mean the difference between eventual resolution of a family's grief and life-long self-blame in such situations.

Assistance may be needed by families in obtaining an autopsy, receiving the correct diagnosis of the cause of death, or arranging for review of the autopsy if desired. Families who have not yet finished paying for the birth expenses may find themselves faced with paying the cost of funeral and burial, hospital emergency department, or ambulance fees. Advocacy regarding the payment of these costs may be needed. Likewise, an advocate may be needed to help the family make funeral arrangements or find financial assistance, adequate housing, help for surviving children, medical assistance, or other basic necessities.

In some cities, the homeless represent a population requiring special services. One SIDS organization has established a new and almost invisible system to meet the need. A funeral director whose establishment normally provides services to the affluent quietly takes care of the burial in cases where there are no financial resources. The same funeral home administers the cemetery plot that was donated to the SIDS organization. A small emergency fund for funerals is nothing new; scrounging support for an entire burial requires a more creative advocacy approach.

Within the service area of any SIDS program, there will be cultural and geographic factors which impact on the ways in which help is needed, offered, or accepted. These factors can range from burial customs, to acceptable funeral services, to ways of grieving for a loved one. It is not uncommon in certain areas for families to bury their infants in the backyard or on their farmland. The custom in some families is to take photographs of the deceased in the casket. Cremation is occasionally preferred, especially by some military families who move frequently. Families have driven their own infants long distances to reach burial sites far removed from their places of residence. Cultural heritage may influence the ways in which a person's grief is expressed, or sometimes held quietly and painfully in one's own heart. Urban and rural factors also influence a person's ways of coping, and may sometimes eclipse cultural characteristics. Anyone in a helping role must make himself or herself aware of the impact of such differing ways of dealing with death. Lack of this knowledge may impede our judgment, the accuracy of our observation, and thus our ability to be effective advocates or caregivers.

Those Who are Engaged in Advocacy

Advocacy efforts can at times be necessary on behalf of professionals, as well as families. Perhaps the greatest service we can provide is the recognition of how devastating this tragic situation is, not only for families, but also for the professionals who have to deal with it. The SIDS organization can often advocate with administrators on behalf of their staff members, in order to make sure they are aware of the difficult nature of this work. For example, an audiovisual developed by the Minnesota SIDS program for EMT personnel has incorporated as part of its basic instructions for dealing with a possible SIDS case the following suggestions for "after care": strenuous exercise, a nutritious diet, and talking about the call ("A Critical Call," 1988).

Those who work regularly with SIDS may almost become immune over time, or perhaps take the devastating nature of this experience as the norm. We are unlikely ever to be unaware of the overwhelming impact of SIDS on families.

However, we must always remind ourselves of the profound effect it has on other professionals, volunteers, and the community at large. It is important to help professionals acknowledge the personal effect which SIDS has on them, and their need to support each other. Some emergency departments have wisely built "staff debriefing" into the routine of their system after a death.

Our advocacy efforts for the needs of the professionals who work with families must extend beyond provision of accurate, up-to-date information, case-by-case consultation, and support. Administrators of the agencies, departments, and organizations with which we work must be made aware of the ways in which SIDS services fit into the existing job descriptions of their staff. They must also be alerted to the support and information needed by their personnel in order to help them do their jobs effectively. There is no one thing which is more important than follow-up with all those involved in each SIDS case, and recognition of both routine and superior efforts on behalf of a SIDS family.

Members of SIDS families can themselves become advocates in important ways. SIDS takes control away from parents, as well as the opportunity to fight for the child they have lost. We need to offer ways for such parents to work for the cause or to offer help so that they have some vehicle for constructive action. This can provide an outlet for their anger and sense of unfairness in the hope that down the road someone else will not have to experience such a profound loss in the same way. Even though such an outlet is not important for all individuals, it is unfortunate when a constructive opportunity is not available to parents who do have this need. Careful channeling of the energies of both recently-bereaved parents and those seasoned by the passage of time is essential. Unless this is achieved, experience has demonstrated that we run the risk of the emotionally wounded trying to help those who are equally emotionally wounded.

Targets of Advocacy

One lesson learned through the evolution of SIDS programming is the critical need for a broad community education effort. It is clear that basic community awareness is the milieu in which all the goals of SIDS advocacy and networking must be met. An enlightened community will not only be a more supportive one for SIDS families, but will be one in which intensive, ongoing efforts to find the answer to the mystery of SIDS will be demanded. Unique groups of dedicated physicians and researchers in many areas have played important roles as advocates for the cause and for research efforts, in addition to playing critical parts in the provision of services. Effective SIDS services must be rooted in accurate, up-to-date medical information. Many committed medical men and women have provided this data for families and professionals over a long period of time with little financial reward or recognition.

There can be no more important focus of long-term advocacy efforts than the need for continued research. It appears that all of the *obvious* possible causes for SIDS have been systematically ruled out by scientific studies to date. The hope for the future lies in renewed commitment, the promise of advanced technology, and the federal appropriation and private raising of the necessary funds to make the goals of prediction and prevention possible.

Sufficient funding is a prerequisite to power and control over our own destiny as a local, national, and international movement. As other children's causes have discovered, the inability of babies and children to vote or provide dollars means that any power that exists must be exercised on their behalf by those of us who so deeply feel their needs. The maxim of SIDS Resources, Inc., in Missouri voices this belief: "Their song will be sung if we sing it." It can legitimately be argued that the cause of SIDS has now come full circle, and that it is time to "sing their song" again in similar ways as it was sung by those parents and their supporters who were the first advocates.

One of the initial results of advocacy in the United States was the involvement of legislators, first in a handful of states, then nationally, and still later on a state-by-state basis in the efforts to provide services for families and to expand research into the causes of SIDS. Across the country, the work of SIDS advocates made possible autopsy legislation in many states. In addition to this critical legislative accomplishment, the inclusion of elected officials gave many of them a feeling of "ownership" or participation in the cause of SIDS. The movement must maintain and build on this sense of concern, at a national and international level, as well as in each state or provincial legislature. This is necessary in order to increase government funding and to continue service programs for SIDS families. One illustration of this need can be found in the existing level of funding for perinatal programs. Although public health officials include SIDS statistics in infant mortality figures in order to call attention to the seriousness of the problem, SIDS is excluded when funds are appropriated for perinatal intervention programs.

NETWORKING

Networking is not a new process or technique. It has been with us in the United States for many years (Froland, et al., 1981). History gives evidence of a strong networking tradition (Collins & Pancoast, 1976). Thus, in the United States in the early 1900s, immigrants were linked up with each other and with necessary resources in ways which advanced the growth of the entire country. More recently, Bott (1971, p. 320) defined a network as "all or some of the social units (individuals or groups) with whom a particular individual or group is in contact." Today, network analysis allows us to define who should be involved in the helping network, as well as what can be gained and in which time frames (Maguire, 1983).

Networking maximizes the use of natural helping systems, sustains advocacy, and endeavors to use professionals more efficiently. Maguire (1983) identified two primary types of networks: natural (informal) and professional (formal). He stated that each of these network types involves multiple connections and chain reactions. In both, the networker serves as a direct linking agent and facilitates additional direct and indirect links. Network members should affect each other in some positive way. Both network strategies define a unit of intervention, establish ways to connect that unit to its appropriate natural or social helping network, and examine ways to support the connection among network members.

Multiple methods are also needed to connect the many individuals who provide service and their organizations into a single effective unit, so that each can communicate and share resources while still maintaining its own special focus. Maguire (1983, p. 97) called this "networking at an organizational level."

The impetus for developing artificial (or formal) networks came from the theory of crisis intervention, which holds that the outcome of crisis in an individual's life largely depends on the availability of assistance immediately after the crisis occurs (Collins & Pancoast, 1976; Rapoport, 1965). Help in time of crisis was often given in the past by a member of the extended family or a close neighbor or friend. In modern urban societies, members of the clergy, physicians, and sometimes law enforcement officers are seen as official caretakers who, if family and friends are not present, may take their place. Many crises occur when relatives, friends, and official caretakers are not available and in situations where informal networks are inadequate. As in the case of SIDS, these situations call for effective linking of both formal and informal systems of support.

PROGRAMS FOR SIDS SERVICES: MODELS OF "TOTAL NETWORKING"

The literature on networking primarily stresses the effective use of informal or natural networks. Although formal or professional networking is recognized as a legitimate approach, there are few descriptions of models, such as are found in effective SIDS organizations, in which the service system is designed around "total" networking or the explicit and systematic integration of formal and informal networks.

Networking with and for Families

The primary focal point of any SIDS service system is necessarily the individuals and families who, without warning, find themselves in the tragic situation of having to cope with the death of a baby. One characteristic of SIDS is that it strikes all racial, ethnic, geographic, economic, or social groups. Thus, the population of individuals and families affected includes all segments of the population as a whole. The death catches each individual and family wherever they were already. For some, this may mean that their lives are relatively intact; for others, the experience with SIDS may add one more tragic layer to a wide variety of pre-existing difficulties.

This diverse nature of the client population's economic, social, and emotional resources explains why, of the persons served initially by SIDS volunteers or professionals, some will and many will not be able to move into a "helping capacity" themselves at a later time. The coping mechanisms that a person has developed previously are the ones which will be at his or her disposal, with varying degrees of effectiveness, at the time of any crisis. It is surprisingly rare for any SIDS family to refuse all services following the death of their baby. Utilization of information and support opportunities by families ranges across a continuum from a one-time counseling visit or telephone interview to ongoing contacts over a long period of time, including consultation through subsequent pregnancies and births.

The foremost consideration is that each person and family first take care of their own needs. At a later time, when some energy may be spared from this task, many families are interested in offering their efforts and assistance to the SIDS organization. A variety of activities are available to ensure that a person's unique experience and capabilities can be matched to the program's needs. The opportunity for parents to talk with someone who has "survived" this overwhelming experience can ease the feeling of isolation and represent "a light at the end of the tunnel." A few parents can provide this invaluable assistance by acting as parent-to-parent contacts. Others play crucial roles as parent facilitators in support group meetings. An educational program is of interest to some who can assist in SIDS presentations to community and student groups. Those who have clerical experience can support the SIDS organization administratively.

SIDS organizations throughout the United States and in other countries have a variety of organizational structures. Some of these organizational models provide a great deal of flexibility in the use of volunteers. Organizations which are structured in such a way as to utilize volunteer boards may provide the opportunity for men and women with business and professional experience to play key roles in advancing organizational goals as directors, members, or officers of advisory or medical boards. Volunteer photographers, graphic artists, carpenters, electricians, and individuals with a variety of other skills help to broaden and deepen the effectiveness of any organization or program. The funding needed in order to ensure quality services provides an additional opportunity for families to involve themselves. The dual purposes of fund raising and expanded community awareness about SIDS offer a challenge that cannot be met without the assistance of volunteers.

There are many lessons to be learned as those of us who care about SIDS endeavor to advance this cause, but the effective utilization of volunteers as part of the SIDS network is critical. Two elements stand out. First, the caution that began this section: people need to take care of themselves before they attempt to use their energies on behalf of others. Second, there is no more important consideration than "matching the right person to the right job."

Networking with and for Professionals

The role of professionals with any SIDS organization is critical in providing effective services and in promoting a progressive organization and a strong network. Their involvement is influenced by how they define their roles. Minimal involvement can encompass inclusion of basic material on SIDS in curricula, or simply reporting a possible SIDS death to the SIDS organization. The exceptional efforts "go the extra mile" toward helping individuals, families, and the cause of SIDS. For example, in one extremely busy trauma center, the nursing supervisor and a head nurse are the two designated people who take turns being called to the emergency room in cases of a possible SIDS death. The staff relies on their leadership and experience. This nursing supervisor has made it a practice to relay in person to the family the medical examiner's diagnosis. If the family has no telephone, she will go to the home.

For the most part, professionals such as physicians, nurses, social workers, funeral directors, coroners, medical examiners, and emergency responders use their expertise and experience to assist families through this tragedy by providing accurate information and support. They also refer the family to a local or area SIDS organization for further services. Involvement by professionals in a SIDS death is personally difficult for many of the same reasons that it is for the parents. The effects of infant death are deeply felt by professionals who not only have chosen their vocation because of their desire to protect or save lives, but in many cases also have to go home to families of their own which include infants and young children. Their training is oriented toward "fixing things," and SIDS is the ultimate "unfixable" situation. The inexplicable nature of SIDS leaves many professionals, as well as parents, asking "what could I have done differently."

One police officer called a SIDS program to report a death that had happened four days earlier. The SIDS staff member was already aware of the death, and was slightly puzzled as to why the officer had waited four days to call. She noted, however, that the officer obviously was still deeply affected by the incident. The explanation was all too painfully typical. The officer was without a partner that night and had arrived at the home before the ambulance. She had been greeted at the front door by the baby's hysterical mother who thrust her dead infant at the officer screaming at her to "do something for my baby." The police officer froze and "forgot everything she knew." She felt she had failed and had "totally blown it." When given the truthful reassurance that anyone in her circumstances might have acted in the same way, the officer felt slightly less disgusted with herself and more willing to consider what she would do differently if there should be a next time. In this case, the officer needed validation and understanding from the SIDS program that she was too embarrassed to seek from her own colleagues.

It is extremely important that professionals have the most accurate and up-to-date information on SIDS and the availability of services. Access to that information is greatly facilitated by: a toll-free telephone number; timely in-service education programs for professionals at both the student and advanced levels; and availability of printed information, visual aids and audiovisuals, conferences, and workshops which provide the opportunity for sharing of experience and expertise—the chance to "pick each other's brains."

Much has been written about the dangers of professional "burnout." An emotionally-charged issue such as SIDS can give new meaning to the experience and implications of "burnout." Dealing on a regular basis with death, let alone infant death, tends to "run down our professional batteries" or "use us up," rather than "burn us out." Yelling at one's family is typically described as one symptom of "burnout." On the contrary, when we are "used up," families are often left in the situation of feeling that being yelled at would be preferable. One of the most valuable contributions of the network approach is that no one, professional or volunteer, has to play "lone ranger" or carry the entire burden individually. As one piece of an effective network, a professional plays a role which builds on those coming before and enhances those which follow. The network experience is like a jumper cable for the professional's battery, aided by ongoing education, consultation, and mutual support.

Networking with and for Community Volunteers

Sudden Infant Death Syndrome touches a multitude of lives and its effects reach far into the community. The role of community volunteers with SIDS programs has been an essential and growing one. Involvement of professionals who want to help in a volunteer capacity is also expanding. Counselors, therapists, physicians, nurses, and other care providers may spend off-duty hours utilizing their unique skills to assist SIDS families. Those who have been indirectly affected by a SIDS death are another group of volunteers who are more and more involved in SIDS organizations. Among these may be friends, co-workers, babysitters, or day care providers. For example, one friend of a SIDS family, deeply touched by the death, was responsible for starting a golf tournament to benefit the cause of SIDS. That tournament and four similar annual events have raised over $50,000 and have provided opportunities for many others to contribute also. Assistance of this sort from volunteers is extremely important because, in addition to the help given by such people, they are often fulfilling personal needs of their own in respect to SIDS.

Experience shows the necessity of providing a wide range of job opportunities for these volunteers. Some opportunities are directly evident in SIDS service roles, but many more are important jobs which allow the volunteer to maintain necessary emotional "distance." Dealing with the emotional layers inherent in the death of a baby is difficult for most individuals. The opportunity to perform a task which is indirectly related to SIDS, such as overseeing the SIDS organization's business as a board member, allows a volunteer to derive satisfaction while, at the same time, leaving intact a sense of self-protection. This consideration is important, not only for individual volunteers, but also for members of community groups, such as Lions, Optimists, or Jaycees. Their sponsorship of special events or donation of time can fill a similar need.

Basic awareness about SIDS can be enhanced greatly as media promotion, volunteer involvement, and public participation combine for a worthwhile cause, frequently in a special fund raising activity. Events which have the potential to become annual activities lend credibility and create recognition for a SIDS program in the community. Experience has demonstrated that a positive, enjoyable activity, such as a golf or racquetball tournament, a children's function, a fashion show, or a flower or bake sale, has the potential for making as many friends for the cause of SIDS as it does money. People seem to find satisfaction through involvement in functions which are enjoyable and which simultaneously give them a sense of helping to serve a worthy cause. A variety of annual events, both by geographic representation and type of activity, can broaden the volunteer and the community awareness base of a SIDS organization.

One additional insight should also be mentioned. Many individuals and businesses cannot offer time or personal involvement, but contributions of funds or merchandise provide a similar sense of satisfaction, as well as critical support for programmatic needs.

The network of volunteers which assists any SIDS program will be most effective not only when a good match is made between the person and the job, but also when flexibility is built into the system. As the experience of volunteers evolves, it is helpful to offer opportunities for ongoing evaluation in order to determine whether the individual's needs are being met, as well as the organization's. Roles can change as personal and programmatic needs evolve. Sometimes the most obvious considerations are neglected, in part because they are so obvious. There is no substitute for recognition, a simple "thank you," and the feeling of ownership in an organization.

Several conclusions may be drawn from this discussion of the SIDS model of total networking.

- Dealing with the entity of SIDS demands a network approach. Services for individuals and families can best be provided by maximizing the effectiveness of the natural networks of which such persons are already a part, and by facilitating the availability and helpfulness of the professional and volunteer networks needed as a result of the SIDS death. One SIDS parent whose daughter died 22 years ago is by profession a nurse and paramedic. She occasionally reminds other parents that, painful as things are today, they cannot begin to comprehend what it was like to lose a baby to SIDS 22 years ago.
- Some individuals, those affected both directly and indirectly by SIDS, can later contribute their time and talents to further the cause. Some can benefit from the services provided at the time of the crisis, but for a variety of reasons can never "give back."
- Both professional and community volunteers can be integral parts of the networking system. Community awareness and fund raising events, as well as other volunteer activities, contribute to the long-term effectiveness of any SIDS program. For example, reports of SIDS deaths from first responders typically outnumber community-originated referrals by a wide margin. As a result of a special awareness event, one SIDS program reported that during a three-month period in the peak incidence season, community referrals on reported cases were the second-most important reporting source (the first being the medical examiner's office).

INTERACTION AND INTERVENTION FOR APPROPRIATE HELPING

The efficacy of any of the efforts described in this chapter can be diluted by lack of regard for a few "red flag" or warning considerations. Some of these have been mentioned previously, but all are important enough to be included in one final list of cautions.

1. Volunteers and organizations both deserve our best efforts to match the right person to the job. It is unlikely that an appropriate helper will be a person who:

- gets involved in the helping effort too soon after a death in his or her own family;
- has too many other pre-existing problems;
- is too emotionally needy;
- has a need to involve himself or herself in "one-upsmanship";
- approaches the loss too intellectually for too long, or is tied into too many theories.

Not everybody can or should be expected to do everything. Control of the volunteer program in this regard is in everybody's best interest.

2. When and where to refer to outside resources is a prime consideration. Anyone involved in the SIDS network has a responsibility to be prepared to recognize and to handle referral needs effectively.

3. A support system for the providers of care is a critical need. We cannot effectively provide care for others in need if we ignore our own personal and emotional needs. Sometimes, we must allow others, including other professionals, to help us.

4. Openness to constructive criticism, the willingness to use mistakes to create better solutions the next time, and the ability to let our programs evolve instead of becoming stagnant or rigid are crucial. Sometimes, intelligent, well-informed risk-taking, not in family services, but in organizational development, is necessary in order to allow the cause to advance.

5. When to terminate, when to allow people to see the need to move on in different professional or volunteer endeavors, is a necessary judgment in any effort, and the cause of SIDS is no exception. At times, a person may need to be moved into a more appropriate role, or to be circumvented. At other times, helpers must be supported and counseled in their attempts to work together. There seem to be no substitutes for honest, gentle directness, the creative ability occasionally to "give people a way out," and sometimes to let people "save face."

CONCLUSION

SIDS services have evolved into a model of total networking. The effective utilization and linking of formal and informal networks provides the best opportunity to assist individuals and families who have been impacted by SIDS, both at the time of the baby's death and later as their needs change. Some of these persons, at a point when all of their energies are no longer needed just to cope with the SIDS experience, may become part of the helping network themselves. Their relatives, friends, and people indirectly affected by SIDS may also play important helping roles. Experience has shown that a variety of opportunities for volunteer involvement is critical, both in order to create a positive experience for the volunteer and also to meet organizational needs. Special events have proven to be prime opportunities for a variety of people to get involved, feel ownership, add to the financial base, and enhance awareness in the community about SIDS and existing resources.

Professionals are more effective when they perform their roles as part of a system of support. Their varying roles, sometimes as volunteers, make possible a consistent, supportive approach to meeting the needs of individuals and families who have been impacted by SIDS. Ongoing educational programs maintain the efficacy of the network.

The cause of SIDS was born in advocacy efforts. These continue to be necessary to assist families, professionals, and the community as a whole. Likewise, they are needed to advance the cause of SIDS and the expansion of research to find predictive and preventive measures. As advocates, we fulfill the maxim, "Their song will be sung if we sing it."

REFERENCES

Bott, E. (1971). *Family and social networks* (2nd ed.). London: Tavistock.

Brager, G. (1968). Advocacy and political behavior. *Social Work, 13*(2), 5–15.

Briar, S. (1967). The current crisis in social casework. *Social Work Practice, 1967* (pp. 19–33). New York: Columbia University Press.

Briar, S. (1968). The casework predicament. *Social Work, 13*(1), pp. 5–11.

Collins, A. H., & Pancoast, D. L. (1976). *Natural helping networks: A strategy for prevention*. Washington, DC: National Association of Social Workers.

"A Critical Call" (1988). Videocassette. Minneapolis, MN: Minnesota Sudden Infant Death Center (see p. 228 below).

Froland, C. D., Pancoast, L., Chapman, N. J., & Kimboko, P. J. (1981). *Helping networks and human services*. Beverly Hills, CA: Sage.

Maguire, L. (1983). *Understanding social networks*. Beverly Hills, CA: Sage.

Rapoport, L. (1965). The state of crisis: Some theoretical considerations. In H. J. Parad (Ed.), *Crisis intervention: Selected readings* (pp. 22–31). New York: Family Service Association of America.

PART IV

SIDS—Summing Up and Looking Ahead

Resources of several sorts are available for those who are interested in or affected by SIDS. In Chapter 12, Richard Pacholski and Charles Corr survey a representative sample of relevant organizations, books, and audiovisuals. In each case, brief descriptions serve to guide readers in selecting those resources which will be most useful in their own particular circumstances. In another way of looking at some of these same resources is provided by Susan Woolsey and Beverley De Bruyn in Chapter 13 through sketches of the development of SIDS-related organizations (private and governmental) and initiatives in the United States and Canada. A retrospective account of the history and animating concerns of these organizations enables readers to appreciate the larger panorama within which SIDS issues are played out in each country and to gain other insights into our present situation. Contrasts between the experiences of these two great countries in North America serve to suggest something of the disparities that are to be found on the even larger international scene.

So much remains to be accomplished in the field of Sudden Infant Death Syndrome that it is all too easy to surrender to dismay in the face of that which is yet to be done. The key to empowerment for the future lies in a realization of that which has already been achieved (mainly in just the past few recent years). Much has been done. Much remains to be done. We are not alone. We are not without resources upon which to call for assistance. The challenge that lies before us is to undertake the good work that needs to be done. This book is designed to help readers shape a constructive response to that challenge.

CHAPTER 12

Existing Resources

Richard A. Pacholski and Charles A. Corr

This chapter identifies and describes SIDS-related resources, focusing on organizations, printed materials (mostly books), and audiovisuals. We sought accuracy in compiling this information, but are aware that addresses, telephone numbers, prices, and other data change. When that happens, the National SIDS Clearinghouse would be a good source for current information.

ORGANIZATIONAL RESOURCES

At the federal level in the United States, the Department of Health and Human Services (through its Office of Maternal and Child Health, in the Bureau of Maternal and Child Health and Resources Development, Health Resources and Services Administration, Public Health Service) operates the Sudden Infant Death Syndrome Program, which coordinates all SIDS-related applied research, supervises program grants, sponsors the services of the National SIDS Clearinghouse, and oversees other SIDS activities.

Of direct interest to readers of this book is the *National SIDS Clearinghouse*, established in 1980 to provide information and educational materials on SIDS, and its many related issues, to health care professionals, community service personnel, SIDS parents, and the general public, as well as to federal, state, and local agencies concerned with SIDS. Publications include fact sheets (on topics, for example, such as theories of causation, medical and legal issues, death investigations, and grief counseling), bibliographies, and referral lists. The Clearinghouse publishes the quarterly newsletter, "Information Exchange," a forum for sharing SIDS-related news on international, national, and state levels. The newsletter is richly informative and exceptionally well written. The Clearinghouse also maintains an automated database and a comprehensive resource collection. A knowledgeable, cordial staff responds to individual requests for information, and makes referrals as needed to regional and local organizations and support groups. Telephone the Clearinghouse at (703) 821-8955; the address is 8201 Greensboro Drive, Suite 600, McLean, VA 22102.

On the state level, since 1981 each state agency administering programs under Title V of the Social Security Act has developed its own SIDS program, determining its own maternal and child health needs and allocating resources accordingly. As of 1988, 92 state-level SIDS programs operate in 50 states, the District of Columbia, and the Virgin Islands. These programs are listed—with names, addresses, phone numbers, and administrators—in the publication, "Directory of Sudden Infant Death Syndrome Programs and Resources," revised and updated by the National SIDS Clearinghouse, May 1988.

To foster collaboration among the various state-level SIDS information and counseling programs and to promote professional growth, the *Association of SIDS Program Professionals* (ASPP) was established in 1987. Now representing SIDS programs in 20 states and Canada, ASPP members work to develop, to improve the quality of, and to expand SIDS programs and related informational and counseling services. The organization thus serves an advocacy role at the same time as it strives to improve communication between SIDS program professionals and other SIDS-related organizations, including self-help parent support groups. For more information, contact Mary McClain, Massachusetts Center for SIDS, Boston City Hospital, Ambulatory Care Center, 5B 29, 818 Harrison Avenue, Boston, MA 02118; telephone (617) 534-5742.

Professionals in the field, as well as SIDS parents, should be aware of the work of *SIDS Family International*, founded in 1987 at the close of an international SIDS conference in Como, Italy. Representatives from 17 nations, including parents and medical/counseling professionals, agreed to continue work on the agenda that brought them together: autopsy identification, standards, and notification; family contact, counseling parents and siblings; research, reporting, and standards for research awards; the proper role of health professionals; and running a volunteer organization. News and information about the activities and members of SIDS Family International is published regularly in the newsletter, "Information Exchange" (published by the National SIDS Clearinghouse). For further information, contact Carrie Sheehan, Western Regional Director, National SIDS Foundation, 915 16th Street East, Seattle, WA 98112; telephone (206) 329-7922.

Funds available for SIDS research, education, caregiving, and counseling have never really been adequate. Indeed, in the United States during the 1980s governmental support declined dramatically. Consequently, several national and regional agencies and services came together in 1988 to establish the *Sudden Infant Death Syndrome Alliance* in order to pool resources and expertise in a coordinated, cooperative effort to raise funds for SIDS. The Alliance concentrates on stimulating and providing financial support for SIDS research. In addition, the Alliance and its member organizations—including the National SIDS Foundation, the National Center for the Prevention of SIDS, the American SIDS Institute, the Council of Guilds for Infant Survival, the Southwest SIDS Research Institute, and SIDS Resources, Inc., in Missouri—offer support to families who have lost babies to SIDS; provide or arrange for clinical services to infants who have experienced apnea and/or are at home on a monitor; and supply up-to-date information on SIDS to the general public, in particular to new and expectant parents. For further information, contact the SIDS Alliance at 10500 Little Patuxent Parkway, Suite 420, Columbia, MD 21044; telephone (301) 964-8000, 800-221-7437 or (800) 638-7437.

The *National Sudden Infant Death Syndrome Foundation* is one of the oldest SIDS-oriented organizations in the United States. Founded in 1962, the not-for-profit Foundation operates through more than 80 local groups of volunteers, composed of concerned citizens, health professionals, and parents who have lost children to SIDS. Its activities include the following:

- Promoting and supporting medical research;
- Helping parents cope with their grief through professional counseling programs;
- Providing medical management for infants who have experienced apnea and/or are at home on a monitor, as well as guidance and counseling support for families;
- Sponsoring training programs for medical, counseling, and other caregiving professionals;
- Educating the general public about SIDS; available for distribution is an extensive collection of pamphlets, brochures, booklets, fact sheets, reprints of timely articles, bibliographies, a quarterly newsletter, audiovisual programs, and ready-made public service announcements for use by local media.

Contact the Foundation for information, referrals, or a printed directory of local chapters. The Foundation shares offices, address, and telephone numbers with the SIDS Alliance (i.e., 10500 Little Patuxent Parkway, Suite 420, Columbia, MD 21044; telephone (301) 964-8000 or (800) 638-7437) and merged with the Alliance in January, 1991.

The National Center for the Prevention of Sudden Infant Death Syndrome has also merged with the SIDS Alliance. Special activities of the National Center included gathering and disseminating information on SIDS to audiences ranging from clinical professionals to the mass media—radio and television stations, newspapers and other periodicals—to prospective parents, to parents of infants who have experienced apnea and/or are at home on a monitor, and to families who have lost a baby to SIDS.

The American Sudden Infant Death Syndrome Institute was founded in 1983 by Alfred Steinschneider (M.D., Ph.D.), an authority on SIDS with a long and distinguished medical and scholarly career. Supported by a combination of private and federal grants, corporate gifts, fees for clinical services, and donations from the public, the not-for-profit Institute is a leading national SIDS organization with a clearly verbalized, three-fold mission:

- Conducting basic research on SIDS;
- Providing specialized clinical services to infants who have experienced apnea and/or are at home on a monitor, and guidance and counseling to parents, on a referral basis;
- Educating a wide range of professionals in the field, holding conferences and workshops for research scientists, health care providers, first responders, social service workers, and pre- and post-doctoral students.

The Institute's research initiatives are multidisciplinary and collaborative, involving Institute staff and investigators around the United States. Underway or planned are studies, for example, of the effectiveness of possible preventive measures; the effects of such measures upon families; pregnancy-related factors in SIDS; refining methods of identifying high-risk infants; and comparative analysis of normal/abnormal control mechanisms in infants.

The Institute's clinics are both a vehicle for translating the latest research findings into improved health care, and a source of new research questions. Services include diagnosis of apneic and high-risk infants, multidisciplinary therapy, training for parents in monitoring their infants, and counseling for families of SIDS victims. Headquarters address is 275 Carpenter Drive, Atlanta, GA 30328; telephone (404) 843-1030, (800) 232-SIDS, or (in GA) (800) 847-SIDS. Another office, housing the counseling division, is located at 1425 S.W. 20th Avenue, Portland, OR 97201; telephone (503) 228-9121.

With goals, activities, and services similar to those provided by the National SIDS Foundation, the *Council of Guilds for Infant Survival* is an umbrella organization for local volunteer "guilds" (made up of SIDS families, concerned individuals, and organizations), affiliates, and regional representatives operating autonomously in most states. The national contact person is Ms Chris Elliott, 9178 Nadine River Circle, Fountain Valley, CA 92708; telephone (714) 968-7623.

Basic clinical research, specialized medical services, and psychosocial counseling are activities of the *Southwest SIDS Research Institute*. Founded in 1984, the Institute is building a nationwide historical database containing extensive epidemiological, perinatal, birth, and full medical histories of SIDS victims.

Parents from around the United States are invited and encouraged to contribute. Simply write or call the Institute. A database containing similar epidemiological and historical information, plus physiological data, on apneic and high-risk infants has also been developed.

Medical care offered to apneic infants includes physical evaluation, laboratory studies, treatment planning, monitoring, follow-up, and telephone support. Individual counseling and group meetings are provided to parents and family members in conjunction with the National SIDS Foundation. In addition, one may call the Institute's hot-line telephone number 24 hours a day for counseling and/or referrals. Printed educational materials and a newsletter are available. Contact Richard A. Hardoin, M.D., Medical Director, or Judith A. Henslee, C.S.W., Program Coordinator, c/o Brazosport Memorial Hospital, 100 Medical Drive, Lake Jackson, TX 77566; telephone (409) 297-4411, ext. 1814.

In Canada, the principal SIDS-related organization is the *Canadian Foundation For the Study of Infant Deaths*, with headquarters in Toronto and chapters in various locations across the country. Founded in 1973 (see Chapter 13), the Canadian Foundation is a private organization which seeks to encourage research, support, and public education in matters related to the sudden death of infants throughout Canada. For additional information, contact the Canadian Foundation at 586 Eglinton Avenue East, Suite 308, Toronto, Ontario; telephone (416) 488-3260. The Foundation's mailing address is P.O. Box 190, Station R, Toronto, Ontario, Canada M4G 3Z9.

Also in Canada, but independent of the Canadian Foundation, is *The SIDS Network Newsletter*, a grassroots project begun in October of 1987 which publishes a quarterly newsletter for SIDS parents from across North America (and with developing contacts in other countries). The newsletter encourages exchange of personal experiences, poetry, and information about literature, meetings, or other useful resources, as well as the establishment of pen-pal contacts and the celebration of subsequent births in SIDS families. For more information or to subscribe to the newsletter, contact Mrs. Gloria Mills, 873 Crowells Street, Oshawa, Ontario, Canada L1K 1X8; telephone (416) 579-6399.

Groups for Bereaved Parents and Families Not Specifically Related to SIDS

As noted in the foregoing discussions of SIDS-related organizations, parents who have lost an infant to SIDS may receive guidance, counseling, and other assistance through a number of governmental and private agencies in the United States. State SIDS programs, for example, if they do nothing else, can readily refer grieving parents to qualified local counselors, local chapters of national SIDS organizations, and/or self-help groups of parents who have lost children. The 80+ local chapters of the National SIDS Foundation, and the many local guilds under the umbrella of the Council of Guilds for Infant Survival, are good sources of help for SIDS parents who can benefit from sharing with others who have "been there."

If no SIDS self-help group is nearby, or if circumstances warrant, local chapters of other groups for grieving parents might be of assistance.

SHARE (a Source of Help in Airing and Resolving Experiences) is a nationwide (indeed worldwide) network of over 200 nondenominational, non-profit support groups *of* and *for* parents who have lost children through miscarriage, stillbirth, or infant death. While the focus of this organization is providing help for parents of babies who never leave the hospital, SIDS parents are welcome, and are encouraged to join. Many do participate in local groups, and do benefit, since their experiences and their needs as grieving parents are in so many ways similar to those of parents who have experienced perinatal loss.

SHARE parents typically meet in regularly scheduled support-group sessions together with counseling and other health-care professionals in or near the sponsoring clinic or hospital. (There are, however, no formal membership, registration, or attendance requirements, no fees, no dues.) Guidance, counseling, and any needed referrals are also available through SHARE by telephone, by correspondence, and by one-to-one contacts. SHARE also distributes educational materials for parents and caregiving professionals—pamphlets, a "bereavement booklet," fact sheets, books, and audiovisuals. A bi-monthly newsletter provides ongoing contact, support, information, and resources. The national office maintains a complete list of support groups, as well as a list of parents who are willing to make initial contact, by telephone or letter, with the newly bereaved. SHARE will happily consult with anyone planning to establish a new chapter; a 70-page manual of information and advice is provided at minimal cost. Contact the national office of SHARE at St. Elizabeth's Hospital, 211 S. Third Street, Belleville, IL 62222; telephone (618) 234-2415 or (618) 234-2120 (ext. 1430).

The other parents' organization that may be of great value to SIDS parents is *The Compassionate Friends* (TCF). TCF provides self-help, counseling, and communication to grieving parents no matter the cause of their children's deaths, no matter the age of the children when they died. Like SHARE, TCF encourages and welcomes SIDS parents to contact them for advice, information, referrals, or simply an attentive ear. TCF members welcome SIDS parents to their meetings, and many do belong to the organization and participate actively. The rapid growth of TCF in recent years—there are literally hundreds of local chapters across the country—attests to the quality and effectiveness of its operational philosophy and activities. Such availability makes it likely that, no matter where a grieving parent lives, someone who has "been there" and is trained to help will be there for them.

Like SHARE, TCF chapters offer support, listening, caring, and friendship in the context of regular but informal meetings and social events, and in one-on-one counseling, in person, in letters, or on the phone. The headquarters organization sponsors periodic national conventions. In addition, it publishes a newsletter and distributes a great many pamphlets, booklets, books, and audiovisual programs (audiocassettes and videotapes). Contact TCF at P.O. Box 3696, Oak Brook, IL 60522; telephone (312) 990-0010.

PRINT RESOURCES

SIDS-Related Literature for Scientists and Researchers

There have been seven major, international SIDS conferences in which scientists and researchers exchanged insights and information. Listed below are the sites and dates of these conferences, together with references to the proceedings volumes which have subsequently been published and which stand as fundamental resources in this field.

Site	Date	Reference
Seattle	Sept. 1963	Wedgwood & Benditt, 1965
Seattle	Sept. 1969	Bergman, Beckwith, & Ray, 1970
Cambridge (UK)	April 1970	Camps & Carpenter, 1972
Toronto	May 1974	Robinson, 1974
Baltimore	June 1982	Tildon, Roeder, & Steinschneider, 1983
Santa Monica	Feb. 1984	Harper & Hoffman, 1988
Como (Italy)	May 1987	Schwartz, Southall, & Valdes-Dapena, 1988

Masterful overviews of the professional journal literature have been provided by Valdes-Dapena in a series of review articles (e.g., 1967, 1977, 1980; Merritt & Valdes-Dapena, 1984). In addition, there is a somewhat dated collection of 27 journal articles from the years 1967–1973, reprinted in book form (Bergman, Melton, & Baker, 1974).

An important contributing author's book edited by Culbertson, Krous, and Bendell (1989) devotes the bulk of its space to epidemiological and pathological data, to theories of etiology and pathogenesis (death mechanisms, airway obstruction, sleep studies, and cardiac dysfunction), and to issues related to infantile apnea and cardio-respiratory monitoring. This might be usefully read alongside the report of two large-scale epidemiological studies in Great Britain (Golding, Limerick, & Macfarlane, 1985).

SIDS-Related Books for General Readers

Three books from England and Australia would be very helpful for health care workers, parents and family members, students, and others who seek an introduction to SIDS. These are an informative handbook by an experienced British physician who helped to found the British Guild for Sudden Infant Death Study (Knight, 1983), and two broad, practical guidebooks by SIDS mothers who speak from their own experiences and from their work with other parents and professionals who have been involved with SIDS (Lord, 1987; Luben, 1989).

Among publications from the United States, there is a helpful research study of SIDS parents and their coping mechanisms (DeFrain, Taylor, & Ernst, 1982), a slim guidebook for parents representing the viewpoint of the National SIDS Foundation (Bergman & Choate, 1975), a general overview by an experienced American pediatrician (Guntheroth, 1989), and an angry book published privately by a SIDS parent (Raring, 1975). In addition, Bergman (1986) has published an admittedly personal account of the mobilization of the political forces that led to the original SIDS legislation in the United States. The appendices to this last volume are particularly useful for reprinting significant documents from this political struggle.

Miscarriage, Stillbirth, and Neonatal Death

Prior to the 1980s, grief related to miscarriage, stillbirth, and most forms of neonatal death tended to be dismissed by many professionals on the mistaken premise that bonding had not yet occurred between parent and child. To acknowledge the importance of such deaths and of the legitimacy of the loss, grief, and mourning experiences which they engender has been an important step forward. A number of books reflect this acknowledgement. Some are based on research studies (e.g., DeFrain, Martens, Stork, & Stork, 1986; Peppers & Knapp, 1980); others draw upon personal experiences (e.g., Berezin, 1982; Borg & Lasker, 1981; Jimenez, 1982). They mean to be helpful in practical ways. All deal with modes of death that precede and are distinct from SIDS, but most will have value for some SIDS parents, families, and helpers.

Parental Bereavement

There are a number of books on parental bereavement, some broader and some narrower than the scope of parental bereavement as it is addressed in this volume. Among the best are: Arnold and Gemma (1983), who offer a sensitive account of the meanings of different kinds of death in childhood; Donnelly (1982), who interviews parents on the nature of their experiences; Klass (1988), who gives special attention to the search for solace through processes of support and self-help groups or psychotherapy; Knapp (1986), who interviewed 155 families to contrast bereavement experiences following a long illness, sudden accidental death, and murder; Rando (1986b), whose contributors in 37 chapters survey implications of the death of a child; and Schiff (1977), who provides practical advice on the basis of her own experiences as a bereaved parent and her interviews with other bereaved parents. Johnson (1987) adds useful advice on counseling bereaved families.

Grollman (e.g., 1982, 1987) has published several well-regarded books intended to be read by grieving persons. In addition, some parents (e.g., Claypool, 1974; Smith, 1974) and others (e.g., Lewis, 1976) have written about their own grief experiences, and Moffat (1982) has assembled an anthology of selections from the literature of mourning.

Loss, Grief, and Mourning

There are a number of good scholarly analyses of grief and bereavement. Worden (1982) combines broad knowledge of the field, brevity, and insight in a handbook which rightly distinguishes between grief counseling and grief therapy. Rando (1984) provides careful analyses of different aspects of grief and mourning. Raphael (1983) explores issues across the life span. Sanders (1989) writes to guide caregivers. And Osterweis, Solomon, and Green (1984) offer a technical account for advanced readers.

Rando's views appear in a somewhat more popular form in a separate publication (1988). The important topic of anticipatory grief, which is so typically precluded by a SIDS death, is examined by Rando and her colleagues in yet another volume (1986a).

Children, Adolescents, and Death

General background on children, adolescents, and death is provided by Wass and Corr (1984a) and Corr and McNeil (1986). Books designed to guide adults in helping young people to cope with death include: Jackson (1965); Jewett (1982); Schaefer and Lyons (1986); and Wass and Corr (1984b). Bernstein (1977) writes for young readers who are coping with loss. And there are two annotated guides to the extensive literature available for children in the area of separation and loss (Bernstein & Rudman, 1989; Wass & Corr, 1984b).

AUDIOVISUAL RESOURCES

General Introductions to SIDS: Basic Background Information

The Sudden Infant Death Syndrome: An Overview and Update

This introduction for general adult and community audiences is presented by Dr. Marie Valdes-Dapena. The package consists of 40 black-and-white slides keyed to two audiotapes (50 minutes), and a 39-page handbook; 1983. Available for a $7.50 rental fee from the SIDS Alliance, 10500 Little Patuxent Parkway, Suite 420, Columbia, MD 21044; telephone (800) 221-7437, (301) 964-8000, or (800) 638-7437.

All About SIDS: Sudden Infant Death Syndrome

This audiocassette (1987, 45 minutes) can be a most useful introduction to SIDS for general adult and community audiences, and certainly for parents. In two-person discussion format, well-paced and articulate, most SIDS-related topics are covered, including the expected basic information as well as some recent research findings. Printed notes accompanying the audiocassette offer a list of resources for further study; several national authorities on SIDS are listed as consultants for this program. Its reasonable price ($9.95) should make All About SIDS a readily distributable counseling and educational tool. Available from the producer, International Learning Institute, P.O. Box 60, Petaluma, CA 94953; telephone (707) 763-1460. Also available from the National SIDS Clearinghouse, 8201 Greensboro Drive, Suite 600, McLean, VA 22102; telephone (703) 821-8955.

Training First Responders

Call For Help

This is a training film for police officers, rescue workers, and emergency room personnel, although a wide range of caregivers will find it valuable. Specific lessons are offered for dealing with cases of SIDS deaths. The film stresses the need for a thoughtful and concerned approach at a time when the family is still in a state of shock and confusion. The manner in which a family is handled at this crucial time can have long-range effects on their future emotional stability. 16mm film, color, 20 minutes, 1976; available for a $7.50 rental fee from the SIDS Alliance, 10500 Little Patuxent Parkway, Suite 420, Columbia, MD 21044; telephone (800) 221-7437, (301) 964-8000, or (800) 638-7437. This film may be purchased for $200.00; contact Order Branch, National Audiovisual Center

(GSA), Washington, DC 20409; telephone (202) 763-1891. For a videotape version of this program, contact the New Jersey Chapter, National SIDS Foundation, 10 Warren Drive, Marlboro, NJ 07746; telephone (609) 890-8008.

Sudden Infant Death Syndrome

This 16-minute videocassette program (1988) is designed to educate law enforcement personnel about the nature of SIDS, proper procedures, and their responsibilities when responding to a SIDS call. Available in Beta and VHS formats, the program is free of charge to anyone who sends two blank videocassettes in the format preferred (one for your copy, the other as a donation to the distributor). Contact Criminal Justice Public Safety Training Center, c/o Ms Geri Horvath, 3055 Brighton Henrietta Town Line Road, Rochester, NY 14623; telephone (716) 427-7710.

A Critical Call

This training videocassette (color, 21 minutes, 1988), designed for emergency responders, follows a paramedic team as it arrives on the scene following a SIDS death. Appropriate actions and words are noted as the team members work with grieving family members; responsibilities of emergency responders are also noted. Topics covered include transporting the victim, providing documentation, dealing with emotional responses of survivors, and understanding the effects of grief on their reasoning and behavior. Besides presenting information about SIDS in general, this program also offers advice on dealing with the "critical incident stress" experienced by emergency responders. An instructor's guide is included. Sale only: VHS, Beta, & ³/₄" = $100.00. Contact Minnesota Sudden Infant Death Center, Minneapolis Children's Medical Center, 2525 Chicago Avenue South, Minneapolis, MN 55404; telephone (612) 874-6285.

SIDS: The First Response

Designed as a training aid for emergency medical technicians, ambulance personnel, emergency room nurses, and other health professionals, this program explains how to differentiate between a SIDS victim and an abused infant, as well as how to respond in a helpful way to the grief crisis situation at home and in hospital. Color videocassette, VHS, 12 minutes, 1983; sale = $175.00; rental = $40.00. Available from Health Science Media Ltd., P.O. Box 798, Horace Harding Station, Flushing, NY 11362; telephone (718) 229-8308.

Your Visit Can Make a Difference

Designed to train public health nurses, this videocassette program (1987) presents the basics of contacting and visiting a newly-bereaved SIDS family as it dramatizes such a visit. An accompanying manual outlines SIDS information, including current research into causal factors; explains emergency responder and public health nurse responsibilities; and gives advice on handling crisis and grief management situations. For further information, contact Lauren Lawson, R.N., SIDS Northwest Regional Center, c/o Children's Hospital and Medical Center, P.O. Box C-5371, Seattle, WA 98105; telephone (206) 526-2100.

Ten Seconds to Respond—An Apnea-Bradycardia Episode

Developed by the SIDS Project in cooperation with James Whitcomb Riley Hospital for Children at Indiana University Medical Center, this 1986 program is designed to train medical staff in suburban and rural hospitals. It guides them in developing team case management approaches to holistic care of infants on apnea monitors. Obtain a free copy of this program by sending your blank VHS videocassette to Barbara Hines, SIDS Project, Indiana State Board of Health, 1330 W. Michigan Street, Indianapolis, IN 46206-1964; telephone (317) 633-8463. Another source: Maryland SIDS Information and Counseling Project, University of Maryland School of Medicine, 10 S. Pine Street, Suite 400, Baltimore, MD 21201; telephone (301) 328-5062.

Responding to Sudden Death: Support and Coping

Developed by Boulder County Hospice in cooperation with the local city police and county sheriff's departments, this audiovisual speaks to problems faced by emergency responders in reporting a death to family members, in offering support to such family members, and in taking care of themselves. Bereaved family members and law enforcement officers share viewpoints; a narrator summarizes important lessons. During the preparation of this videotape, one member of the production team experienced the death of her teenage daughter in an automobile accident involving a drunken driver. Her comments on the help that she received from a police officer are a striking feature of this presentation. Color videocassette, 25 minutes, 1985; sale = $375.00 for VHS or $395.00 for ¾"; rental = $60.00 (VHS only). Contact Boulder County Hospice, 2825 Marine Street, Boulder, CO 80303; telephone (303) 449-7740.

Parents and Counselors Respond to SIDS Losses

You Are Not Alone

Parents who have lost children to SIDS, caregivers, and general audiences are reminded that causes of the syndrome remain unknown, and that nothing can be done to prevent a death from SIDS. Specific advice is offered on dealing with emotional and other responses of parents, siblings, relatives, and friends. The dramatized cases of several couples who have lost a child to SIDS illustrate typical emotional progression from confusion to anger to understanding and acceptance. 16mm film, color, 25 minutes, 1976; available for a $7.50 rental fee from the SIDS Alliance, 10500 Little Patuxent Parkway, Suite 420, Columbia, MD 21044; telephone (800) 221-7437, (301) 964-8000, or (800) 638-7437. This film may be purchased for $285.00: contact Order Branch, National Audiovisual Center (GSA), Washington, DC 20409; telephone (202) 763-1891. For a videotape version of this program, contact the New Jersey Chapter, National SIDS Foundation, 10 Warren Drive, Marlboro, NJ 07746; telephone (609) 890-8008. This older film, and the one that follows, may be dated in their instructional techniques and visual styles (we chuckle now at the miniskirts and bouffant hair-dos), but the core content remains accurate. The contemporary world still awaits a definitive SIDS audiovisual.

After Our Baby Died: Sudden Infant Death Syndrome

This well-made, impressive film, winner of a blue ribbon in mental health at the 1976 American Film Festival, was created to help professionals and others who come into contact with SIDS parents to better understand the syndrome. Parents are interviewed, and offer telling lessons and insights for caregivers. The film stresses the importance of counseling SIDS parents at the time of loss, and offers helpful advice to improve the quality of that counseling. 16mm film, color, 21 minutes; available for a $7.50 rental fee from the SIDS Alliance, 10500 Little Patuxent Parkway, Suite 420, Columbia, MD 21044; telephone (800) 221-7437, (301) 964-8000, or (800) 638-7437. This film may be purchased for $210.00: contact Order Branch, National Audiovisual Center (GSA), Washington, DC 20409; telephone (202) 763-1891. For a videotape version of this program, contact the New Jersey Chapter, National SIDS Foundation, 10 Warren Drive, Marlboro, NJ 07746; telephone (609) 890-8008.

Sudden Infant Death Syndrome . . . A Family's Anguish

The Colorado SIDS Program developed this 15-minute audiovisual in 1986 to meet the need for an up-to-date audiovisual program for SIDS parent support, professional training, and community education. Medical and statistical information is presented by SIDS researcher and author, Dr. J. Bruce Beckwith. Family issues are presented through interviews with parents—including a single parent—who have lost children to SIDS, with surviving siblings, and with a day care provider. A useful program for many audiences, such as, parent support groups, caregiver education (medical, counseling, human service, clergy, and funeral service), and general community groups. Available for rental ($45.00) or sale ($195.00) in audiocassette tape/slide format or videocassette; contact Colorado SIDS Program, 1330 Leyden Street, Suite 134, Denver, CO 80220. Telephone (303) 320-7771; in Colorado, (800) 332-1018.

A Cradle Song: The Families of SIDS

The most recent (1988) of SIDS-related audiovisuals in this grouping is a help-ful choice for parent-counseling and general community education. In 26 min-utes, it reviews the current state of knowledge about the syndrome and an-alyzes the very special grief experienced in families who have lost babies to SIDS. Historical, medical, scientific, and counseling information about SIDS—including, for example, a helpful discussion of the value of apnea monitors and the advantages of self-help parent groups—is presented by experienced, artic-ulate doctors, researchers, and caregivers. Interspersed coherently throughout the program are interviews with many SIDS parents, who describe emotional responses at various stages in their grieving process. They tell of their shock and frustration trying to understand the cause of their children's totally unex-pected deaths, and of the concomitant guilt feelings they developed and the shame they were made to feel by uninformed outsiders. The reactions of sib-lings and grandparents are touched upon, too. Then the emphasis shifts to the work of the National SIDS Foundation and, finally, to the healing process. A well-spoken narrator provides continuity; transitions between segments make listening and learning very easy. Background music enhances the program's dramatic impact. Although a few of the parents' comments seem mumbled and sketchy, the viewer is invariably moved by their frankness and willingness to share, and comes away from the program satisfied both by its art and its con-tent. Available for rental ($50.00/day, $100.00/week) or sale ($295.00) in any video format from Fanlight Productions, 47 Halifax St., Boston, MA 02130; tele-phone (617) 524-0980.

Parents and Counselors Respond to Perinatal Losses: Insights and Information Applicable to SIDS Situations

Some Babies Die

This remarkable film about stillbirth and neonatal death can be used effec-tively in SIDS counseling situations, helping caregivers to help parents survive this most painful event of their lives. A medical-counseling team in Australia is filmed working with Tess—who has just lost her newborn—and her three sur-viving children. Though on-camera, these people are themselves—no mug-ging, no faking, no self-consciousness. The conduct of the caregiving staff in these stressful circumstances teaches important lessons by example about ef-fective medical and counseling interrelationships with patients on personal levels. Some Babies Die illustrates the effectiveness of a totally open and hon-est approach to the realities of death and suffering. Tess and her children are not simply allowed, but are encouraged to hold, cuddle, and talk to the dead newborn. They say goodbye. Reality sinks in directly, in an atmosphere of total mutual trust. The bereaved are not told what they "should" do, but are helped to understand what they are feeling, and what particular methods they may choose to get themselves successfully through the experience. The caregiving philosophy is to trust the family members to do what is important for themselves, then support them during and after. Counselors, medical caregivers, and general adult audiences, particularly self-help and support groups of parents who know the anguish of neonatal death, will find this film profoundly moving, deeply enriching, and inspiring. *Some Babies Die* (color, 54 minutes, 1986) is available for sale (16mm film = $850.00; videocassette, all formats = $450.00) or for rent (film, 3/4" U-matic, or 1/2" VHS = $60.00) from University of California, Extension Media Center, 2176 Shattuck Avenue, Berkeley, CA 94704; telephone (415) 642-0460.

Empty Arms: Reaching Out to You

This is a "parents' video guide" after miscarriage, stillbirth, or neonatal death. Produced by Sherokee Ilse, a perinatal bereavement professional who has herself suffered a miscarriage, a full-term stillbirth, and an ectopic pregnancy, this 1988 program addresses the reactions and needs of parents in the first hours after their loss. Advice is offered about seeing and holding the deceased infant, creating mementos and memories, saying goodbye, planning the funeral service, going home without the baby, and facing the empty nursery. Information is provided about dealing with the typical, not always helpful, reactions of relatives, friends, and co-workers, about differences in mourning styles of father/mother or male/female, and about the special needs of single parents. Parents who have lost a child present all this information and advice in the program, and emphasize the crucial importance of seeking out local professionals, whether counselors or institutional support staff, and self-help organizations. Indeed, professional staff themselves should view this richly informative program and consider its use as part of their ongoing work with the bereaved. The 30-minute videotape is conveniently divided into two segments. Sale = $200.00; rental = $50.00. Wintergreen Press, 4105 Oak Street, Long Lake, MN 55356; telephone (612) 476-1303.

Empty Arms: The Caregiver's Role—Pregnancy and Infant Loss

This audiovisual is especially designed to train medical professionals, funeral directors, clergy, mental health personnel, and support group leaders to work more effectively and more knowledgeably with parents who have suffered perinatal loss. Sherokee Ilse was videotaped as she presented a day-long seminar at Vanderbilt University Hospital in April, 1988. The three two-hour videotapes that constitute this package are structured as follows:

Tape 1	Segment A:	Introductions, setting the stage, protectionism vs. preparation, support for the caregivers;
	Segment B:	Building the dream, when does bonding and preparation for parenthood begin, why the death of a baby/child is difficult, measuring grief, love and loss;
Tape 2	Segment C:	Reproductive losses, the statistics and the aftermath (including such losses as infertility, miscarriage, stillbirth, infant death, adoption, abortion, SIDS, loss of the perfect birth experience or perfect baby), funeral/memorial services, disposition of the remains;
	Segment D:	Common reactions—men, women, children, grandparents, families, including resistant families;
Tape 3	Segment E:	Immediate decisions, options and needs, the caregiver's role, and memories—their importance and suggestions on how to maximize their creation;
	Segment F:	Discharge, follow-up, care for caregivers, and wrap-up.

This program has been approved for CEU credit by the nursing associations and boards of funeral directors of several states. Related written materials (pre/post tests, objectives, handouts, certificates, and full instructor qualifications) are available at extra charge ($25.00). Sale, full set of three tapes = $500.00; singly = $200.00 each; rental/preview, applicable to purchase = $200.00. Wintergreen Press, 4105 Oak Street, Long Lake, MN 55356; telephone (612) 476-1303.

When a Child Dies

Candid interviews with two bereaved couples and a bereaved mother, each of whom lost their child in different circumstances (leukemia, car accident, and SIDS), offer insights into grief and suggestions for helping. The particularly destructive nature of parental grief is explained, as well as the attendant rage, frequent loss of religious faith, and stress between spouses. Recalling their experiences, the interviewees offer suggestions for interacting in a helpful manner with bereaved parents, whether one is a family member, friend, neighbor, or medical or mental health professional. This prize-winning program (Mental Health Film Festival, American Film Festival; color, 24 minutes, 1980, 16mm or videocassette format) was funded by and is available from the National Funeral Directors Association, 11121 West Oklahoma Avenue, Milwaukee, WI 53227; telephone (414) 541-2500. VHS format, sale only = $80.00; 16mm film, rental only, no charge (except return shipping) for 30-day period. The 16mm film version may also be rented for $17.00 from Western New York

SIDS Center, Department of Pediatrics, University of Rochester Medical Center, 200 Fairport Village Landing, Fairport, NY 14450; telephone (716) 223-5110.

The Anguish of Loss

This is an unusual resource for bereavement counselors, for the bereaved themselves, and for anyone trying to understand the nature and effects of loss. The program consists of a set of 59 slides—photographs of clay sculpture depicting the pain of bereavement—and an audiocassette of music arranged as background for the slide show. The pieces of sculpture were created by artist Julie Fritsch after the death of her son, Justin, in 1986, as an outlet for her pain. An accomplished artist, Ms Fritsch has captured in her works the universal human dimensions of the anguish of loss. Sale, slide set and audiocassette (about 15 minutes) = $160.00 (plus postage, insurance, and CA tax). Julie Fritsch, 607 Harriet Avenue, Aptos, CA 95003; telephone (408) 688-7990. (Photographs of the sculpture are also available in book form, 56 pages, 1987, ISBN 0-9609456-5-2, $8.95.)

Memories

Parents who have experienced miscarriage, stillbirth, and neonatal deaths share their experiences and feelings. Nine situations are presented. A narrator discusses the implications of each one; further questions for the viewers of the program then follow. Situations include a mother expressing both shock and detachment when news of her child's death is related to her, and parents discussing both the negative and positive experiences surrounding the deaths of their infants. Studying the program, caregiving professionals will enrich their awareness of the needs and feelings of grieving parents; grieving parents themselves may be helped by viewing and listening to the words of others who have been there. Color, 27 minutes, 1984. Available from Health Sciences Consortium, 201 Silver Cedar Court, Chapel Hill, NC 27514; telephone (919) 942-8731. Sale, videocassette, all formats = $385.00 for non-members/$192.50 for HSC members; rental = $80.00/$40.00; preview = $30.00/$15.00.

To Touch Today: A Study of Neonatal Death

This is a videocassette study of parental reactions to neonatal death. The focus is on how caring professionals can help parents: by encouraging them to touch and hold the infant, and to take pictures of the infant both before and after death; by teaching parents about the nature and effects of the mourning process; and by putting parents in touch with self-help support groups. The tape explains how caregivers can determine the nature and intensity of the grief parents are experiencing by assessing bonding, the gestational stage at which loss occurred, and the length of time since the loss. It explores stages of mourning and how parents can be helped through them. Color, 24 minutes, booklet, 1984. Available from Health Sciences Consortium, 201 Silver Cedar Court, Chapel Hill, NC 27514; telephone (919) 942-8731. Sale, videocassette, all formats = $385.00 for non-members/$192.50 for HSC members; rental = $80.00/$40.00; preview = $30.00/$15.00.

Death of the Wished-for Child

Glen W. Davidson, Professor of Thanatology at Southern Illinois University Medical School, interviews a mother who lost her child at birth and who developed emotional problems because of errors in intervention made by her caregivers. Dr. Davidson makes quite clear what should be said and done in such situations. This was not a SIDS loss, of course, but this now-classic program can be most helpful for the insights it provides into the nature and effects of grief, and for the techniques of effective grief management it demonstrates. A valuable film for all caregiving professionals. Color 16mm film and videocassette, 28 minutes, 1979. Film version is available from O.G.R. Service Corporation, P.O. Box 3586, Springfield, IL 62708; telephone (217) 793-3322. Sale = $300.00; rental = $40.00. Or Maryland SIDS Information and Counseling Project, University of Maryland School of Medicine, 10 S. Pine Street, Suite 400, Baltimore, MD 21201; telephone (301) 328-5062.

A Child Dies and The Grieving Family

These two videocassettes were designed as a series for nursing education, but they could be used separately and in other contexts; each is in color, is 28 minutes long, and comes with a study guide. In A Child Dies (1988), two nurse clinicians report on their extensive experiences with dying children and family members. They outline typical feelings and responses in the grieving process, and they stress the importance of active listening. Interspersed are interviews with family members. The Grieving Family (1987) then applies these insights, offering nurses a kind of "checklist" of actions they can take to assist the bereaved family: for example, supporting parents, siblings, and other family members as they say goodbye, helping with funeral arrangements, and advising on other decisions that have to be made after the death. Throughout, the program also offers guidelines to nurses for dealing with their own feelings. Available from the American Journal of Nursing Company, Educational Services Division, 555 W. 57th Street, New York, NY 10019-2961; telephone (800) 223-2282; in New York, call collect, (212) 582-8820. Sale, both programs = $450.00; purchased separately = $275.00 each; rental = $60.00 each.

Touch the Snow

Rarely presented in thanatological audiovisuals is the topic of sibling grief in the very young. This filmstrip/audiocassette program (color, 32 minutes, 1982) tells the true story of the effects of the death of her 10-month-old sister upon a two-year-old girl, and how the parents learned to understand. This program is especially effective in addressing, at a child's level, what death is, the nature and manifestations of grief, issues of guilt and blame, remembering, and living once again. The lessons offered here would be very useful in SIDS counseling and education activities. Available for sale only at $25.00 from The Centering Corporation, P.O. Box 3367, Omaha, NE 68103-0367; telephone (402) 553-1200.

Thumpy's Story: A Story of Love and Grief Shared, by Thumpy, the Bunny

A children's story for children of all ages, 3 to 103, available in a number of formats: English and Spanish language story book ($5.95), coloring book ($4.95), workbook ($8.95) [instructional and therapeutic, subtitled "My Story of Love and Grief by _____"], audiocassette ($4.50; 9 minutes) and video-cassette, both in English and Spanish. Thumpy, as a sibling, shares an experience of grief when his sister, Bun, unexpectedly dies. Questions, anger, bargaining, searching for answers—the whole Bunny family reacts to their loss. Thumpy's mother and father model sharing their grief and support with their children. In time, Thumpy's hurts ease, but Thumpy does not forget Bun, and does not stop questioning. The story, in whatever format one uses, can be an effective teaching and counseling tool for children who have lost young siblings, no matter the cause. It can be an excellent means of opening communication within a family or in a classroom. It can raise community awareness of a child's need to be involved, and of the real pain children experience following a death of any significant other. In the videocassette (9 minutes, VHS, 1988; available for purchase @ $125.00 or rental @ $25.00), the text of the story is narrated by actress Wenda Shereos. The soft, lifelike, watercolor artwork of the book, highly evocative in its own right, is translated faithfully to the video medium. Orders to Prairie Lark Press, P.O. Box 699-F, Springfield, IL 62705. Information from SHARE, St. Elizabeth Hospital, 211 S. Third Street, Belleville, IL 62222; telephone (618) 234-2415.

When Bad Things Happen to Good People

This 60-minute videocassette (VHS only, 1986) of Dr. Harold Kushner lecturing on the subject of his book by the same title is available to individuals for $43.20 (institutions should inquire). Contact WTVI Video, 42 Coliseum Drive, Charlotte, NC 28205; telephone (704) 372-2442.

A videocassette of an episode of "Donahue" featuring bereaved parents (1986) is available from the New Jersey Chapter, National SIDS Foundation, 10 Warren Drive, Marlboro, NJ 07746; telephone (609) 890-8008.

Audiovisuals from National Conferences

1. National SIDS Foundation 25th Anniversary Conference, 9/87. For information on available videotapes made at the conference, contact Western New York SIDS Center, 200 Fairport Village Landing, Fairport, NY 14450; telephone (716) 223-5110.
2. Annual "SIDS Community Conference," Children's Hospital of Philadelphia, sponsored by the Philadelphia SIDS Center and the Philadelphia Area Chapter of the National SIDS Foundation, 6/11/88. Videotapes are available of these presentations: (a) "Evaluating and Monitoring the High Risk Infant," Alan Spitzer; (b) "Changes in Couples—Relationships After a Child's Death," Carol Cobb-Nettleton; (c) "Spirituality and Grief," panel. Contact Philadelphia SIDS Center, 321 University Avenue, Philadelphia, PA 19104; telephone (215) 222-1400.
3. A conference in Columbus, Ohio, "Interprofessional Approach to SIDS," 6/20/88, co-sponsored by Ohio Department of Health, Columbus Children's Hospital, and Ohio Chapter of the American Academy of Pediatrics. For information on presentations available on videotape, contact Ohio SIDS Program, Perinatal and Infant Health Unit, Bureau of Maternal and Child Health, P.O. Box 118, Columbus, OH 43266-0118; telephone (614) 466-3543 or (614) 466-4716.
4. The Sixth National Conference on Miscarriage, Stillbirth and Newborn Death: "A Special Grief: The Death of a Baby," 9/23-24/88, Redwood City, CA. Some two dozen audiocassette tapes of presentations on a wide range of related topics are available for $10.00 each (shipping included) from MC-CPOP, Stanford University Medical Center, 750 Welch Road, Suite 120, Palo Alto, CA 94304; telephone (415) 723-5763.

REFERENCES

Arnold, J. H., & Gemma, P. B. (1983). *A child dies: A portrait of family grief.* Rockville, MD: Aspen.

Berezin, N. (1982). *After a loss in pregnancy: Help for families affected by a miscarriage, a stillbirth, or the loss of a newborn.* New York: Simon and Schuster.

Bergman, A. B. (1986). *The "discovery" of sudden infant death syndrome: Lessons in the practice of political medicine.* New York: Praeger.

Bergman, A. B., & Choate, J. (1975). *Why did my baby die?: The phenomenon of sudden infant death syndrome and how to cope with it.* New York: Third Press.

Bergman, A. B., Beckwith, J. B., & Ray, C. G. (Eds.) (1970). *Sudden infant death syndrome: Proceedings of the Second International Conference on Causes of Sudden Death in Infants.* Seattle: University of Washington Press.

Bergman, A. B., Melton, J. W., & Baker, R. E. (1974). *Sudden unexpected death in infants.* New York: MSS Information Corp.

Bernstein, J. E. (1977). *Loss and how to cope with it.* New York: Seabury.

Bernstein, J. E., & Rudman, M. K. (1989). *Books to help children cope with separation and loss* (3rd ed.). New York: Bowker.

Borg, S., & Lasker, J. (1981). *When pregnancy fails: Families coping with miscarriage, stillbirth, and infant death.* Boston: Beacon.

Camps, F. E., & Carpenter, R. G. (Eds.) (1972). *Sudden and unexpected deaths in infancy (cot deaths): Report of the Proceedings of the Sir Samuel Bedson Symposium held at Addenbrooke's Hospital, Cambridge.* Bristol: John Wright & Sons Ltd.

Claypool, J. (1974). *Tracks of a fellow struggler: How to handle grief.* Waco, TX: Word Books.

Corr, C. A., & McNeil, J. N. (1986). *Adolescence and death.* New York: Springer Publishing Co.

Culbertson, J. L., Krous, H. F., & Bendell, R. D. (Eds.) (1989). *Sudden infant death syndrome: Medical aspects and psychological management.* Baltimore: The Johns Hopkins University Press.

DeFrain, J. D., Martens, L., Stork, J., & Stork, W. (1986). *Stillborn: The invisible death.* Lexington, MA: Lexington Books, D. C. Heath.

DeFrain, J., Taylor, J., & Ernst, L. (1982). *Coping with sudden infant death.* Lexington, MA: Lexington Books, D. C. Heath.

Donnelly, K. F. (1982). *Recovering from the loss of a child.* New York: Macmillan.

Golding, J., Limerick, S., & Macfarlane, A. (1965) *Sudden infant death: Patterns, puzzles, and problems.* Somerset, England: Open Books Publishing Ltd.; Seattle, WA: University of Washington Press.

Grollman, E. A. (1987). *Living when a loved one has died* (2nd rev. ed.). Boston: Beacon Press.

Grollman, E. A. (1982). *What helped me when my loved one died.* Boston: Beacon Press.

Guntheroth, W. G. (1989). *Crib death: Sudden infant death syndrome* (2nd ed.). Mount Kisko, NY: Futura Publishing Co.

Harper, R. M., & Hoffman, H. J. (Eds.) (1988). *Sudden infant death syndrome: Risk factors and basic mechanisms.* New York: PMA Publishing Corp.

Jackson, E. N. (1965). *Telling a child about death.* New York: Hawthorn.

Jewett, C. L. (1982). *Helping children cope with separation and loss.* Harvard, MA: Harvard Common Press.

Jimenez, S. L. M. (1982). *The other side of pregnancy: Coping with miscarriage and stillbirth.* Englewood Cliffs, NJ: Prentice-Hall.

Johnson, S. E. (1987). *After a child dies: Counseling bereaved families.* New York: Springer Publishing Co.

Klass, D. (1988). *Parental grief: Solace and resolution.* New York: Springer Publishing Co.

Knapp, R. J. (1986). *Beyond endurance: When a child dies.* New York: Schocken.

Knight, B. (1983). *Sudden death in infancy: The 'cot death' syndrome.* London: Faber & Faber.

Lewis, C. S. (1976). *A grief observed.* New York: Bantam.

Lord, J. D. (1987). *When a baby suddenly dies: Cot death—the impact and effects.* Melbourne: Hill of Content.

Luben, J. (1989). *Cot deaths: Coping with Sudden Infant Death Syndrome,* (2nd ed.). London: Bedford Square Press.

Merritt, T. A., & Valdes-Dapena, M. A. (1984). SIDS research update. *Pediatric Annals, 13,* 193–207.

Moffat, M. J. (Ed.) (1982). *In the midst of winter: Selections from the literature of mourning*. New York: Random House, Vintage Books.

Osterweis, M., Solomon, F., & Green, M. (Eds.) (1984). *Bereavement: Reactions, consequences, and care*. Washington, DC: National Academy Press.

Peppers, L. G., & Knapp, R. J. (1980). *Motherhood and mourning: Perinatal death*. New York: Praeger.

Rando, T. A. (1984). *Grief, dying, and death: Clinical interventions for caregivers*. Champaign, IL: Research Press.

Rando, T. A. (1988). *Grieving: How to go on living when someone you love dies*. Lexington, MA: Lexington Books, D. C. Heath.

Rando, T. A. (Ed.) (1986a). *Loss and anticipatory grief*. Lexington, MA: Lexington Books, D. C. Heath.

Rando, T. A. (Ed.) (1986b). *Parental loss of a child*. Champaign, IL: Research Press.

Raphael, B. (1983). *The anatomy of bereavement*. New York: Basic Books.

Raring, R. H. (1975). *Crib death: Scourge of infants—shame of society*. Hicksville, NY: Exposition Press.

Robinson, R. R. (Ed.) (1974). *SIDS 1974: Proceedings of the Francis E. Camps International Symposium on Sudden and Unexpected Deaths in Infancy*. Toronto: The Canadian Foundation for the Study of Infant Deaths.

Sanders, C. (1989). *Grief: The mourning after*. New York: John Wiley.

Schaefer, D., & Lyons, C. (1986). *How do we tell the children*. New York: Newmarket.

Schiff, H. S. (1977). *The bereaved parent*. New York: Crown.

Schwartz, P. J., Southall, D. P., & Valdes-Dapena, M. (Eds.) (1988). The sudden infant death syndrome: Cardiac and respiratory mechanisms and interventions. *Annals of the New York Academic of Sciences, 533*.

Smith, A. A. (1974). *Rachel*. Wilton, CT: Morehouse-Barlow.

Tildon, J. T., Roeder, L. M., & Steinschneider, A. (Eds.) (1983). *Sudden infant death syndrome*. New York: Academic Press.

Valdes-Dapena, M. A. (1967). Sudden and unexpected death in infancy: A review of the world literature 1954-1966. Pediatrics, 39, 123-138.

Valdes-Dapena, M. A. (1977). Sudden unexplained infant death, 1970 through 1975: An evolution in understanding. *Pathology Annual, 12*, 117–145.

Valdes-Dapena, M. A. (1980). Sudden infant death syndrome: A review of the medical literature 1974–1979. *Pediatrics, 66*, 597–614.

Wass, H., & Corr, C. A. (1984a). *Childhood and death*. Washington, DC: Hemisphere.

Wass, H., & Corr, C. A. (1984b). *Helping children cope with death: Guidelines and resources* (2nd ed.). Washington, DC: Hemisphere.

Wedgwood, R. J., & Benditt, E. P. (Eds.) (1965). *Sudden death in infants: Proceedings of the conference on causes of sudden death in infants*. Bethesda, MD: U.S. Department of Health, Education, and Welfare, Public Health Service, National Institutes of Health, National Institute of Child Health and Human Development. P.H.S. Pub. No. 1412.

Worden, J. W. (1982). *Grief counseling and grief therapy: A handbook for the mental health practitioner*. New York: Springer Publishing Co.

CHAPTER 13

Current Services and Organizations: Springboard to the Future

Susan F. Woolsey and Beverley De Bruyn

This chapter reviews the history and current situation of concerns that are related to Sudden Infant Death Syndrome (SIDS). In so doing, it focuses specifically upon services that are required for bereaved families and upon organizations that have been established to provide such services in the United States and in Canada. The purpose of this review is to bring us to the point of being able to look toward the future in an informed and intelligent manner.

THE UNITED STATES

The Past

In order to look to the future, it is necessary to make a brief excursion into the past. As early as the 1950s, some researchers became interested in the phenomenon of what was then called "crib death." However, it was not until the 1960s that organized efforts got underway in the area of SIDS in the United States. In 1962, the Jed Roe Foundation was established, which later evolved into what is now the National Sudden Infant Death Syndrome Foundation. About the same time, The Guild for Infant Survival was begun by Saul and Sylvia Goldberg. These two organizations were instrumental in bringing together parents, friends, relatives, and interested professionals who spearheaded the push to see that hearings were held in the United States Congress about what was now called "Sudden Infant Death Syndrome."

Bergman (1986) has graphically and effectively described this process in terms of what he calls the "practice of political medicine." His description may become required reading for other groups that wish to "move Congress." In the end, after several years of hard work that included congressional hearings over a two-year period, the Sudden Infant Death Syndrome Act (PL 93-270) was passed in 1974. As a result of this legislation, two major directions were taken: funds were directly allocated to fund research toward finding possible causes of SIDS; and there was a mandate to establish information and counseling projects throughout the United States. Staff members in local and regional SIDS information and counseling projects could take pride in their work because their objectives had been established by SIDS parents themselves through the national legislative process. These objectives were as follows:

- To ensure that autopsies were conducted on every infant and child that died suddenly and unexpectedly;
- To have Sudden Infant Death Syndrome used as the diagnosis of death;
- To ensure that parents were informed of the cause as soon as possible after the death;
- To have information and counseling available for all families affected by Sudden Infant Death Syndrome;
- To provide information and education for all those who came in contact with SIDS families.

Responsibility for implementation of objectives established by the SIDS Act was given to the United States Department of Health, Education, and Welfare (HEW), Division of Maternal and Child Health (MCH). A recommended model for establishment of Information and Counseling Projects was developed, and requests for proposals were sent out. By 1975, grants had been awarded to 24 projects. All of them were set up to meet the designated objectives, but there were some variations among them as to how they would accomplish these tasks. Many believe that this was a strong point, since each project then had "possession" of its own program and there was leeway for creativity that would not have been possible if the programs were rigidly prescribed.

There were many ups and downs within the SIDS projects, depending upon their individual circumstances. Where there was a strong SIDS parent group prior to establishment of the federally funded program, it was not uncommon to have tension between the parent group and the associated SIDS project group. Prior to the establishment of the information and counseling program, SIDS parents often had received rather insensitive treatment from professionals, many of whom still do not have an understanding of parental bereavement, grief, and mourning processes. Frequently, it took a great deal of effort to work through these unresolved feelings in order for the SIDS parents' groups to develop trust and a working relationship with the new SIDS information and counseling projects. At the same time, the projects had a good deal to learn from the experiences of the SIDS parents.

Through the early years, the Department of Health, Education, and Welfare (now the Department of Health and Human Services) was directly responsible for the overall SIDS information and counseling program. Organizations and institutions wishing to develop information and counseling projects were invited to submit proposals directly to HEW. As awards were made and the projects were starting up, HEW provided a number of support services to assist them. These included publication of educational movies and printed materials, ongoing consultation, periodic conferences on selected topics, and annual meetings which included the parent groups, researchers, and federal program personnel. All of these services helped to maintain a close communication network among those engaged in SIDS activities.

In addition, federal guidelines at the time included the requirement to subcontract to minority small businesses for a certain number of services. For example, one of those contracts was with a group hired to establish and maintain the SIDS Information Clearinghouse. Another group was selected to study the operation and functioning of the information and counseling projects. Staff members in the projects often mentioned that they were frustrated in their efforts to deal with these "outside" organizations because considerable time was required for their orientation to topics related to SIDS, as well as to the complex nature of relationships within the SIDS network. These groups also had frequent staff turnover which further compromised consistent follow through and satisfying communication.

With the exception of the SIDS Information Clearinghouse and grants from HEW for a very few selected services, direct support from the federal level was discontinued with the consolidation of MCH services at the beginning of the 1980s. As a result, monies for Maternal and Child Health categorical programs are awarded directly to individual states, leaving them free to decide for themselves how they wish to allocate these resources.

Some states decided to discontinue their SIDS information and counseling projects, or to reduce their funding drastically. In some cases, the SIDS projects were modified to include all cases of infant death in a given state. In at least two states, all cases of sudden death of children were included. Where at one time there were 46 SIDS projects across the country, there are now only about 22. Another negative result is that there no longer is a centralized, coordinated, networking system in the area of SIDS.

To help maintain communication among the existing SIDS projects, in 1987 professional staff members formed the Association of SIDS Program Professionals, through which they hope to maintain and support their mutual interests. There have been some very positive results coming out of the consolidation decision. For example, the states of Missouri, Colorado, Wisconsin, Ohio, Pennsylvania, and New Jersey have begun to develop programs which include both SIDS parent groups and program professionals from the former federally funded SIDS projects. They are incorporating and operating individually within their states—quite successfully. More recent events will be discussed below.

Immediate, Sensitive Care and Information

Provision of immediate, sensitive care and information must remain the goal of everyone who is interested in helping all newly bereaved SIDS families. Nevertheless, the very first objective of the 1974 SIDS Act and the foundation upon which all of this depends—the provision of autopsies for all babies who die suddenly and unexpectedly—has still not been realized. Some states do not yet require automatic autopsy in such cases. But when there is no autopsy, the question of cause of death remains an open one. In addition, without a centralized system for case finding, those interested in contacting newly bereaved families have no established procedure upon which to depend.

Furthermore, with the recent, well-intentioned emphasis upon inquiry into and prevention of child abuse, SIDS families are again being subjected to more intense scrutiny and investigation than is warranted. This was an experience which heightened feelings of parental guilt and self-blame in the period prior to the passage of the 1974 SIDS Act, and which complicated subsequent grief and mourning. It would be unfortunate if our society were to return to that sad state of affairs. Moreover, in some states now, every infant death is required to undergo an investigation by already-overworked child protective service departments.

Another side effect of this trend is that many medical examiners, who were making immediate diagnoses of SIDS after the SIDS Act was established, are now deciding to defer making a final diagnosis until all laboratory examinations are completed. This makes it impossible for the family to be aware of a diagnosis before the funeral of their child. Diagnosis may be delayed for a month or two, thus impairing the ability to intervene positively at an early stage.

An important function of the local and regional SIDS information and counseling projects was to provide training and education for all levels of emergency personnel. In the present circumstances, it is likely that care provided by such personnel will begin to deteriorate since their usual focus is on technology with the goal of saving lives. Many rescue teams are made up of volunteers. The nature of their work leads to very rapid turnover and constant retraining. The local and regional SIDS projects had the visibility and ability to keep reminding emergency personnel of SIDS-related issues. When services received by families were evaluated by SIDS projects, it was possible for the project staff to provide follow up with a particular rescue squad, police department, emergency room, member of the clergy, or funeral director when it was apparent that support or continuing education was needed.

There is a very wide variation in individuals that a family is likely to deal with in the emergency room of a hospital. In addition to physicians and nurses, these individuals might include auxiliary staff, parent advocates, parents on call, a psychiatric liaison person, or a member of the clergy. There are pros and cons concerning all of these models, but the point is that without an organized system to ensure training and support, the emphasis on provision of sensitive and thoughtful care for families experiencing a SIDS death will diminish.

Local and regional SIDS projects also provided a consistent referral system. Each one had established a system for learning about new cases and then contacting the bereaved families. Before the federally funded SIDS projects were set up, referrals tended to be rather hit or miss. Some SIDS parent groups relied upon reading obituary columns of newspapers, or upon word-of-mouth information. Newly bereaved parents are very unlikely to hunt for help in circumstances which for them are unanticipated, foreign, and disempowering. Thus, in order to ensure that they receive help, it is necessary for some form of organized referral system to exist, as well as to have in place organized and reliable helping systems.

The concept of self-help is wonderful in circumstances for which it is appropriate. However, experience in the field has demonstrated that SIDS parent groups or chapters do not always have a large enough core group of available parents to do the hard work of making contact with all newly bereaved families. In addition, the quality of parent ability varies greatly and many bereaved parents are neither able nor interested in undertaking this work. In fact, for most bereaved parents, there is a tension between having them available to assist other parents who find themselves in a similar situation and enabling them to grow and go on with their lives. There is a great need to provide activities which use the zeal of parents to do something. But that something is not necessarily providing one-to-one support for other newly bereaved parents.

Another related aspect which is now causing concern is that there is no longer a federal government priority in the United States to continue SIDS information and counseling projects. All programs for children tend to be neglected by those in power since children have no money and cannot vote. There is also a widespread societal perception that not much is lost when an infant dies.

It is interesting that there are conflicts among medical caregivers stemming from the belief that all infants should live. However, medical professionals and the health system have concentrated resources on perinatal programs, which are very expensive in emotional, social, and monetary terms. One result of such emphasis is that some infants' lives appear to be "worse than death."

Beyond that, expensive perinatal programs drain human, societal, and fiscal resources from care that is needed in the remainder of infancy beyond the newborn period or the first month of life. This has led to calls for a reexamination of our priorities in this area.

Social and Emotional Support for the Bereaved and Their Helpers

In the past, SIDS projects expended a large amount of energy in the training of health care professionals, the clergy, and others who related to a bereaved family. Of course, some of that type of training was and still is being done by others, but surprisingly little emphasis in professional and other modes of education is placed upon teaching the skills necessary for assisting the bereaved population. Even though loss, grief, and bereavement are fundamental human experiences, most medical, nursing, and social work schools do not require courses of this nature.

Some possibilities for enhancing support have already been explored. For example, the LaLeche League and the Childbirth Education Association have both expressed interest in offering bereavement support to parents who lose infants. However, even though they earnestly wish to provide such services, the main focus of these organizations is on promoting life, and it may prove that confrontation with death is too great a threat to their primary work.

What about churches? Bereavement outreach seems to be a natural program for a church or other religious community. Yet, it has been discovered that very few churches have any kind of organized program in this area. Those that do are typically more in touch with needs of their older parishioners or community members. One young widower found that after his wife died following a long-term illness, no one from his church spoke to him about her. After staying away from church for a couple of years, he decided to start a bereavement outreach program himself. It was so successful that he was invited to start one in another church in his town. There are some churches taking the lead or seizing the initiative in this area, but there is still very much to be done.

Another possibility appears to be working with retirees or, in the case of SIDS, grandparents. Here we have found that, in general, there is an unwillingness to become involved. When looking to volunteer groups for providing consistent and quality support, a great deal of work will need to be done. A number of questions occur in this regard: Is there a general attitude of selfishness in our society these days? Is death too close to some and therefore a threat? Is there a lack of a sense of community or social responsibility? Has our focus on technology, and the belief in a quick fix for everything, raised our level of impatience? Has the technical age led us to no longer be interested in the humanities and in the potential for common bonds with our fellow human beings?

One last note: bereavement work does require a certain sense of commitment, flexibility, openness, availability, and some passionate feelings for the importance of what one is doing.

Some Unanswered Questions for Future Planners

Is it an advantage or a disadvantage to limit the service population only to SIDS families, or should programs look toward including all infant deaths or all deaths of children? Is it possible to develop a concrete, universal model for helping bereaved families when human beings are all so very individual and different? With the widespread changes in available funds in the United States, will we lose what has been gained? Is there a need for a new groundswell movement such as the one 20 years ago? Or can we meet the needs of bereaved families in the future on a regional, state, and/or local basis? Do we not need some centralized, coordinated networking system at the national level?

A New Level of Sophistication and Cooperation

As compared with the early years after the SIDS Act of 1974, there is a different level of sophistication and cooperation between SIDS parents and professionals in the United States. In part, this has come about as a result of decreased federal and state funding. It has also arisen from shared experiences through the years. In the recent past, both SIDS parents and SIDS professionals have come to respect what each has to offer, and a team spirit has developed in some areas that encourages creativity and initiative on the part of individuals and groups. Having to deal with the political system has also helped to increase respect for the different backgrounds and skills which are required.

In addition, it has recently become necessary to care for many very ill persons, at least in part, at home. At the same time, the emerging hospice movement has demonstrated that it can be both feasible and desirable to care for dying persons and their families in the home. All of this has raised awareness within communities concerning the need for services to families experiencing deaths. Improved education about the implications of death, dying, and bereavement is beginning to bring about promising changes in our society.

For example, there has been a natural ripple effect arising from the work done by community-based SIDS and hospice programs. Many hospitals have recently established positions for mental health liaison persons in their emergency rooms, although most are only available during daytime hours and on-call evenings and nights. In working with hospitals, it has been found useful to mention that it is good public relations for them to ensure that bereaved persons receive thoughtful and sensitive support. Often, bereaved families speak in great detail about their emergency room experiences, whether positive or negative. With the present competition among hospitals, this, in some cases, has moved them to consider establishing or improving such services.

Problems to Face Now

Because of reduced federal funding in the United States, nearly all of the SIDS information and counseling projects are being required to spend more time and effort in raising money to support themselves. The skills to provide information and counseling for bereaved families are very different from those related to raising money. Thus, programs are having to develop those skills, add a new group of staff, advisory, or board persons with such skills, or hire professional fund raisers. Without a centralized authority (e.g., the Department of Health and Human Services), there is a lack of support—not just financial—for the former SIDS information and counseling projects. Thus, they have felt isolated and less well informed in the last few years.

In 1987, the Association of SIDS Program Professionals was formed by nurses, social workers, and other professionals who have been working in the SIDS area. This was intended to help fill the gap that such professionals were feeling. The Department of Health and Human Services is still available to provide consultation and some limited funds to support meetings. That assistance has been valuable to this rather small group of about 40 members.

As mentioned earlier, many states have discontinued their SIDS projects completely. This leaves affected families with very poor (if any) services when their babies die. This need is too big for only small, sometimes very widely scattered groups of parents.

Through the years, there has been a proliferation of SIDS-related organizations, each begun to address particular needs. There are the National SIDS Foundation and the Council of Guilds for Infant Survival; both are parent and mutual help organizations. There are about 20 SIDS information and counseling projects. Some have evolved into incorporated programs with professional staff members combined with the SIDS parent organization. These incorporated programs often are forced to raise a large percentage of their funding through their own individual efforts. There is the American SIDS Institute, the Southwest SIDS Research Institute, and the former National Center for the Prevention of SIDS.

In addition to these national organizations, a number of states also have SIDS institutes or some other programs devoted to the study of SIDS. This situation has inevitably led to much duplication of effort, competition, and a great deal of confusion, not only for the staffs of these organizations, but also for newly-bereaved parents and their friends and relatives. It makes for, if not an impossible, at least a very undesirable situation.

A New and Hopeful Sign

In 1988, representatives of all national SIDS organizations came together at several meetings to discuss ways in which they might begin to address some of the problems identified in this chapter. They decided to form the SIDS Alliance and to join together for the purposes of fund raising. They also hired the staff of the National Center for the Prevention of SIDS which subsequently merged with the SIDS Alliance. In January of 1989, the National SIDS Foundation and the SIDS Alliance agreed to begin to share office space and some staff and equipment. In January of 1991, the Foundation also merged with the SIDS Alliance. These moves will help realize a significant savings of money which can now be spent supporting research rather than duplicating efforts by the three organizations. Having one umbrella organization should remove many stumbling blocks which formerly took great amounts of energy and which tended to confuse those outside the field who were confronted by a many-headed cacophony of voices. Those involved in serving the needs of SIDS research, family support, and community education will now be freed to meet the objectives shared by all of the groups in a more adequate and efficient manner.

CANADA

The organizational history of the Canadian Foundation for the Study of Infant Deaths (CFSID) may be similar in some respects—while different in others—to that of many SIDS organizations around the world. Consequently, a description of the background, structure, and work of the CFSID may have value beyond the borders of Canada.

The Canadian Foundation for the Study of Infant Deaths: Past

The Canadian Foundation for the Study of Infant Deaths was incorporated under the Canada Corporations Act and registered as a charitable organization on February 8, 1973. Its genesis as a national voluntary SIDS movement may be unique. There had been just one local parents' group in Canada, already active without any provincial or national affiliation, which had been established in Toronto in 1972. At the same time, in the United Kingdom, principals of the Foundation for the Study of Infant Deaths were taking an interest in the needs in Canada. A bridge was already in place between those countries in that Sir Max Aitken, a Canadian industrialist and benefactor, had established his center of operations in England, while still maintaining active involvement in Canadian affairs. Peter Camps, son of the internationally famous British forensic pathologist, Francis E. Camps, having been an English child evacuee during the Battle of Britain, had returned to live in Canada as a financial expert in stocks and bonds.

The initial funding of the Canadian Foundation and part of its governance came to be provided under British auspices, with Mr. Camps as a Vice-President and Executive Director. There was a quickly assembled Scientific Advisory Committee made up of ten academic specialists in pediatrics, pathology, and public health selected from across Canada. Of these, Dr. Sydney Segal, who has been the source of this archival information, still remains with the Foundation as a fount of wisdom and guidance. The Foundation's immediate target was the production of what was to be the fourth and most comprehensive international symposium on SIDS (following earlier meetings in Seattle in 1963 and 1969, and in Cambridge, England, in 1970). The 1974 symposium was hosted by the new CFSID in collaboration with its first chapter, the original Toronto parents' group. The announced purpose of the meeting was "to associate together those who have specially studied the subject with experts in other fields and disciplines who have limited knowledge of the problem."

Shortly after the 1974 symposium, the CFSID began its expansion to include additional parent chapters across Canada. Subsequent annual national conferences were held in a greatly reduced fashion in different cities across Canada. However, within a year or two the appetite for national SIDS services created by the CFSID began to outstrip its resources. There was no government subsidy. Financial and administrative deficits occurred in the attempts to meet the expectations of both Canadian researchers and parents' groups. Peter Camps overstrained his own health in trying to maintain the standards which his father had established as a contribution to SIDS, and both he and the CFSID had to be rescued.

The Foundation's salvation was achieved in 1976 by a financial grant from its friends in the U.K. Its administration was taken over by members of the local chapter in Toronto, and a new Scientific Advisory Committee and a wholly Canadian Board of Directors were created. In this way, the CFSID was delivered from its creditors, its modest annual conferences were continued, and it began to pursue a program of producing informational pamphlets that were appropriate to a Canadian readership.

With a working board established, financial stability was felt to be within reach and eventually sufficient confidence was achieved in 1984 to qualify for some federal government operating funds. However, at no time did the CFSID receive the equivalent in service funds corresponding to the federal and state support provided so substantially up to that time in the United States. All this while, funding for research related to SIDS was sufficient only for financial support of studentships, rather than for the total costs of major research projects. The latter were left for the standard government peer-reviewed systems.

Important as had been the contribution of partially salaried members of the Toronto Chapter, individuals who had provided dedicated coordinating services, the first major stride within the CFSID followed the appointment in 1984 of a professional national Executive Director to unify its far flung chapters for better cohesiveness and motivation for common needs, and the confidence of a close and competent hand on the administration and promotion of the organization.

The Canadian Foundation for the Study of Infant Deaths: Present

At present, the CFSID is a small national organization which is in a stage of transition and growth. Its approximately two dozen local chapters are run by volunteers who, as a group and because of the circumstances of their involvement, usually are younger than those in similar positions in many larger, non-profit, voluntary organizations. It has a non-partisan and responsive head of staff, with an extremely small, part-time support staff. It shares the problems and challenges of being a national organization in a geographically large and diverse country with many larger, health-related, charitable organizations, such as the Canadian Cystic Fibrosis Foundation, the Canadian Cancer Society, or the Canadian Heart Foundation. Volunteers, staff, and involved professionals (e.g., social workers and nurses), however empathetic, usually look at problems with slightly different viewpoints, and tensions have the opportunity to exist within and between all levels as in all organizations.

Currently, the CFSID is trying to escape from the problems of its history. It had seemed to be on the brink of financial ruin from its inception in 1973 until about 1985. The Foundation has had a low profile in the public eye, almost to the point of invisibility, but not a low public image where it and its work have been known. Even when the CFSID lacked professional managers and administrative staff, it nevertheless made a creditable effort in fulfilling its mission.

The mandate of the CFSID is to provide accurate information and emotional support to families of babies who have succumbed to Sudden Infant Death Syndrome, to present programs of public information and awareness, and to promote and support research activities into the cause or causes of SIDS.

The CFSID is proud of being a self-help, mutual-support organization, but it also carries the heavy burden of trying to educate the public, and, in particular, of attempting to fund research activities. Some other health-related organizations have made a decision to emphasize one or the other of these priorities, but not all.

Local Chapters and the National Office

There are over 20 official chapters or affiliates of the Foundation whose levels of activity span a broad spectrum. While in the past, to some observers, there may have appeared to be little differentiation between the national office in Toronto and the Toronto Chapter, this is no longer the case. Because of financial and geographical constraints, national CFSID Board of Directors meetings are held infrequently (approximately one per year). This is, in reality, not an unusual situation, especially in small, voluntary organizations. Nevertheless, it does seem to cause feelings of alienation, particularly in those board members located away from the national office. Consequently, an Executive Committee (whose members are not necessarily the officers of the Board) has been established to oversee the day-to-day operations of the Foundation.

There are the usual challenges of managing relationships among national, local chapter, and individual levels, as in all voluntary organizations. Sometimes it appears that each local chapter of the Foundation believes that its situation and problems are so different from the other chapters that it requires unique and special treatment. The trick is to help each chapter benefit from its individuality without having the administrative nightmare of 20 different sets of rules and regulations for 20 different chapters. Internal communication is vital to encourage a feeling of participation in a partnership where everyone has a voice and works for the common good.

It might be surprising for an outside observer to learn that the CFSID has several "one-parent" chapters in smaller centers. But it would then probably not be surprising that a major challenge of the organization is continuity, or rather, the lack of it. However, even in large centers, continuity of chapter organization is a problem as a result of the demographics of the volunteer population which represents the Foundation at the local level. As a consequence of this, "spotty" service implementation exists across the country.

Parent Volunteers

Parents of babies who die of SIDS are typically young persons who are at the start of their careers. As a result, they are often unable to provide as much financial help to the CFSID as they might if they were older or more well established. These parents frequently have young families of other children for whom they must care. Consequently, many of them lack much time to help the Foundation in any volunteer capacity, even should they desire to do so.

Death has frequently been termed the last taboo in Western society. In fact, it is often difficult to interest someone who has not had a very close personal involvement with SIDS deaths in the work of the Foundation on a voluntary or supportive basis. SIDS families themselves sometimes wish not to become very involved with the work of the Foundation, as they feel it is too sharp a reminder of their loss. Those persons who may have an interest, but who have not had a baby die in this way, may not be considered to be sufficiently empathetic or motivated by some SIDS parents. In contrast, interested and enthusiastic persons with no personal SIDS connection have been known to become frustrated with what they feel is passivity and an unwillingness to act on behalf of vital SIDS issues on the part of some of those personally afflicted. It is, in fact, true that a non-SIDS parent cannot really understand how it feels to lose a baby this way, and the long-term mental debilitation this grief may bring.

The relative youth of the leadership volunteers, especially in the chapters, is both an asset and a liability. Whereas relatively young volunteers are more open than many other people to new and different ideas, they frequently do not bring wide experience to their positions. They may rush in where angels fear to tread, but are less apt to say, "we tried that ten years ago, and it didn't work." They are easily discouraged in fund raising, taking rejection personally.

An Umbrella Resource Agency

Until recently, the CFSID has had very little opportunity, or necessity, to share its perceived expertise in providing emotional support to SIDS parents. Up until now, it has been the "umbrella" for all Canadian SIDS support work through its local chapters. SIDS support groups unaffiliated with the CFSID, and not necessarily seeking to join it, do sporadically spring up. They might freely avail themselves of the educational literature and audiovisual aids provided by the Foundation, but may not contribute to it financially.

It seems ironic that while the United States is now embarking on an "umbrella" SIDS group approach that has been the long-time Canadian norm, Canada may possibly be undergoing an evolutionary process in this regard.

Local Initiative

The CFSID sometimes finds that the only way of coping with their grief for some newly bereaved SIDS parents is their wish to provide emotional support for others. Some of these parents find it hard to believe that this may be an inappropriate time for them to attempt to give such emotional support. It is at this point that people may try to set up independent support groups. Others may focus their attention with much zeal on one aspect or other of SIDS issues and concerns, such as electronic monitoring or fund raising for research. However, it must also never be forgotten that every SIDS support organization that has ever been established has owed its existence to the untiring and often thankless efforts of one or more grieving parents.

Fund Raising

It cannot be denied by any person who has tried to expand the financial resources of the Foundation that intense external competition exists for funding from both the public and private sectors. There is a very strong desire to provide support services, and thus, of course, the necessity to receive charitable donations. This conflict between the need to seek adequate funding and the mandate to provide caregiving is faced by all of the major charities, as well as other organized grief support groups, or various other agencies which minister to the needs of parents who have suffered a child's death. In fact, some of the Foundation's professional resource persons themselves must deal with other such groups in their work lives and may find it difficult not to have feelings of divided loyalties.

SIDS in Canada in general (e.g., research) and the CFSID in particular, have never received any substantial government financial assistance. There is no tradition of lobbying government because until very recently, any activity along this line could cost a charitable organization its federal registration.

A Self-Help, Mutual-Support Organization for Bereaved Parents

A description of the CFSID reveals what the organization is and can be used to compare it to what it is not. The Foundation is a self-help, mutual-support organization which believes that a bereaved person can best be helped by someone else who has gone through the same ordeal. It is not usually a situation where a grieving parent becomes part of a social worker's case load or where professional therapy is considered to be indicated for normal grief. It is to be hoped, however, that CFSID support parents and groups learn to recognize when a particular person's grief goes beyond what they can help as personal "befrienders," and when to make a referral to professional help.

The CFSID provides personalized service in the form of individual parent-to-parent contact, over the telephone, at each other's homes, and sometimes right in the hospital where the SIDS baby is taken. Although there are group meetings, people may attend as few or as many as they want. There is no set series of "classes" with a beginning and an end that one is expected to attend. Although every chapter has professionals that can be called upon, the SIDS parents themselves normally provide the emotional support. They can provide information and emotional support as only someone can who has earlier walked in the shoes of the newly-bereaved parents.

International Initiatives

In 1987, the *SIDS Family International*, an informal association of worldwide, volunteer-driven SIDS support groups, was formed. Challenges and problems which individual leaders had felt to be particular to their group alone were discovered to be common to SIDS groups around the world. Countries the size of Denmark shared ideas with countries the size of Canada or Australia. Many groups had had shaky beginnings; most are still struggling for funding. However, the mutual support focus was paramount in them all.

The future of SIDS groups lies here, in the common bond of those who have lost a child and wish to help others finds a way out of this pain.

CONCLUSION: A VISION FOR THE FUTURE

In the best of all possible worlds, of course, there would be no SIDS. However, we have not yet reached the point of even knowing definitely what SIDS is, let alone how to prevent it. Thus, at present, those of us who wish to help must focus upon our shared desire to help affected families recover in the healthiest way possible. We know that healthy recovery is determined by whether or not bereaved family members have a realistic perception of what has happened, as well as by their individual coping skills and the quality of their social support systems. Obviously, we cannot change their coping abilities during the crisis time right after an infant dies. But there is much that we can do to influence their perception of the event by ensuring that they receive sensitive care and accurate, concrete information about SIDS, about what happened to the baby, and about what is happening to them. In addition, we can help to mobilize their own social support systems and to provide or engage them in larger networks of social support.

Our objectives should still be the same as those so wisely established by the writers of the SIDS legislation in 1974 in the United States. It is not necessary to reinvent the wheel. There is a growing cadre of well-trained and experienced SIDS parents and professionals who are available to continue the work. At the very least, we should ensure that each family receives quality social support during their recovery after the death of their baby.

Would it not be truly remarkable if, under the umbrella of the new SIDS Alliance in the United States, of national organizations in Canada and in many other countries, and of the SIDS Family International around the world, interested persons could come together and organize enough local groups to: (1) provide adequate support to families who are bereaved as the result of having an infant or child die suddenly and unexpectedly; (2) raise enough funds to support those efforts; and, in addition, (3) raise the millions of dollars (whether directly or through pressure upon governmental agencies to place appropriate emphasis upon SIDS research) that are necessary to continue research efforts? There is strength in numbers and a house united will not fall.

It is truly a new era for the SIDS movement in the United States, Canada, and around the world. One can hope that we will begin to reap the benefits of the efforts and experiences of the past for the betterment of all. There is much well-documented research to demonstrate that unresolved grief is one of the most debilitating conditions experienced by human beings, and that the loss of an infant or child is one of the worst types of bereavement. May all who read this book commit themselves to increasing their efforts toward this preventive mental health effort in the first place, and, in the long run, to identifying, explaining, screening for, and preventing the causes of Sudden Infant Death Syndrome.

REFERENCE

Bergman, A. B. (1986). *The "discovery" of Sudden Infant Death Syndrome: Lessons in the practice of political medicine.* New York: Praeger.

INDEX